Confidentiality and the Law

BRIAN C. REID

MA(Cantab), LLM(Lond), Barrister

WATERLOW PUBLISHERS

First Edition 1986

Waterlow Publishers
Oyez House, PO Box 55
27 Crimscott Street
London SE1 5TS
A division of Pergamon Books Ltd

ISBN 0 08 039236 9

British Library Cataloguing in Publication Data

Reid, Brian C.
Confidentiality and the law.—(Waterlow practitioner's library)
1. Confidential communications—England
I. Title
344.2063'3 KD7518

Printed and bound in Great Britain by
A. Wheaton & Co Ltd, Exeter, Devon

Preface

The present work has a fairly modest aim. It is to treat the role played by the concept of confidence, in the widest sense, in the law as a whole. Confidential information in the ordinary sense of trade secrets and the like occupies only a part, albeit an important part, in that field.

Brian C. Reid

Middle Temple
London E.C.4

April 1986

Contents

Table of Cases

Table of Statutes

Table of Statutory Instruments and Conventions

CHAPTER 1

General Introduction

EQUITABLE ORIGIN

1.01 In an old 16th-century rhyme concerning the Chancellor's power, quoted by the celebrated legal historian Maitland in his lectures on *Equity*,[1] it is stated that:

> "These three give place in court of conscience,
> Fraud, accident, and breach of confidence."

The rhyme reflects the historical nature of the law's concern and involvement with questions of confidence; the root is old although the full flowering of the tree is more recent.

1.02 Moreover, confidence (in the sense of confidentiality or secrecy, as opposed to assuredness or optimism) can still today be regarded, in the broadest sense, as constituting an equitable concept. In 1967, for example, Denning M.R. in *Seager v. Copydex*,[2] a case involving an inventor of a carpet-fixing device licensing its use to a potential manufacturer, was able to say:

> "The law on this subject does not depend on any implied contract. It depends on the broad principle of equity that he who has received information in confidence should not take unfair advantage of it."

And the Law Commission in 1974[3] even felt constrained to admit on the topic of breach of confidence:

> "There is a continuing doubt as to the ultimate legal foundation on which the whole jurisdiction rests."

STATUTES AND TERMINOLOGY

1.03 The result is that no statute currently exists which promulgates generally the law of confidence, or even the somewhat narrower topic constituted by the law of breach of confidential information. This is not

1 *Equity (Two Courses of Lectures)*, Cambridge University Press (1910), page 7.
2 [1967] R.P.C. 349 at 368; [1967] F.S.R. 211; [1967] 1 W.L.R. 923; [1967] 2 All E.R. 415.
3 Working Paper No. 58 on "Breach of Confidence" (1974).

to say that statute law ignores the matter entirely; individual statutes may well refer to "confidential information", or its equivalent, in connection with their own statutory purposes.

1.04 Thus, section 3(5) of the Checkweighing in Various Industries Act 1919[4] provides that:

> "(5) If any checkweigher or representative of workmen appointed under this Act, or the regulations made thereunder, divulges any *trade secret* or other information with regard to the employer's business, he shall be liable on summary conviction ..... unless he proves that the *trade secret* did not come to his knowledge or the information was not acquired by him in the course of the exercise of his powers under this Act." (emphasis added)

1.05 A more recent example is provided by section 87(5) of the Food Act 1984[5] in relation to powers of entry upon premises:

> "(5) If any person who, in compliance with this section . . . is admitted into a factory or workplace, discloses . . . any information obtained by him in the factory or workplace with regard to any manufacturing process or *trade secret*, he shall, unless the disclosure was made in performance of his duty, be liable . . ."

1.06 "Trade secret" was a term widely used in the common law of the Victorian and post-Victorian eras to denote technological manufacturing information of the kind which would nowadays tend to be classified under the wider term of "confidential information". Its continued retention by Parliament in such contexts is to be noted.

1.07 "Know-how", a term still classified as late as 1974 by the Shorter Oxford English Dictionary as a slang term of United States origin, has become more prevalent since the end of World War II. It is now widely used as a synonym for confidential information of a technological character, particularly information concerning the practical day-to-day working of a patented invention. The term can be found in, for example, section 386 of the Income and Corporation Taxes Act 1970,[6] in relation to the tax treatment of dealings in know-how; sub-section (7) even includes a formal definition of the term, for those tax purposes, as follows:

> "(7) In this section "*know-how*" means any industrial information and techniques likely to assist in the manufacture or processing of goods or materials, or in the working of a mine, oil-well or other source of mineral

4 9 & 10 Geo. V c. 51.
5 1984 c. 30.
6 1970 c. 10.

> deposits (including the searching for, discovery, or testing of deposits or the winning of access thereto), or in the carrying out of any agricultural, forestry or fishing operations." (emphasis added)

It is also a standard expression in matters of European law arising under the Treaty of Rome. For example, it occurs throughout the block exemption for patent licences recently promulgated by the European Commission in relation to Article 85(1) of the Treaty as a description for the information associated with the exploitation of the invention which may also pass with the patent licence. Article 1(4) of this Regulation,[7] for instance, refers to:

> "an obligation on the licensee not to manufacture or use the licensed product, or use the patented process *or the communicated know-how*, in territories within the common market . . ." (emphasis added)

1.08 The term is, however, essentially a word of chameleonic character; outside the purely technological sphere, it is sometimes used (as in *Amway Corporation v. Eurway International*[8] (see Chapter 3) to denote subject-matter of a character which cannot be protected under the head of confidential information. In other words it can, depending on the context, have mutually converse meanings. Such aphorisms as:

> "Information which is merely 'know-how' will not be protected."[9]

should therefore be treated with care. In this book, usage of the term is accordingly generally avoided, for sake of clarity.

1.09 The modern trend is, generally speaking, to use the term "confidential information" together with corresponding associated terms like "duty of confidentiality" or "breach of confidence" as appropriate. This reflects the increasing usage of these terms in case and statute law, and in legal literature generally.

1.10 Section 46(4) of the Copyright Act 1956,[10] for example, provides that:

> "(4) Nothing in this Act shall affect the operation of any rule of equity relating to *breaches of trust or confidence*." (emphasis added)

This formal statutory acknowledgement of the equitable nature of the action for breach is noteworthy.

1.11 Section 42(3) of the Patents Act 1977[11] is another instance. This

7 Regulation No. 2349/84, [1984] O.J. L219/15 to 24.
8 [1974] R.P.C. 82; [1973] F.S.R. 213.
9 *Halsbury's Laws of England* (4th Ed) Vol. 16, Para. 1455.
10 4 & 5 Eliz. II, c. 74.
11 1977 c. 37.

preserves the employee's duty of confidentiality in respect of any invention made by him:

> "Sub-section (2) above shall not be construed as derogating from any *duty of confidentiality* owed to his employer by an employee by virtue of any rule of law or otherwise." (emphasis added)

This provision is discussed further in para 6.02, *post*.

1.12 Examples in delegated legislation are provided in the Fire Services (Discipline) Regulations 1948,[12] which provide that:

> "A member of a fire brigade commits an offence against discipline if he is guilty of—
>
> . . .
>
> (b) *Breach of confidence,* that is to say, if he divulges any matter which it is his duty to keep secret."

and in the Public Trustee Rules 1912,[13] which provide that:

> "Subject as aforesaid the Public Trustee shall observe *strict secrecy* in respect of every trust or estate in course of administration by him." (emphases added)

1.13 All these examples must, however, be regarded as constituting mere local statutory crystallisations of a pervasive overhanging general equitable concept. To evaluate the scope of such statutes or other legislation reliance may well have to be placed on the case-law concerning the equitable concept. It is the tax statute which represents the exception proving the rule in this connection, by incorporating its own formal definition. In certain areas (for example banking) there may, moreover, be overlap between the general law of confidence and specific statutory provisions (see Chapter 4).

OTHER INCIDENTS

1.14 Although the action for breach of confidence has equitable origins, it should not be overlooked that the confidential information itself normally constituting the subject-matter of the action—the substratum which engenders the action in a given case—has also proprietary incidents of its own. It is probably true to say that it does not rank as property (real or personal) in the strict sense of the word as used in English law. But it is in practice bought and sold, licensed and assigned, just as other marketable commodities (in the widest sense of that word) are. Such dealings will have tax and commercial legal implications for those involved in them. The information may also be regarded as

12 S.I. 1948 No. 545, Schedule.
13 Statutory Rules and Orders 1912 No. 348, Para. 29(2).

property for other statutory purposes; in the bankruptcy case of *re Keene,*[14] for example, it was held that the bankrupt had to reveal to his trustee a secret formula that had never been committed to writing, since it formed part of the assets of his business. Nevertheless, to quote again from the Law Commission:

> "... the nature of confidential information is such as to place it in a category of its own ..."[15]

SCOPE AND DEVELOPMENT

1.15 It will be appreciated from the foregoing that confidence and its limits—In what circumstances and how does it arise? What kind of subject-matter does it protect? How far can the law assist in its maintenance and compensate for its loss?—is a topic of considerable significance in commercial and industrial spheres of activity. But the topic is not limited to such spheres; it can arise also in a wide range of what might be regarded, compendiously, as individual spheres of activity, for example in the conduct of a law-suit, the relation between a professional person and his client, or as between pupil and teacher. The communication(s) involving the confidential material may, again, have been oral and/or written; there is little difference in principle so far as mode of transmission is concerned, although proof of exactly what was passed and to whom may be more difficult in the former instance than in the latter.

1.16 Nevertheless, the case-law on the subject as a whole has tended to develop separately along the two avenues outlined above. The division will be followed in this book. The first part (Chapters 2 to 6), therefore, deals principally with breach of confidence in relation to information of commercial and/or industrial value; in short, with what was in earlier times often referred to as the law of trade secrets generally. The second (Chapters 7 to 14) deals *seriatim* with separate aspects of the law of confidence as viewed more widely, including confidentiality as between lawyer and client, doctor and patient and journalist and "mole", the Official Secrets Acts and the new Data Protection Act; this list is not exhaustive.

1.17 But the division should not be taken as meaning that the two halves of the modern law are to be regarded as totally different animals or, as Kipling said, as if:

14 [1922] 2 Ch. 475.
15 *Breach of Confidence* (Cmnd. 8388), Para 2.10.

"East is East and West is West and never the twain shall meet"[16]

Much of the substratum of the law is common. The division reflects, rather, the historical evolution of the case-law; and in a field where law is essentially judge-made rather than statute-made, it is the cases which tend to dominate.

1.18 The third part of the book (Chapters 15 to 16) is concerned primarily with the procedural aspects of the subject—action for breach of confidential information, remedies, interlocutory relief and the like. As such, it is common to a great extent to the substantive law outlined in the first and second parts.

16 "The Ballad of East and West"

CHAPTER 2

Breach of Confidential Information (Trade Secrets)—Historical Outline

FOUNDATIONS

2.01 The foundations of the modern action for breach of confidence in relation to trade secrets (in the widest sense of the word) can be seen in a series of early Victorian cases in the Courts of Equity concerning patent medicines. In an era when modern scientific medicine had hardly emerged, and quackery flourished, the commercial scope for a successful product was naturally very considerable. It was not surprising that numerous disputes arose over successful secret formulae. An equivalent today might be the formula of the syrup used for the manufacture of a cola-type soft drink, or of a new perfume.

PATENT MEDICINES—THE TRILOGY

2.02 *Williams v. Williams*[1] in 1817, although not the earliest case to be found in the reports, may be mentioned first. This was a dispute between father and son in respect of certain remedies invented by the father, for the cure of eye diseases. The Lord Chancellor (Lord Eldon) was doubtful about the ability of a Court of Equity to protect subject-matters of this kind:

> ". . . upon general principles, I do not think that the Court ought to struggle to protect this sort of secrets in medicine. The Court is bound indeed to protect them in cases of patents, to the full extent of what was intended by the grant of the patent, because the patentee is a purchaser from the public, and bound to communicate his secret to the public at the expiration of the patent. Then, whether the principle can be extended to such a case as this—whether a contracting party is entitled to the protection of the Court in the exercise of its jurisdiction, to decree the specific performance of agreements, by restraining a party to the contract from divulging the secret he has promised to keep, that is a question which *would require very great consideration*. But the present case is not one which calls for determination of it. If the defendant has already disclosed the secret, the injunction can be of no use ..." (emphasis added)

1 3 Mer. 157 at 160.

2.03 The attitude reflected by these remarks was in keeping with Lord Eldon's well-known conservatism, under which it has been remarked that:

> "... it was apparent that Equity was the direct negation of what the term had implied when the Court of Chancery was first established."[2]

2.04 *Green v. Folgham*[3] in 1823 related to "Dr. Johnson's Ointment for the Eyes". The original owner of the recipe had assigned it on the marriage of his daughter to trustees in trust for her and her husband for life, with eventual sale of the secret (on the latter's deaths) for the benefit of any grandchildren. But upon the husband's death, his wife destroyed the recipe and orally communicated its contents to the eldest son only. A dispute between that son and his younger brothers and sisters (the remaining grandchildren) arose. The Vice-Chancellor (acting in Chancery—the events took place prior to the fusion of the Courts of Law and Equity in 1875) directed that the parties proceed to a trial at law to determine the value of the secret. The defendant's argument,[4] citing the *Williams* case, *supra*, that there could be no property in a mere verbal secret, appears to have fallen on stony ground; the tide had turned in favour of protection, although it still had far to travel before it reached a high-water mark.

2.05 *Morison v. Moat*[5] in 1851 involved a substance known as "Morison's Universal Medicine" (its composition is not recorded). Dispute arose between the respective sons of the original inventor of the recipe and his subsequent partner; the partner had improperly communicated the secret to his own son. By this date the Vice-Chancellor was prepared to say flatly:

> "... there was, according to the authorities to which I have referred, *a perfect right*, on the part of Morison against Moat, to restrain him from divulging the secret."[6]

and:

> "The case then in this stage stands thus: The Defendant admits that the secret was communicated to him by Thomas Moat. His allegation, that he acquired a knowledge of it by acting as partner in the concern, is disproved; and it is shown, that if he did acquire such knowledge, he did do surreptitiously. The question then is whether there was an equity against him; and I am of opinion that there was. It was clearly a *breach of faith* and

2 Keeton, *An Introduction to Equity*, Pitman (5th Ed, 1961) at 28.
3 1 Sim. & St. 398.
4 At 403.
5 9 Hare 241.
6 At 261

of contract on the part of Thomas Moat to communicate the secret. The defendant derives under that breach of faith and of contract and I think he can gain no title by it."[7] (emphasis added)

2.06 The important point is that the breach of faith was actionable in itself, quite apart from there being a breach of the partnership agreement under which Thomas Moat had originally acquired his knowledge of the formula.

Prince Albert v. Strange

2.07 *Prince Albert v. Strange*[8] in 1849 may also be mentioned at this stage. This is not quite so much because of the extent of its contribution to the law, but more because the eminence of the plaintiff (Prince Albert, Consort of Queen Victoria) and public interest in its subject-matter (royal sketches) has ensured its continuing notoriety. As stated by the Lord Chancellor at the commencement of his judgement continuing the injunction:

> "The importance which has been attached to this case arises entirely from the exalted station of the Plaintiff, and cannot be referred to any difficulty in the case itself."[9]

2.08 The decision does, however, make it clear that an action for breach of confidence can be brought against a third party further down the chain of communication and with whom the original owner of the confidential matter had no direct connection. The facts were that Prince Albert and Queen Victoria periodically made for their own amusement various etchings of subjects of private and domestic interest. Some of the plates had been sent to a printer for making impressions; occasionally copies of one or other of these would be given by their Royal Highnesses to friends in the royal entourage. A dishonest employee of the printer had apparently surreptitiously taken further copies for his own use and these had eventually reached the defendants, who were intending to display them publicly for gain. The defendants were obviously strangers (in a legal sense) to Prince Albert; but quite irrespective of any question of property rights, the Court was prepared to give relief on wider grounds:

> "but this case by no means depends solely upon the question of property, for a breach of *trust, confidence,* or contract *would of itself* entitle the Plaintiff to an injunction."[10] (emphasis added)

7 At 263.
8 1 Mac. & G. 25.
9 At 40.
10 At 44.

2.09 A well-known modern application of the third-party liability rule is contained in *Duchess of Argyll v. Duke of Argyll* (discussed more fully in Chapter 13).[11] The injunction was granted here both against the Duke (to restrain him from making further communications to the newspaper) and the newspaper itself (to restrain it from publishing the contents of any such further communications). Whereas there had been a pre-existing relation between the Duke and Duchess, which served to give the Duchess certain rights of marital confidence, there was none between Duchess and newspaper.

VICTORIAN (AND POST-VICTORIAN) DEVELOPMENT

2.10 From the mid-19th century onwards the Courts developed trade secrets law on a substantial scale. The impact of large-scale industrialisation spurred its importance; the fusion of law and equity in 1875 (already mentioned) facilitated its practical application. Amongst the numerous decisions there may be mentioned, in chronological order:

Table 1

Case	*Subject-matter*	*Date*
Estcourt v. Estcourt Hop Essence[12]	Hop substitute	1875
Merryweather v. Moore[13]	Dimensional tables for fire engines	1892
Powell v. Birmingham Vinegar Brewery[14]	Yorkshire Relish	1897
Lecouterier v. Rey[15]	Chartreuse	1910
Amber Size & Chemical v. Menzel[16]	Resin size for paper making	1913
Rex Co. and Rex Research Corporation v. Muirhead and H.M. Comptroller-General of Patents[17]	Insecticides	1926
British Industrial Plastics v. Ferguson[18]	Aminoplastic moulding powders	1938

11 See para 13.25 *post*.
12 L.R. 10 Ch. 276.
13 [1892] 2 Ch. 518.
14 14 R.P.C. 720; [1897] A.C. 710; 66 L.J. Ch. 763; 76 L.T. 792.
15 27 R.P.C. 268; [1910] A.C. 262; 70 L.J. Ch. 394; 102 L.T. 293; 26 T.L.R. 368.
16 30 R.P.C. 433.
17 44 R.P.C. 38.
18 56 R.P.C. 271.

2.11 Not all of these involved just simple improper acts of behaviour by former employees, partners, successors or the like of a kind which might be considered generally akin—bearing in mind the growth of the large corporation as a business entity over this period—to those present in the early Victorian cases first mentioned. The whole concept of trade secrets is given a wider recognition, and relied upon in further fields of law.

2.12 The *Powell* decisions, for example, arose in the context of a passing-off action. The plaintiff had a long-standing reputation for his "Yorkshire Relish" sauce, of a secret composition; the defendant put on the market his own brand of a similar (although not identical) product, calling it "Holbrook's Yorkshire Relish". The fact that it was not quite the same as the existing product, even though it was no doubt a perfectly satisfactory sauce in its own right and was clearly denominated by the defendant merely as his own version of the product, weighed heavily with the Court in finding that there had been passing-off. The accompanying trade secret had, as it were, served to expand the aura of protection accorded under common law to the plaintiff's trade mark.

2.13 In the *Lecouterier* decision, registered trade marks (to "Chartreuse" for liqueurs) were involved. There had been a compulsory dissolution in France of the original monastery of La Grande Chartreuse. The monks had then taken their secret process for making the liqueur with them to Spain. The House of Lords upheld their right to have the name of the French liquidator expunged from the Register as owner of the marks, in rectification proceedings under section 90 of the Patents, Designs and Trade Marks Act 1883[19] and to injunct him and his assignees from continuing to use the mark on liqueurs. To quote from the leading speech of Lord Macnaghten, at page 275:

> "But two things that belonged to them—the *secret* of their manufacturing process and the reputation which their liqueurs had acquired in foreign countries, and notably in England—were *incapable of being seized or confiscated*. . . .
>
> Then followed a warfare in England waged with varying success. On the one hand were the monks and La Union Agricola, on the other M. Lecouterier, the liquidator appointed by the French Court to wind up the affairs of the dissolved monastery, and with the liquidators were the purchasers from him calling themselves La Compagnie Fermière de la Grande Chartreuse. The monks fought to preserve the *remnant of their property which was beyond the reach of French law*. The liquidator and the purchasers from him, who were not in possession of the monks's secret, strove to supplant them in the English market by adopting their insignia and representing that they were the proprietors of the 'genuine' liqueur, 'the old and world-renowned liqueur Chartreuse'. . . .

19 46 & 47 Vict. c. 57.

> To me it seems perfectly plain that by the very nature of things a law of a foreign country, and a sale by a foreign Court under that law, cannot affect property not within the reach of the foreign law, or the jurisdiction of the foreign Court charged with its administration."

The monks' victory thus hinged, at root, upon the commercial significance of their secret recipe.

2.14 Indeed, it was not unknown for trade secret law to be regarded in then contemporary text books as part of trade mark law generally, on the basis that it provided a case "analogous" to that of trade marks. As put in Sebastian's *Law of Trade Marks*, 4th Edition (1899):

> "In addition to the cases in which there has been an infringement of trade mark properly so called, a *variety of cases* have been decided in which the Court has restrained the practice of *fraud* by one person at the expense of another, the means adopted to perpetrate the fraud *resembling to some extent the infringement of a trade mark*, but yet being distinguishable therefrom." (at 247)

After discussion under this head of such topics as trade names, passing-off, trade libel (and also a passing reference to the *Prince Albert* decision), he comes to trade secrets and defines them as follows:

> ". . . the general rule may be stated as being that any person who has, without the use of unfair means, become acquainted with the mode of compounding a *secret unpatented preparation*, may make and sell the compound, provided that he does not lead the public to suppose that his preparation is the manufacture of the original discoverer or of his successors in business; . . .
>
> On the other hand, where the knowledge of the *secret process* has been acquired by means of a breach of trust, neither the person who has committed the breach of trust, nor anyone to whom he has imparted his discovery, will be allowed to make use of the information so surreptitiously acquired." (at 287–8; emphases added)

2.15 What is interesting about these remarks is their restriction as regards type of subject-matter coming within the concept of "trade secret". Although the law has clearly progressed beyond the protection of patent medicines and the like only, there is not yet the recognition that technological subject-matter generally can be protected under it. No direct reference is made to mechanical devices or drawings or engineering industries generally. Such expansion had still to come, in the 20th century.

MODERN FORMULATION

2.16 The modern law can be regarded as starting with the formula adopted by Lord Greene (Master of the Rolls) in 1948 in *Saltman*

Engineering v. Campbell Engineering,[20] relating to drawings of tools for the manufacture of leather punches. The defendants had used drawings, originally given to them by the plaintiffs for purposes of fulfilling a contract for the supply of leather punches, for their own subsequent purposes as well. Lord Greene's formula was:

> "If a defendant is proved to have used confidential information, directly or indirectly obtained from a plaintiff, without the consent, express or implied, of the plaintiff, he will be guilty of an infringement of the plaintiff's rights."

So far as the application of this formula is concerned, Lord Greene's judgement makes two further points of importance.

2.17 Firstly, as regards the prerequisite for the information to be confidential. This was explained as follows:

> "The information, to be confidential, must, I apprehend, apart from contract, have the necessary quality of confidence about it, namely, it must *not* be something which is public property and public knowledge. On the other hand, it is perfectly possible to have a confidential document, be it a formula, a plan, a sketch, or something of that kind, which is the result of work done by the maker upon materials which may be available for the use of anybody; but *what makes it confidential is the fact that the maker of the document has used his brain* and thus produced a result which can only be produced by somebody who goes through the same process."[21] (emphasis added)

Hence the fact that the defendants could notionally have made the drawings themselves, or via a third party, by reverse engineering from the leather punch already on the market (ignoring for the moment any copyright complications) was to no avail. By dispensing with this step, and relying on drawings direct from the plaintiffs, they had come under an obligation to them.

2.18 Secondly, the judgement makes it clear that the parties do not necessarily need to have been in pre-existing contractual relation for the obligation of confidence (and hence the potential action for breach of confidence) to arise. Lord Greene put it thus:

> "The main part of the claim is based on breach of confidence, in respect of which a right may be infringed without the necessity of there being any contractual relationship. I will explain what I mean. If two parties make a contract, under which one of them obtains for the purpose of the contract or in connection with it some confidential matter, even though the contract is silent on the matter of confidence the law will *imply an obligation* to treat that confidential matter in a confidential way, as one of the implied terms of the contract; but the obligation to respect confidence is *not* limited to cases where the parties are in contractual relationship."[22] (emphasis added)

20 65 R.P.C. 203 at 213
21 At 215.
22 At 211.

In other words, the existence of a formal contractual obligation to respect confidence provides the plaintiff with a bonus to his claim; it may give him a second arrow to his bow, but he may equally well have been able to succeed already with his first arrow represented by the equitable obligation.

2.19 The fact that the equitable obligation alone may suffice can be of substantial significance in practice. Frequently, the parties will not have considered properly, or formally arranged, their mutual positions before passing over the confidential information. Two large multi-national corporations, considering entry into an agreement for exchange of confidential information relating to, for example, the manufacture of instant coffee, probably will of course have done so. They are likely to have been well aware of the advantages of clarity in business relationships and to have entered accordingly into a comprehensive written contract on the matter as a whole, incorporating provisions for maintaining secrecy; if one improperly reveals a relevant item of information to a third party, the action by the other injured party can then be grounded in breach of contract in any event. Likewise, each such corporation will probably have taken covenants from its scientific employees, via their contracts of employment, not to reveal secret details of their current research into the manufacture of the product; if such an employee hands over the vital information as to processing conditions to a competitor, he would be in breach of his employment contract also. But an amateur power boat enthusiast or the like working at the weekend in his domestic garage is unlikely to have made any such formal arrangement with his collaborator from next door. And it is he who is probably in greater need of protection, since it is he who is less likely to have legal considerations at the forefront of his mind. The rule that contract is not essential therefore makes good sense.

2.20 A somewhat more recent formulation is that given by Megarry J. in the *Coco v. A. H. Clark (Engineers)*[23] decision, in 1968, concerning moped engines. The plaintiff appears (from the somewhat sparse information given in the judgement) to have been a solo designer and to have had informal arrangements only with the defendant company whom he wished to interest; contractual documents were prepared in draft but never executed.

2.21 For cases not governed by some pre-existing contract, *Coco* spells out the elements of the action as follows:

23 [1969] R.P.C. 41 at 47.

> "... *three elements* are normally required if, apart from contract, a case of breach of confidence is to succeed. *First*, the information itself, in the words of Lord Greene, M.R. in the *Saltman* case on page 215, must "have the necessary quality of confidence about it. *Secondly*, that information must have been imparted in circumstances importing an obligation of confidence. *Thirdly*, there must be an unauthorised use of that information to the detriment of the party communicating it." (emphasis added)

2.22 This formulation may be regarded more as a re-statement of the *Saltman* formula rather than as any fresh declaratory rule, although the emphasis upon the need for the transmission of the information to have occurred in confidential circumstances (as well as the information being confidential *per se*) is a useful gloss.

2.23 An owner of confidential information can of course decide voluntarily to abandon its confidentiality and put it into the public domain instead. If he does, then a party to whom he subsequently makes the same revelation in purported confidence and who is unaware of the pre-existing publication, may well be under no duty to maintain confidence; this is a matter of degree, depending on the circumstances of the antecedent publication; if the confidential matter relates, for example, to a method of de-licing sheep and thereby improving their wool publication in the standard veterinary textbook or in the national press may be one thing but publication in an obscure Tasmanian sheep-farmers' journal, or in 19th century patents and extracts from the *Weavers' Gazette* (as in *Courtaulds v. G. Hattersley*[24]) quite another.

2.24 Reference may be made finally in this chronology to the contemporary Irish decision in *House of Spring Gardens v. Point Blank*, where the ethical substratum of the law is again underlined, as follows:

> "The Court, it should be borne in mind, is being asked to enforce what is essentially a moral obligation."[25]

2.25 The serial nature of the *Coco* test (which is in effect a series of hurdles which the plaintiff must jump successively if he is to succeed) has made it popular with the Courts. The triple group of requirements—confidential quality + communication in confidence + unauthorized disclosure—is accordingly elaborated upon in the succeeding Chapters 3 to 5, in individual turn.

24 I.P.D. 7117.
25 [1983] F.S.R. 213 at 253.

THE FUTURE

2.26 As for the future, the 1980 Report of the Law Commission on *Breach of Confidence*[26] recommended the wholesale sweeping away of the present common law action for breach of confidence and its replacement by a new statutory tort of breach of confidence. Whether this would be intrinsically desirable (and certainly Parliament has not yet enacted any such statute) is perhaps more debatable. Granted that there is a certain degree of uncertainty as to precisely how far the present action extends, nevertheless it has up to now exhibited a substantial flexibility and ability to cope with the changing demands for redress by those affected by a breach of confidence. This might be lost if the law were rendered statutory; a statute, unless revised regularly, inevitably imports an element of fossilisation into the law. This is quite apart from the room for argument that is bound to exist as to the interpretation of the actual words employed in the statute, even if (as would appear likely, bearing in mind the format of the draft Bill written by the Law Commission and reproduced in the Appendix) the general intention of the statute is to follow the existing common law. In the meantime, of course, it is the latter which controls.

26 Cmnd. 8388.

CHAPTER 3

Confidential Quality

TYPES

3.01 The case-law illustrates the wide range of types of commercial and/or industrial information which the Courts are now prepared to consider as protectable in principle. It is not even essential that the information be of a technological character—relevant, say, to the operation of an industrial process, or building of a machine, or formulation of a product—although naturally a large proportion of the cases are so concerned. And whether or not the action for breach of confidence will succeed may well depend upon whether or not the other elements of the action are fulfilled as well.

3.02 The following list (in alphabetical order) in Table 2 of mainly contemporary cases (including both successful and unsuccessful, interlocutory and final, allied with other causes of action, instances) is only partial but may prove helpful. The list (in chronological order), already given in Chapter 2 (Table 1) in relation to the historical developement of the action provides further examples.

Table 2

Case	*Subject-matter*	*Date*
Aveley Cybervox v. Boman[1]	Language laboratory design	1974
Coral Index v. Regent Index[2]	List of betting customers	1969
Cranleigh Precision Engineering v. Bryant[3]	Swimming pool fittings	1964
Dunford & Elliott v. Johnson & Firth Brown[4]	Merchant bankers' report	1976
Fraser v. Thames Television[5]	Idea for television series	1982
Harrison v. Project & Design[6]	Home stair lifts	1977

1 [1975] F.S.R. 139.
2 [1970] R.P.C. 147.
3 [1966] R.P.C. 81; [1965] 1 W.L.R. 1293; [1964] 3 All E.R. 289.
4 [1978] F.S.R. 143; [1977] 1 Lloyd's Rep. 505.
5 I.P.D. 6127
6 [1978] F.S.R. 81.

Case	*Subject-matter*	*Date*
Industrial Furnaces v. Reaves[7]	Furnace design	1969
Jarman & Platt v. Barget[8]	Report by cost and management accountants	1976
Mustad v. Dosen[9]	Fish hooks	1928
Nicrotherm v. Percy[10]	Pig weaners	1957
Potters-Ballotini v. Weston-Baker[11]	Manufacture of ballotini (small industrial glass beads)	1976
Saltman Engineering v. Campbell Engineering[12]	Tools for leather punches	1948
Schering v. Falkman[13]	Side effects of drug	1981
Seager v. Copydex[14]	Carpet grips	1967
Terrapin v. Builders' Supply[15]	Portable buildings	1959
Thomas Marshall (Exports) v. Guinle[16]	Trade officials in Iron Curtain countries; supply sources in Far East	1978
Underwater Welders & Repairers v. Street & Longthorne[17]	Cleaning ships' hulls	1967
Vernon v. Universal Pulp Containers[18]	Disposable bed pans	1980

PROOF OF CONFIDENTIAL QUALITY

3.03 Two principal questions normally arise:

(a) How is the confidential information to be characterised or defined?
(b) Is the information truly confidential?

They will be considered in turn.

Characterisation

3.04 As to characterisation, this may have been carried out in tangible form (for example, by means of documents, models and the like) or intangible (for example, by means of oral disclosure). Documents in this

7 [1970] R.P.C. 605.
8 [1977] F.S.R. 260.
9 [1963] R.P.C. 41; [1963] 3 All E.R. 416.
10 [1957] R.P.C. 207.
11 [1977] R.P.C. 202.
12 65 R.P.C. 203.
13 [1982]QB 1; [1981] 2 W.L.R. 848; [1981] 2 All E.R. 321.
14 [1967] R.P.C. 349; [1967] 1 W.L.R. 923; [1967] 2 All E.R. 415.
15 [1967] R.P.C. 375.
16 [1979] F.S.R. 208; [1978] 3 W.L.R. 116; [1978] 3 All E.R. 193.
17 [1968] R.P.C. 498; [1967] Lloyd's Rep. 364.
18 [1980] F.S.R. 179.

context include of course not merely conventional types of document such as reports, memoranda, lists, specifications and drawings but also those of a more exotic kind, for example representations of computer programs, magnetic tape and microfilms.

3.05 Take again the case (see Chapter 2) of confidential information relating to the manufacture of instant coffee. Suppose one company, ABC GmbH in West Germany (licensor), enters into an agreement with another company, DEF Ltd in the United Kingdom (licensee), whereby the former agrees to provide the latter with information concerning the manufacture of Kofflös. The relevant information is likely to be conveyed from one company to the other by a combination of documents (recipes, schedules for treatment time and condition of the starting coffee beans, drawings of apparatus for expanding the ground-up treated beans into porous granules, drawings of packing machinery and the like), supplemented by oral disclosures to the licensee's production manager when he visits the licensor's plant to inspect the process in operation. Information of the first kind is precisely defined by the contents of the documents themselves. The bounds of information of the second kind may be less certain; there could be dispute over exactly what was revealed (particularly if the conversations were carried on through an interpreter, or partly in the course of entertainment); the licencee's production manager may also have accidentally seen during his factory tour rather more than he was supposed to—say, also the German company's apparatus for making their companion instant tea product Löstee, quite outside the licence arrangement.

3.06 It follows that it may well be easier to restrain the improper use of documentary information than that of verbal information. Similar considerations arise in the converse situation of an independent inventor offering some new developement of his to a company. To avoid the possibility of subsequent dispute between them as to exactly what was revealed, the company may refuse to consider the confidential material until the inventor has filed a patent application and then look only at that. Not infrequently, it happens that the company is already working along the same lines in its own R & D department. By crystallising the information provided by the outside inventor in this fashion, it is then possible for the company to show (if that should ever prove necessary) exactly how far they had already premeditated the information in their own laboratories.

Truly confidential

3.07 As to the information being truly confidential, the test must be to some extent objective. Merely stamping a document "CONFIDENTIAL" will not make its contents confidential if they are to be found already in the standard textbook concerning the manufacture of instant coffee. Self-delusion on the part of the person asserting confidentiality is not enough. Likewise if the contents are only marginally different from what is already known—unless of course that marginal difference, say in respect of treatment temperature or duration, represents the key to commercial success. Generally, there must be some substantial element of novelty involved in the information. But a collection of individual already known pieces of information can provide a confidential whole; the very act of piecing them together may have produced something new and valuable. So can information obtained on analysis—say, of a traditional herbal remedy, or an alloy—which was always potentially available but not actually ascertained until the analysis had first been performed.

3.08 It may well be more difficult to assert confidentiality in respect of information outside the technological sphere, other of course than that of the strict facts and figures variety. Consider the case of a new fast food product being exploited by franchising. The instructional material given to potential franchisees as regards marketing is almost bound to be of an inherently more diffuse nature than the instructional material relating to the cooking of the special sauce whereby the advantage, *qua* savour, over the competition is obtained. Moreover, marketing techniques have been the subject of prolonged research and application in recent times; there must be a limit as to what is really new in the field.

3.09 Some of these points are reflected in the quartet of cases to be discussed below—*Stevenson Jordan & Harrison v. Macdonald & Evans*[19] (1951); *Amway Corporation v. Eurway International*[20] (1973); *Yates Circuit Foil v. Electrofoils*[21] (1975); and *Thomas Marshall v. Guinle*[16] (1978).

3.10 In *Stevenson Jordan & Harrison*, it was sought to restrain the publication of certain lectures which had been written by the author when in the employment of a business management concern, based upon expertise which the writer had there acquired. The book was to be called *Flexible Budgetary Control and Standard Costs*, with the sub-title "Cost

19 (1951) 69 R.P.C. 10; [1952] 1 T.L.R. 101 C.A.; partly reversing (1951) 68 R.P.C. 190—see para. 5.28 *post*.
20 [1974] R.P.C. 82; [1973] F.S.R. 213.
21 [1976] F.S.R. 345.

Control for Management". The attempt failed, the Court of Appeal commenting:

> "There is, so far as the energies of learned counsel have been able to discover, no case in the books corresponding in anything like the material particulars with the present case; . . ." (at 14)

3.11 This approach was followed in the *Amway* case involving, *inter alia*, United States sales literature in relation to a business of direct selling of cleaning materials via distributors (some 200,000 in the United States). A director of the defendants had acquired the literature during a visit to the United States plaintiff, and had subsequently relied upon its teachings in setting up a rival similar business in the United Kingdom. On application for interlocutory relief, the Court was influenced by the difficulty which would arise in framing the injunction; the requisite certainty as to what was to be prohibited (and hence in turn as to what was still permitted to be done) would be hard to pinpoint. It went on to add:

> "I am not satisfied that the plaintiffs' literature ever came into the hands of defendants under any confidential badge; but, even if it had it seems to me that it is merely know-how which the plaintiffs cannot keep exclusively to themselves. It is know-how which the law does not protect, . . ." (at 87)

3.12 *Yates Circuit Foil* concerned alleged secret processes for the continuous production of copper foil by electrodeposition using the insoluble anode method, in an action against former employees who had become involved in running a competitive concern. The Court made it very clear that it felt that the quantum of secrecy present had been exaggerated by the plaintiffs. To quote just two extracts from the lengthy judgement delivered:

> "It may well be that in the end the most important secret in this field, as in other fields, is that there is *nothing* so very secret in what anybody is doing, but the mere fact that nobody knows what anybody is doing may have some commercial advantage to it." (at 357, emphasis added)

and:

> "If one takes the secret features—and I do not pause to go through them again—the vast majority of these allegedly secret features are features which are inevitably going to be found in a conventional copper foil plant, produced by somebody who knows the literature and who has perhaps taken the trouble to visit a plant to see how others are operating." (at 393)

3.13 *Thomas Marshall (Exports) v. Guinle* was again an action against an ex-employee, this time a former managing director who had resigned around half-way through a 10-year service contract to set up in competition. The field was that of clothing imports; confidential information as to sources of supply, state officials and the like in Eastern Europe and the Far East was involved. The Court here essayed a definition as to how the existence (or not) of confidentiality was to be tested:

> ". . . I think . . . that *four elements* may be discerned . . . *First,* I think that the information must be information the release of which the owner believes would be injurious to him or of advantage to his rivals or others. *Secondly,* I think the owner must believe that the information is confidential or secret, i.e. that it is not already in the public domain. It may be that some or all of his rivals already have the information, but as long as the owner believes it to be confidential I think he is entitled to try and protect it. *Thirdly,* I think that the owner's belief under the two previous heads must be reasonable. *Fourthly,* I think that the information must be judged in the light of the usage and practices of the particular industry or trade concerned." (at 229–230)

3.14 This test clearly poses both a subjective hurdle (elements (1) and (2)) and an objective hurdle (elements (3) and (4)). What was probably decisive on the facts here was the intrinsically more precise nature of the information involved, as compared with that in the *Stevenson Jordan & Harrison* or *Amway* cases. The identity of a given influential official represents a particular; principles of salesmanship represent a generality.

3.15 It may be mentioned in passing that the *Coco* and *Thomas Marshall* decisions were both pronounced by the same Court (Megarry J, the latter in his capacity as Vice-Chancellor). Both enunciate what might be regarded as a mathematical approach to the issues they address—in *Coco,* the three elements of the cause of action for breach of confidence and in *Thomas Marshall* the four elements (more correctly, sub-elements) of the first *Coco* element (the need for confidential quality). Although such mode of approach should not be pursued to a point of absurdity in any given case (the law in this area—even though it may concern mainly scientific subject-matters—not yet itself being a scientific theorem), there is no doubt that they assist understanding of the same and exert a clarifying influence. More recently, the technique has been adopted in the important case of *Faccenda Chicken v. Fowler,* in relation to confidential information acquired by employees: this is discussed at para. 3.31 *post* in this chapter and also in Chapter 4 at paras. 4.29ff.

EMPLOYEES

3.16 Actions brought by an employer against an ex-employee for subsequent improper use of confidential information acquired by him during his previous tenure of employment constitute one of the most important avenues whereby the law of confidential information has become developed. This is not altogether surprising. The situation arises, at least potentially, on a daily basis in commercial and industrial life. Many of the decisions already discussed in this chapter reflect its occurrence. But its very importance justifies a fuller analysis.

Ex-customers

3.17 The simple case on the facts, which will accordingly be dealt with first, is that of the ex-employee on the sales side walking out with a list of customers and then either soliciting those customers himself directly, or indirectly via his new employer or by selling the list to a rival. The Court has in the past tended to regard such information as inherently confidential (and hence protectible) even if the list does not exist in written tangible form but has been memorised by the ex-employee.

3.18 An early instance is to be found in *Robb v. Green*[22] in 1895. The plaintiff's business lay in procuring the eggs of game birds (particularly pheasants) and in the subsequent hatching, rearing and sale of such birds. He had numerous customers, mainly country gentlemen and their keepers, whose residences were spread out widely over the country. The defendant, his former manager, had surreptitiously copied the list of names and addresses and subsequently solicited their custom for his own business; he was held liable in damages. A similar approach was often taken in cases involving retail trades rounds—say that of a fishmonger, or dairyman as in *Wessex Dairies v. Smith*[23] (1935); given, for example, a large housing estate it may naturally be of considerable value to know which houses (a) are interested in salmon and turbot (b) never go beyond kippers and smoked haddock (c) buy fish merely for the cat and (d) eat meat and poultry only. A more unusual situation was presented in the *Coral Index* case cited in Table 2 (para. 3.02 *ante*), involving the previous office manager in charge of the Coral Index whereby Stock Exchange punters could gamble on whether the Financial Times Index would go up or down; the action failed here (at least at interlocutory stage) for the reason that no written list appeared to have been made, and as for memory a distinction had to be drawn between deliberate memorisation (which would be improper) and inevitable memorisation (which could hardly be helped, bearing in mind the very nature of the job).

3.19 Whether such a restrictive approach will continue to be applied in the future is by no means clear; bars on competition tend, in the widest

22 [1895] 2 Q.B. 315; 64 L.J.Q.B. 593; 73 L.T. 15; 11 T.L.R. 517.
23 [1935] 2 K.B. 80; 153 L.T. 185; 51 T.L.R. 439.

sense, to be looked at more narrowly nowadays than heretofore; and it can be argued, particularly in the case of the ordinary commodities of daily life, that all should be free to trade always with all the populace. The 1985 *Faccenda Chicken* decision, although not overruling as such the *Robb* line of authority, suggests that it would be unwise to assume henceforth that customer lists will automatically be regarded as possessing confidential quality. The *Coral Index* decision in 1970 can be looked at as being the straw in the wind in this respect; the Court there, by drawing the distinction between conscious and unconscious memorisation, was certainly not being over-astute in the former employer's favour.

Skilled employees

3.20 More complex situations can arise with employees engaged professionally on the technical or scientific side of a business. A balance has to be struck between the two conflicting principles:

(a) that an employer is entitled to protect his legitimate trade secrets; and
(b) that the employee cannot be prevented from continuing to practise his trade or profession.

3.21 The employee on the one hand may have been highly skilled already before he came to the employer—indeed, that may have been the very reason why he was hired in the first place. Moreover, he may have become more skilled during his employment in the natural course of his career developement; a person of this type is fully entitled to keep up-to-date with the progress of the art by reading technical journals, attending conferences and symposia, going on refresher courses and the like. The employer on the other hand may also have a somewhat exaggerated view of the degree of confidence extant in his own production techniques.

3.22 Similar complexity can arise with employees who, although not engaged directly with technical or scientific aspects, are nevertheless in positions of administrative or managerial responsibility where they acquire information of commercial value concerning their employer's business. For an unskilled employee, on the other hand, the conflict and hence the need to strike a balance may not arise at all, since it may be difficult to regard him as having a trade or profession as such.

3.23 In terms of the *Coco* elements of an action for breach of confidence, principle (a) above enters primarily into the first element (confidential quality, or not) and principle (b) into the second and third elements (obligation of confidence, or not; unauthorized use, or not, respectively). However, a clear demarcation between the three elements is not so easily drawn in cases of possible action for breach by employees (including ex-employees). Ordinary considerations of employment law supervene. It has also to be remembered that much of the case-law concerning employees pre-dates the *Coco* decision; hence the majority of the precedents are not couched in terms of the *Coco* analysis. Conceptually, it may be easiest to reconcile the *Coco* approach with the employee situation by looking primarily at the confidential quality issue; for if (1) the relevant information is held to lack confidential quality in the first place (because it forms instead part of the employee's own legitimate reservoir of skill and knowledge), then subsequent issues as to obligation and unauthorised use necessarily disappear; but if (2) the information *is* held to be confidential because it comes outside the bounds of that reservoir, then those subsequent issues do arise and have to be determined in turn. The remainder of this chapter will accordingly deal mainly with confidential quality, with treatment of other employee considerations (including permissible scope of restrictive covenants in respect of confidential material) being postponed to the succeeding Chapter 4.

Skill v. secrets

3.24 A clear dividing line was drawn in 1916 in the leading case of *Morris v. Saxelby*[24] in the following manner:

> "Trade secrets, the names of customers—all such things which in sound philosophical language are *denominated objective knowledge*—these may not be given away by a servant; they are his master's property and there is no rule of public interest which prevents transfer of them against his master's will being restrained. On the other hand, a man's *aptitudes, his skill, his dexterity, his manual or mental ability*—all those things which in sound philosophical language are not objective, but *subjective*—they may and ought not to be relinquished by a servant; they are not his master's property—they are his own property; they are himself." (at 714, emphasis added)

3.25 Lord Shaw's remarks here provide a fuller version of the same objective/subjective distinction which he drew a few years earlier in the equally well-known case of *Mason v. Provident Clothing and Supply*.[25] Other cases in this line of authority include *Amber Size & Chemical v. Menzel*[26] (manufacture of "Amber" size); *Litholite v. Travis &*

24 [1916] 1 A.C. 688; 85 L.J. Ch. 210; 114 L.T. 618; 32 T.L.R. 297.
25 [1913] A.C. 724; 82 L.J.K.B. 1153; 109 L.T. 449; 29 T.L.R. 727.
26 30 R.P.C. 433.

Insulators[27] (manufacture of electrical insulators); *Terry v. Reddaway*[28] (waterproof coverings for wires); *Sorbo Rubber Sponge Products v. Defries*[29] (manufacture of rubber sponge articles); *Reid and Sigrist v. Moss and Mechanism*[30] (gyroscopic turn indicators); *British Industrial Plastics v. Ferguson*[31] (aminoplastic moulding powders); *Triplex v. Scorah*[32] (manufacture of safety glass), as well as the *Yates Circuit Foil*[21] case already discussed (at para. 3.12); this list is not intended to be exhaustive in any event.

Acquisition during Employment

3.26 But it is clear that the mere acquisition of further skill and knowledge as such from the employer during the course of employment does not necessarly mean that any trade secret has been imparted. The point is taken in the early case of *Sir W. C. Leng v. Andrews*[33], where it was said:

> "That doctrine does not mean that an employer can prevent his employee from using the skill and knowledge in his trade or profession which he has learnt in the course of his employment by means of directions or instructions from the employer. That information *and that additional skill* he is entitled to use for the benefit of himself and the benefit of the public who gain the advantage of his *having had such admirable instruction.* The case in which the Court interferes for the purpose of protection is where use is made, not of the skill which the man may have acquired, but of the *secrets of the trade* or profession . . ." (at 773–4, emphases added)

3.27 Likewise, further skill and knowledge acquired by the employee from sources other than the employer, even though useful and valuable for purposes of the employer's business, may not necessarily become confidential in the hands of the employer. Indeed, if gleaned by the employee from publicly available sources, the knowledge may well, by definition, be intrinsically incapable of ranking as secret at all. This was the point taken in the *Triplex* case, as follows:

> ". . . That information which was open to the public—information which he acquired, as I have suggested, by reading technical papers and finding in a technical paper suggestions, possibly useful suggestions, with regard to the making of safety glass—it would be his duty to communicate to the Company; but to suggest that, because he communicated to the Company

27 30 R.P.C. 266, 532.
28 33 R.P.C. 269.
29 47 R.P.C. 454.
30 49 R.P.C. 461.
31 58 R.P.C. 1.
32 55 R.P.C. 21; [1938] Ch. 211; [1937] 4 All E.R. 693; 157 L.T. 576; 54 T.L.R. 90.
33 [1909] 1 Ch. 763.

> information which he had acquired in that way, he was to be *thereby debarred* from making any use of the information so acquired, seems to me to go far beyond what the law allows . . ." (at 28, emphasis added)

3.28 The employer may run into similar difficulty if he never makes it clear to the employee in the first place that he is being rendered privy to a trade secret. As pointed out in *Bjorlow (Great Britain) v. Minter*,[34] involving an allegedly secret process for the waterproofing of suède calf/kid:

> "I think it is a matter of strong comment, as regards the alleged secrecy, that quite plainly, according to the evidence, the Plaintiffs took *no steps whatever*, as far as I can see, to *impress* upon anybody that there was here any important secret which they desired to preserve." (at 324, emphasis added)

3.29 A frequently cited modern pair of contrasting cases as to the skill v. secrets distinction generally, is provided by *Underwater Welders and Repairers v. Street and Langthorne*[17] (in 1967) and *Printers and Finishers v. Holloway*[35] (in 1964). To quote from the subsequent analysis of the two in *United Sterling Corporation v. Felton and Mannion*[36]:

> ". . . it seems to me that the distinction between the two cases is this. In *Printers and Finishers* there was no secret feature of the plaintiff's flock printing process which was *readily separable from Holloway's general knowledge of the flock printing process* and from his *acquired skill* in manipulating a flock printing plant. This led Cross J. to the conclusion that a man of average intelligence and honesty would not think there was anything improper in Holloway subsequently placing his memory of particulars of the plaintiff's process at the disposal of his new employer. In *Underwater Welders* the learned judge reached the conclusion that, for the purposes of the motion before him, he ought to conclude that the Gardella process did involve *some particular secret characteristic* although it was not identified in the evidence before him; therefore, no doubt, such particular secret characteristic was *readily distinguishable from the managing director's general knowledge* of the business of cleaning ships' hulls." (at 172–3, emphasis added)

3.30 Much naturally depends, therefore, upon the precise circumstances of each individual case. Reconciliation of the conflicting interests of employer and employee is never easy, and the precise point at which the balance is to be struck may also change in any event from time to time; policy considerations have their role to play here, just as in many other branches of the law of confidentiality.

34 71 R.P.C. 321.
35 (No. 2) [1965] R.P.C. 239; [1964] F.S.R. 236; [1965] 1 W.L.R. 1; [1964] 3 All E.R. 731.
36 [1974] R.P.C. 162; [1973] F.S.R. 409.

Faccenda Chicken v. Fowler

3.31 In the recent case of *Faccenda Chicken v. Fowler*[37] the Court of first instance attempted a fresh synthesis of the principles applicable to assessment of the confidential quality of information imparted to and/or acquired by employees; the dispute concerned sales information by way of names and addresses of customers, timing of deliveries, prices paid and details of delivery routes taken, in the trade of selling fresh chickens to retailers; the principal defendant had been the plaintiff's former sales manager and largely instrumental in building up a successful van sales operation for him, prior to setting up his own competing business with the assistance of other former salesmen. The information was valuable, and of easily memorisable kind. No restrictive covenants had ever been taken from any of the employees. The Court suggested that information acquired by the employee during the course of employment could be split up into three categories, as follows:

(i) information which because of its trivial character or easy accessibility from public sources cannot be regarded by reasonable persons or by the law as confidential;
(ii) information which the employee must treat as confidential (either because he is expressly told it is so or because from its character it is obviously confidential) but which once learned necessarily remained in the employee's head and became part of his own skill and knowledge applied in the course of his employer's business; and
(iii) specific trade secrets which, even though necessarily requiring to be learnt by heart by the employee, could not possibly be lawfully used for anyone's benefit but the employer's.

3.32 It is as yet too early to tell whether the *Faccenda* analysis will become (in suitable cases for its application) a standard touchstone as to confidential quality. It is of course not entirely comprehensive in any event. An employer may be mistaken *in limine* as to what is already in the public domain in the particular art in question; public availability is essentially the converse of confidentiality, and as its area increases, so may (not necessarily must, since there may be a question as to the circumstances of the public availability) the area of confidentiality be correspondingly eroded. Alternatively, the employer may have failed to make it clear that he regarded the information as confidential at all; this was the pitfall in the *Bjorlow (Great Britain)* case mentioned above (at para. 3.28). But it does have the attraction of providing a kind of formula.

37 [1985] F.S.R. 105.

3.33 A possible example of future applicability can be seen in the case of secret formulae for liqueurs and the like. Assuming for purposes of argument that the monk is the employee of the monastery abbot (alternatively, taking the instance of the gin-distillery employee), then:

(i) the knowledge that herb X or seed Y gives flavour Z may well be available from standard works on botany and/or pharmacognosy;

(ii) the ability which the monk acquires over the years in achieving maximum efficiency for the extractive distillation of the active principles of herb X or seed Y from the appropriate plants or bushes in the monastery garden may well form just a mere part of his own skill and knowledge, and hence be transferable with him when he changes his Order;

(iii) the precise combination of herbs and/or seeds, and their respective relative amounts, which provide the unique quality of the liqueur in question and represent the key to the monastery's commercial success, may in contrast be a legally protectible trade secret.

CHAPTER 4

Obligation of Confidence

SITUATIONS

4.01 The situations in which an obligation of confidence arises may be, generally, conveniently grouped into:

(a) express contractual provision;
(b) employer/employee relations; and
(c) other miscellaneous situations.

EXPRESS CONTRACTUAL PROVISION

4.02 Express contractual provision will normally be present whenever a formal agreement, say a licence agreement, concerning the confidential information has been drawn up. There may be some uncertainty of course as regards the true scope of the agreement terms or as regards ancillary matters on which the agreement is silent—for example, as to what happens when the agreement expires, or upon bankruptcy of the licencee, or upon state requisition of the licencee's works, or failure to pay the royalties due. Much may depend on the degree of particularisation with which the agreement document has been drawn up; normal principles of contract law, for example those to the effect that the parties' prior negotiations do not generally rank as an aid to construction of the contract terms *(Prenn v. Simmonds*[1]*)*, or that the parties' conduct under the contract is likewise not an aid *(Schuler v. Wickman*[2]*)*, may also be applicable. But as to the central fact of the existence of confidence, and hence contractual obligation, there is unlikely to be very much doubt.

4.03 A good example of the problems arising on construction of an express contract is provided by the case of *Beecham Group v. Bristol Laboratories*,[3] involving the manufacture of semi-synthetic penicillins. The critical clause in the contract read:

1 [1971] 3 All E.R. 237.
2 [1973] 2 All E.R. 39
3 [1978] R.P.C. 521.

"Disclosures: Beecham hereby agrees: (1) to disclose and furnish to International all such particulars and information as it or its subsidiaries or affiliates may have concerning secret processes, secret methods, secret formulae, cultures, strains, enzymes and other confidential know-how and materials now owned by Beecham or its subsidiaries or affiliates relating to the subject matter;"

4.04 The eight nouns "secret processes . . . confidential know-how and materials" were clearly intended to provide a comprehensive net for all relevant information which the licensor (Beecham) had in this field, and of potential value to the licensee (Bristol). Did they suffice to catch also a confidential Beecham proposal to make a certain semi-synthetic penicillin (identified by the chemical formula of its constituent side-chain amino-acid)? The confidential proposal had in fact been communicated to Bristol in the normal course of implementation of the agreement—perhaps without any very serious thought on the part of Beecham as to whether it was embraced by the contract terms; in real life, a scientist tends not to have a lawyer constantly at his side. It was held not, essentially for the reason that in the pharmaceutical field—where so much is empirical and the properties of a compound are never known until it has actually been made and tested—information is that which is *in esse* rather than *in posse*. The eight nouns needed to be viewed, and construed, in that light. Nor did the mere fact that communication had actually occurred compel the conclusion that the information was embraced. It could perfectly well be regarded as gratuitous information, given to the other party on a common-sense basis so as to avoid duplication of research effort.

Equitable additions

4.05 The *Beecham Group* case illustrates another point as well—namely, as to how an equitable obligation of confidence can—in appropriate circumstances—be grafted on to contractual obligations. The equitable obligation can therefore affect the practical position of the parties, although it does this not so much by modifying the construction which would otherwise be given to the contract terms themselves but rather by working outside, and additional to, the contract.

4.06 Specifically, the contract here had an "entire agreement" clause, couched in as correspondingly comprehensive terms as the "information" clause already quoted, as follows:

"Entire Agreement and Amendments: This agreement contains the entire understanding of the parties with respect to the matter herein contained. There are *no* restrictions, promises, covenants or undertakings other than those expressly set forth herein, and *no* rights or duties on the part of either party hereto are to be *implied or inferred* beyond those expressly herein provided for." (emphasis added)

4.07 It might be expected, therefore, that there was no possibility of any further obligations being held to apply. Not so, since the proposal to make the semi-synthetic penicillin (which turned out subsequently to be the fore-runner of the leading antibiotic, amoxycillin) was outside the agreement terms in the first place; likewise the further information, on other proposed penicillins, which had also passed between the parties. On all this additional subject-matter, which had actually passed even though not contractually required to be passed, the equitable obligation of confidence imputed by the common law would have bitten. As put by Lord Diplock in the House of Lords:

"This information would no doubt be confidential in the sense that it was *not to be communicated to outsiders,* lest their knowledge of what Beechams thought to be the most promising line of research might help them anticipate Beechams in finding a new penicillin whose exceptional therapeutic qualities would justify protection by a selection patent."[4] (emphasis added)

4.08 An equitable obligation of this kind would also have relevance as regards pre-contract negotiations. During the course of such negotiations confidential information may well have been mutually disclosed by the parties which falls outside the scope of the eventual contract; the potential licensee may, for example, decide in the end that he is really only interested in using the furnace for the manufacture of glass fibres and not for the manufacture of rockwool fibres as well, even though both techniques were shown to him in confidence when he first toured the licensor's factory, and have the concluded agreement limited accordingly. So far as rockwool is concerned, it is likely that there would then be an enforceable equitable obligation against the licensee in respect of both (a) disclosure of the technique by the licensee to outside third parties and (b) subsequent use of the technique by the licensee himself in years to come when he changes his mind as to commercial prospects.

4.09 Similarly, if the negotiations prove abortive and no contract is eventually executed, equitable obligations would be likely to bite on the material revealed at this stage. It is of course frequently impossible to persuade a licensee or the like to take a complete pig in a poke. He may well—and quite reasonably—insist upon gaining some degree of knowledge about the body of confidential information involved before deciding whether to enter into an agreement to pay royalties or to purchase.

4 At 578.

Lacunae

4.10 As for the instance when the express contract between the parties is silent on the point in issue—in other words, the instance where the agreement, although perfectly good in its own right, has failed to make provision for all the matters which it should have done—a pair of cases illustrating contrasting approaches of the Court may be taken.

4.11 In the first, *Torrington Manufacturing v. Smith & Sons,*[5] the agreement provided that in the event of unilateral determination by the licensor (which had taken place) the licensee should retain the right to use the licensor's confidential information in the manufacture of articles (fans) the subject of the licensor's patents and registered designs. But the licensee was concerned at this time to use that confidential information in the manufacture of other fans which were *not* the subject of any such patent or registered design. The agreement, although exhaustive in other respects, had a complete lacuna on this point. What was the position? It was held that the licensee's rights in this respect had accordingly to be determined by the general law, and that hence the licensee could be restrained from deriving any advantage from information originally received by him exclusively for the purposes of the agreement. The equitable obligation could be added on to the contractual obligation, just as in the example discussed in *Beecham Group v. Bristol Laboratories* (paras 4.03ff *supra)* of possible disclosure to third parties of the gratuitously passed information.

4.12 In the second case, *Regina Glass Fibre v. Schuller,*[6] an existing clause in the agreement was stretched so as to bridge the gap instead. The agreement, a combined patent and confidential information agreement, had expired in due course by effluxion of time. The issue was whether the licensee had a continued right, post-termination, to use confidential information as to improvements which the licensor had communicated to him whilst the contract was running; the contract lacked any proper post-termination provisions. The matter was one of considerable seriousness to the licensee, since if he were unable to continue using those improvements his whole business would have to close down; they had, in the course of time, become essential rather than just preferable options. The improvements clause read, in material parts:

> "*During the continuance of this Agreement* Mr. Schuller shall be entitled to continue research in connection with glass fibre making but if he shall make develop acquire or become entitled to any improvement upon the process

5 [1966] R.P.C. 285.
6 [1972] R.P.C. 229; [1972] F.S.R. 141.

> the same shall forthwith be communicated to the Company and if required to do so Mr. Schuller shall grant to the Company for its own use only . . . the free and exclusive rights to use the same in the British Commonwealth (except Canada) and other territories as aforesaid." (emphasis added)

4.13 It was held that the preamble "During the continuance of this agreement" related to the time during which the licensee could require a grant to be made and not to the time for which the right, when granted, was to last. The Court was clearly heavily influenced by the potential disaster which would otherwise occur to the licensee. To cite the judgement of Denning M.R.:

> "That is a result which cannot have been intended by the parties. Rather than give the agreement such a construction, I would give it the meaning that the right to use is to be granted to the company indefinitely, without being liable to termination." (at 234)

Termination

4.14 The *Regina Glass Fibre* case illustrates vividly the need for the draftsman of a confidential information agreement to consider, and deal properly with, the status of any information which has passed between the parties under the agreement once that agreement has come to an end (as it normally does sooner or later). Both information communicated initially, and during the running of the agreement, may have to be accommodated. In the absence of any express provision, the *Regina Glass Fibre* decision makes it clear that there is no automatic termination under common law of the right to use communicated information once the agreement itself has terminated.

4.15 In the past, this aspect of the confidential information agreement has tended to be ignored. Thus, a few years prior to *Regina Glass Fibre,* Lord Upjohn in *National Broach & Machine v. Churchill Gear Machines*[7] observed, in relation to the "improvements" clause of a combined patent licence and confidential information agreement which on its strict wording led to a result (on termination) which seemed harsh upon the licensee, that:

> "But in drafting Clause 10 the draftsman probably never really contemplated what would happen in the closing months of the agreement. His mind was fixed upon the situation arising during the currency of the agreement . . ." (at 112)

In short, parties now neglect this question at their peril.

7 [1967] R.P.C. 99; [1966] F.S.R. 394; [1967] 1 W.L.R. 384.

EMPLOYER/EMPLOYEE RELATIONS

4.16 The relation between employer and employee may well be covered as such in the employee's contract of employment (in which case there is overlap—from the classification standpoint—with the express contractual kind of situation). Almost certainly that is to be expected today in the case of a scientific, technical or other skilled employee working in a professional or quasi-professional position in a substantial organisation—a commercial company, a nationalised industry, the civil service, a research council or institute and the like. The general law can then be regarded as stepping in simply to curb any excessively wide restrictions in the contract, or to bridge any gaps in the same, in relation to confidence. Alternatively, if the contract of employment is quite silent as to the matter of confidential information (as may well be so in case of employees of lower rank or ones who would not normally be expected to have any access to confidential information, say the canteen hand), then the general law necessarily has entire control in this respect. These matters will now be elaborated upon.

4.17 So far as contractual employer/employee relationships are concerned, the issue of obligation is obviously closely bound up with that of confidential quality in the first place. If the information, although labelled by the employer as "confidential", is not truly capable of being so regarded, then naturally an employee can hardly be under any obligation concerning it; any contract provision having such effect is unlikely to be enforceable. Similarly, if the contract purports to put the employee under an obligation of such kind as may unreasonably interfere with the subsequent normal practice elsewhere of the employee's profession, as opposed to restraining him from revealing or using trade secrets properly so called of the employer, an excessively wide restrictive covenant is liable to be struck down, as being injurious to the public interest, in this area of employment law just as much as it may be in other areas where little question as to trade secrecy (apart maybe from the names of customers) could arise—say, for example, employees in the fields of hairdressing, tailoring, legal executives, or song-writing. Reference should be made to standard works on contract and employment law for a fuller treatment of the general position.

4.18 For trade secrets, width of permissible restriction as regards the taking-up of future employment needs to be distinguished also from width of permissible restriction as regards maintenance of the previous employer's secrets. Long (or even perpetual) times may be justified in the latter instance, but not the former.

4.19 Further distinction may be needed to be drawn between the ex-employee who wishes to sell information acquired during his previous employment (assuming that it is of knowledge and experience type—say, to repeat the example given in Chapter 3, the skill acquired by the monk over several years in maximising the yield from extractive distillation of the monastery's herbs) and the ex-employee who just wishes to continue to use that information in his new employment. This could be done either by labelling the information as a trade secret strictly so-called for sale purposes, but merely as knowledge and experience for continued use purposes; alternatively, by regarding the obligation of the ex-employee as higher in the former as compared to the latter case.

Covenant cases

4.20 Many of the cases already mentioned in Chapter 3 in relation to confidential quality (or not) of the information and knowledge acquired by the employee during the course of his employment arose originally in the context of a dispute as to validity (or not) of a restrictive covenant weighing the employee down with burdensome restrictions and obligations as regards future employment by others. In the present chapter, in contrast, the matter is approached more from the standpoint of the intrinsic validity (or not) of the restriction or obligation—that is to say, assuming confidential quality of the information in the first place. But the demarcation is not exact, for reasons already given in Chapter 3.

4.21 In *Morris v. Saxelby*,[8] for instance, there was in issue the validity of a clause in an engineer's service contract requiring that:

> ". . . he will not at any time during a period of seven years from the date of his ceasing to be employed by the company whether under this agreement or otherwise howsoever either in the United Kingdom of Great Britain of Ireland carry on either as principal agent servant or otherwise alone or jointly or in connection with any other person firm or company or be concerned or assist directly or indirectly whether for reward or otherwise in the sale or manufacture of pulley blocks hand overhead runways electric overhead runways hand overhead travelling cranes or any part thereof or be concerned or assist as aforesaid in any business connected with such sale or manufacture."

A preceding clause, requiring that he:

> ". . . shall not during his employment nor at any time afterwards divulge nor communicate to any person corporation or firm any information which he may receive or obtain in relation to the company affairs and customers and all instructions drawings notes and memoranda made by the employee or which may come into his possession while engaged as aforesaid shall be the exclusive property of the company." (at 690)

8 [1916] 1 A.C. 688; 85 L.J. Ch. 210; 114 L.T. 618; T.L.R. 297.

would, in contrast, although not actually at issue in the litigation, have had a much better chance of being upheld. The former clause has the effect of excluding the employee from subsequently practising his professional skill, in the field involved, for a considerable fraction of his working life; the latter, at least on its face, is restricted to subsequent improper dissemination of the employer's secrets.

4.21a *Mason v. Provident Clothing and Supply*[9] involved a covenant in the contract of a representative for a company supplying clothing and the like on a "check and credit" system; an attempt to justify a three-year restriction on subsequent employment in the same field, on a trade secrets basis, failed. It was pointed out that:

> "It appears, however, from the rules for canvassers, which are printed, that what is required is simply a fair share of intelligence and industry, with the accompaniment of a persuasive manner." (at 742)

4.22 *Commercial Plastics v. Vincent*[10] involved the employment contract of a plastics technologist in the calendered plastics sheeting industry. It was held that there was inherently confidential information extant for which protection could be claimed:

> "The defendant would not remember the minute details recorded in the mixing specifications, but he would be likely to remember in general terms what was the problem and what was the solution . . . the defendant would be *likely,* when the need arose, to *dredge up from the recesses of his memory* the particular secret which, while he was in the plaintiffs' employ, he had found appropriate to deal with the customer's requirements." (at 642)

The restrictive covenant failed, however, since it was wider than needed in the circumstances—being, for example, world-wide whereas in fact protection outside the United Kingdom was not required by the employer.

4.23 Other cases in this vein include *Technograph Printed Circuits v. Chalwyn*[11] (former development manager for manufacturers of printed circuit boards) where a two-year restrictive covenant against subsequent employment with a competitor except with consent in terms of:

> "Such consent shall not however be unreasonably withheld" (at 343)

was (in interlocutory proceedings) regarded as proper; *Standex International v. Blades*[12] (former employee of director status, in mould-

9 [1913] A.C. 274; 82 L.J. K.B. 1153; 109 L.T. 449; 29 T.L.R. 727.
10 [1965] 1 Q.B. 623.
11 [1967] R.P.C. 339; [1967] F.S.R. 307.
12 [1976] F.S.R. 114.

engraving field); *Potters-Ballotini v. Weston-Baker*[13] (former general manager and works manager of ballotini manufacturers); and *Underwater Welders & Repairers v. Street and Longthorne*[14] (former diver in employment of licensee).

Non-covenant cases

4.24 Leading cases on the instance where the common law may be prepared to imply an obligation of confidence over and above any explicit terms of the employment contract include *Robb v. Green*,[15] *Wessex Dairies v. Smith*[16] (already mentioned in Chapter 3 at para. 3.18 in relation to customer lists) and *Hivac v. Park Royal Scientific Instruments*.[17] *Hivac* concerned highly skilled employees (in the manufacture of miniature valves for deaf aids) who worked in their spare time for a newly founded rival concern. It was held that this was in breach of an implied term of their employment contract, even though it was clear that in fact no item of confidential information had been disclosed or utilised by the employees involved. *Faccenda Chicken v. Fowler*, discussed later at paras 4.29ff, is also in this category.

Good faith

4.25 The justification for the intervention of the common law in such instances can be regarded as rooted in the inherent duty of good faith of an employee towards his employer. And the more senior the employee is so may the level of that duty correspondingly increase. The company director or the like is liable to be viewed more narrowly in this connection than the canteen hand or furnace man.

4.26 Thus in *Worthington Pumping Engine v. Moore*[18] (a patent case), the defendant was the general manager of the United Kingdom branch of the United States parent corporation; the relationship between him and the parent was described as being of:

> ". . . the closest and most confidential character . . ."

The Court had little difficulty in concluding that patents which he had taken out during the course of his employment in the field were held by him as trustee on behalf of the corporation, and expressed itself in wide terms as regards the ownership of rights in technological improvements:

13 [1977] R.P.C. 202
14 [1968] R.P.C. 498; [1967] F.S.R. 194; [1967] Lloyd's Rep. 364.
15 [1895] 2 Q.B. 315; 64 L.J. Q.B. 593; 73 L.T. 15; 11 T.L.R. 517.
16 [1935] 2 K.B. 80; 153 L.T. 185; 51 T.L.R. 439.
17 [1946] Ch. 169; [1946] 1 All E.R. 350; 115 L.J. Ch. 241; 172 L.T. 422; 62 T.L.R. 231.
18 20 R.P.C. 41; 19 T.L.R. 84.

"I think that he would not have been acting in accordance with the *good faith implied in his contract* had he kept back *new ideas or details of construction* suggested or carried out in the ordinary course of business between the parties . . . with a view to his personal profit at the expense of the Plaintiff Corporation. It appears to me that the degree of good faith due from the Defendant to the Plaintiff Company was little, if at all. less than that *required from a partner* towards the firm of which he is a member." (at 46, emphasis added)

4.27 In *Bell v. Lever*[19] (outside secret speculations of directors in the cocoa market), there is the well-known passage in Lord Blanesbury's speech:

". . . the company has no concern in his profit and cannot make him accountable for it unless it appears—this is the essential qualification—that in earning that profit he has made use either of the property of the company or of some *confidential information* which has come to him as a director of the company." (at 194, emphasis added)

4.28 An example in ordinary trade secret law of the *Bell v. Lever* principle is to be found in *Aubanel and Alabaster v. Aubanel*[20] (manufacture of sectional pipe coverings), wherein it was said:

"It seems to me that the *dangers* of a director using confidential information (acquired as director) to assist him in the competing business and the *difficulties of avoiding* such use of any confidential information, are *considerable,* but I must accept the proposition that such competition is permissible. But solicitation of the company's customers is another matter. The function of a director is to supervise the carrying on of the company's business for the benefit of the company and its shareholders and to advance these interests. How can it be compatible with this function that the director should depreciate the value and progress of the company's business by asking the company's customers to cease to deal with the company and to deal with him in his competing business instead? It seems to me that this *cannot be proper behaviour by a director.*" (at 346–7, emphasis added)

Faccenda Chicken v. Fowler[21]

4.29 The Court of first instance had attempted in this contemporary decision (as already mentioned in Chapter 3 at para. 3.31) a fresh synthesis as to the principles applicable to assessment to confidential quality (or not) of information acquired by the employee in the course of his employment. In the Court of Appeal, a wider and more comprehensive synthesis of the employee's position (including also the impact of the employee's duty of fidelity) was enunciated. Again, it is not at present clear whether the approach laid down is always to govern in future; there

19 [1932] A.C. 161.
20 66 R.P.C. 343.
21 [1985] F.S.R. 105 (High Court); The Times, 11 December 1985 (Court of Appeal).

is still the prospect of a definitive House of Lords decision to come. The inter-relation of the Faccenda approach to the substantial body of traditional case-law on the topic, canvassed earlier in this Chapter, has still to be fully worked out. But the formula is there.

4.30 The relevant principles were held by the Court of Appeal to be:

(1) Where the parties were or had been linked by a contract of employment, the employee's obligations were to be determined by the contract between him and the employer.

(2) In the absence of any express term, the employee's obligations in respect of the use and disclosure of information were the subject of implied terms.

(3) While the employee remained in the employment, the obligations were included in the implied term which imposed a duty of good faith on the employee. It was to be noted that the extent of the duty of fidelity varied according to the nature of the contract and would be broken if an employee made or copied a list of his employer's customers for use after his employment ended, or deliberately memorised such a list.

(4) The implied term which imposed an obligation on the employee after the determination of his employment was more restricted than that imposed by the duty of fidelity. The obligation not to use or disclose information might cover secret processes of manufacture, designs or special methods of construction, and other information of a sufficiently high degree of confidentiality as to amount to a trade secret. The obligation did not extend to information only "confidential' in that any unauthorised disclosure would be a clear breach of the duty of fidelity.

(5) To determine whether any particular item of information fell within the implied term so as to prevent its use or disclosure by an employee after his employment had ceased, it was necessary to consider all the circumstances of the case.

The principles thus draw a distinction between the covenant case (principle (1)) and the non-covenant case (principles (2)–(5)).

4.31 As regards the former, the Court went on to say that a restrictive covenant would not be enforced, i.e. would not be regarded as valid by the Court, unless the protection sought was reasonably necessary to protect a trade secret or to prevent some personal influence over customers being abused in order to entice them away. This is quite reasonable. The earlier law would also tend to decline to enforce any covenant which went beyond the legitimate interest being required to be protected of the employer.

4.32 As regards the latter, the Court elaborated in particular as to the matter which would be relevant under principle (5) in relation to "all the circumstances". These were:

(a) The nature of the employment. A high obligation of confidentiality might be imposed where the employment was in a capacity where "confidential" material was habitually handled.
(b) The nature of the information. Information would only be protected if it could properly be classed as a trade secret or as material which was in all the circumstances of such a highly confidential nature as to require the same protection as a trade secret.
(c) Whether the employer impressed on the employee the confidentiality of the information.
(d) Whether the relevant information could be easily isolated from other information which the employee was free to use or disclose. The separability of information was not conclusive, but the fact that the alleged "confidential" information was part of a package and that the remainder of the package was not confidential was likely to throw light on whether the information in question was really a trade secret.

4.33 They left open the question of whether an ex-employee who wished to sell information acquired during his previous employment should be treated differently from one who merely wanted to continue to use the information for his own benefit in the practice of his trade or profession. This point has already been mentioned. It is suggested that there is certainly substantial justification for taking a less liberal attitude towards the selling ex-employee than the using ex-employee.

4.34 On the facts in *Faccenda* (already given at para. 3.31 and involving the continued use of sales information by a senior ex-employee who had made no covenant in this respect in his previous employment contract), it was held that there was no implied term restricting such use.

4.35 *Faccenda* can accordingly be regarded as showing that the Court, in the present judicial climate, is not over-anxious to inhibit the bettering by employees of their position in life. A striking illustration of this, albeit in a rather different context to that of the *Faccenda* kind, is to be found in the other recent decision (1982) of *G.D. Searle v. Celltech,*[22] where information as to the names, aptitudes, characters, and specialisations of the plaintiff's employees (highly qualified research scientists in the genetic

22 [1982] F.S.R. 92.

engineering field) was refused protection—notwithstanding the great commercial value of the information to a rival concern who was trying to hire personnel in the field with a view to rapid build-up of a smooth-running competitive research team. The point was taken that there is now no rule of law or equity which restrains a competitor from seeking out the servants of another and offering them employment, provided that he does not go so far in his solicitation as positively to procure a breach of the servant's contract. The subject-matter involved (names, aptitudes and the like) went really to assisting this seeking-out, rather than to filching any property as such properly belonging to the employer.

OTHER MISCELLANEOUS OBLIGATIONS

4.36 In the third and miscellaneous group, the law has developed over the years essentially through individual precedents. Day-to-day commerce can give rise to an almost infinite variety of relationships between business parties; some are, inherently, of more private nature than others. Yet frequently nothing is stipulated, either in writing or orally, as to confidentiality.

Business relationships

4.37 Consider a typical export transaction. A Governmental import agency in a remote underdeveloped country writes to a United Kingdom confirming house enquiring whether it can accept an order for 20,000 bicycles; the latter, because it lacks itself any connection with manufacturers of products of this kind, forwards the enquiry to another confirming house (possibly in return for a commission should the business go through). Has there been a breach of confidence by the first confirming house? It would seem unlikely, unless of course the original enquiry had been specifically marked "Confidential". It is difficult, in the ordinary course of events, to see what proprietary interest the import agency could have in keeping secret the knowledge that it wished to purchase bicycles; indeed, if anything, the publicity might encourage a more competitive tender. *Contra,* perhaps if the enquiry had been for 20,000 machine guns instead; almost certainly, if the enquiry had been for mustard-gas, because of the unfavourable publicity which might then accrue to that country's Government should the news that it was interested in buying chemical warfare weapons leak out. The question of whether there would then be a defence of "public interest" available to an action for breach of confidence is quite separate.

4.38 An example of an ordinary business communication was involved in *Tett v. Drake & Gorham*.[23] The plaintiffs (who were water-softening engineers) had written a letter to suppliers of mineral substances for use in water-softening plant, enquiring as to prices and adding:

> "We have been using a certain type of mineral for some time past and have not found it completely satisfactory . . ." (at 493)

The letter was divulged to a third party, competitors of the plaintiffs, who publicised its contents at the Ideal Home Exhibition, Olympia and thereby affected the plaintiffs' orders at the same. It was held that there had been no breach of confidence. According to the report:

> "It was a somewhat indiscreet letter for the plaintiffs to write and in the absence of it being marked private or confidential it could not be assumed that it was either made or accepted as a confidential communication." (at 495)

Bankers

4.39 The position of the banker is also often of some importance. It was discussed in *Tournier v. National Provincial and Union Bank of England*.[24] The plaintiff there was a travelling salesman and a customer of the bank, but his account was in overdraft; the bank had drawn a cheque in favour of the plaintiff, in amount well above the overdraft, but the plaintiff had paid this over to a bookmaker instead. This information was conveyed by the bank to the plaintiff's employers, who promptly gave him notice. Had the bank exceeded the bounds in so acting? On the first page of the pass book issued by the bank to the plaintiff there was (as usual) the statement that:

> "The officers of the Bank are bound to secrecy as regards the transactions of its customers." (at 463)

It was held that they had. After pointing out that there could be circumstances in which disclosure could be enforced for other reasons, Atkin L.J. continued:

> "But the bank is entitled to secure itself in respect of liabilities it incurs to the customer, or the customer to it in respect of liabilities to third parties in respect of the transactions it conducts for or with the customer. It is *difficult to hit upon a formula which will define the maximum of obligation which must necessarily be implied.* But I think it safe to say that the obligation not to disclose information such as I have mentioned is subject to the qualification that the bank have the right to disclose such information when, and to the extent to which it is *reasonably necessary for the protection of the bank's*

23 [1928–35] Macg. Cop. Cas. 492.
24 [1924] 1 K.B. 461; 93 L.J. 449; 130 L.T. 682; 40 T.L.R. 214.

> *interests,* either as against their customer or as against third parties in respect of transactions of the bank for or with their customer, or for protecting the bank, or persons interested, or the public against fraud or crime. I have already stated the obligation as an obligation not to disclose without the customer's consent." (at 486, emphasis added)

4.40 It follows from the Court's final comment that where the customer asks the bank to provide a reference there is, in principle, an implied consent to disclose information in relation to his account. The question of precisely how far the bank can go in such case—for example, can it reveal the fact that five years ago it had to "bounce" a cheque drawn by the customer, knowing that such revelation would cast doubt upon the customer's credit-worthiness—is often one of some nicety.

4.41 In cases involving bank fraud or the like, a sterner approach may be taken. Thus, in *Bankers Trust v. Shapira*,[25] a third party bank with whom the defendants had assertedly deposited some of the fraud proceeds was compelled to give discovery of all relevant transactions and correspondence. Lord Denning commented:

> "Owing to his fraud, he is disentitled from relying on the confidential relationship between him and the bank." (at 1282)

4.42 The Banking Act 1979[26] has a limited degree of statutory impact in addition. Under section 19 of this Act, there are certain restrictions on the subsequent disclosure of customer information obtained by the Bank of England in exercise of its general supervisory jurisdiction under the Act.

Partners

4.43 Some other common situations also merit consideration. Relations between business partners are likely to be taken as fiduciary, in line with the *Worthington Pumping Engine* dicta (see para. 4.26) even if no formal partnership agreement exists; hence information as to the secret ingredients used by a pair of Cornish farmers' wives in the manufacture of their well-known "Carantock" pasties or "Indian Queens" violets perfume cannot be revealed by one to the detriment of the other; even the state of next year's order books on these products might be protected.

Professional advisers

4.44 Likewise, in relations between professional advisers and their

25 [1980] 1 W.L.R. 1274.
26 1979 c. 37.

clients; the surveyor who is instructed by a local politician to negotiate the purchase of a derelict farm in a Green Belt area because the latter has got wind of an impending change in regional planning policy under which that land would be re-zoned for housing, to his great potential profit, cannot publicise that news; nor can the stockbroker, instructed by his client to go out and buy a large stake in a publicly quoted company, immediately announce that news and the identity of his client to the world at large. This is so even in the absence of any formal contract between the professional man and his client—which is often absent in any event, particularly if the arrangement was entered into over the telephone. The obligation is inherent in the nature of the relation.

Officious bystander

4.45 In *Coco v. Clark*,[27] the Court attempted to enunciate a general approach to the question of implied obligation of confidence in terms of the notional officious bystander. This can be of value in instances where the arrangements between the parties are of a kind falling outside any of the existing precedents;

> "If the reasonable man is overworked, so is the officious bystander; but just as he provides a convenient touchstone for implied terms in contracts, so I think he may perform some useful function in relation to the implied obligation of confidence. If he had said to the parties at the outset, 'Do you not think that you ought to have an express agreement that everything you are discussing is confidential', I think the parties would have testily suppressed him with a common *'But it obviously is'*." (at 50, emphasis added)

4.46 The plaintiff here had done some research (as already mentioned in Chapter 2) on a new moped design; he had had a batch of pistons to his design made for him. The defendant company had expressed interest, and over the course of the next three months the plaintiff showed them his prototype and also supplied them with such relevant information, drawings and other aids towards production of the moped such as a list of possible suppliers of parts. The defendant company in its turn did a certain amount of work also on the plaintiff's ideas, and also put forward before him certain draft documents regulating the financial and other arrangements between them. These were never signed, however; nor were terms otherwise agreed between them.

4.47 In these circumstances, the Court had little difficulty in coming to a conclusion on behalf of the plaintiff so far as the existence of the legal obligation was concerned:

27 [1969] R.P.C. 41; [1968] F.S.R. 415.

"The *circumstances of the disclosure* in this case seem to me to be *redolent of trust and confidence*. Business men naturally concentrate on their business, and very sensibly do not constantly take legal advice before opening their mouths or writing a letter, so that business may flow and not stagnate. I think the court, despite the caution which must be exercised before implying any obligation, must be ready to make those implications upon which the sane and fair conduct of business is likely to depend.

. . .

In the case before me I would imply a term if there were a contract, and so, *a fortiori,* I imply the equitable obligation." (at 51, emphasis added)

NEGLIGENCE

4.48 Negligence can be regarded as something of a postcript to the general topic of obligation of confidence. A simple example is represented by the case of the licensee under a confidential information licence agreement who carelessly reveals too much concerning the secret process to a third party visitor to his factory, or who leaves exposed on his desk at the close of the day a document revealing the vital formula which is then picked up that evening by the cleaners and passed on to another rival. This is not to suggest that such occurrences are frequent. A licensee who is paying a substantial royalty for the use of confidential information is usually at pains to safeguard his investment.

4.49 Where there is a formal contract governing the use of the confidential information, it is naturally likely that there will be present an express term requiring the licensee (or the like) to maintain confidentiality of the relevant material. Thus, the contract in the *Beecham Group* case (paras. 4.03–07 *supra*) also contained a provision to the effect that:

"Any and all secret processes, secret methods, secret formulae, cultures, strains, enzymes and other confidential know-how and materials relating to the Subject Matter disclosed or furnished by Beecham to International . . . shall, for a period of five years following the date of this agreement be *maintained in confidence by International* to the best of its ability, . . ."

Accordingly, a negligent act by International along the lines indicated above would have involved a contractual breach in any event. That breach would have given the licensor a right to sue for damages or other relief.

4.50 But where there is no associated contractual breach, then reliance may have to be placed instead (to the extent possible) on an action for negligence arising from a common law duty of care in respect of the confidential information. Thus, in the *Beecham Group* case, this avenue might have been the only one available in the event of possible loss by International of gratuitously communicated confidential information (coming outside the formal contractual definition contained in this clause) on which only an equitable obligation of confidence would have arisen.

4.51 The commercial case of *Weld-Blundell v. Stephens*[28] involved a letter written by an investor to an accountant concerning a requested investigation into the affairs of a company into which he had placed a substantial sum of money, and containing defamatory comments in respect of some of its present management. It was held that a duty to keep secret the contents of the letter had arisen, and that such duty had been breached by the accountant's omission in this respect; the omission had led to libel damages being awarded to the defamed persons against the investor.

4.52 There would seem in principle no reason why the *Weld-Blundell* approach should not be extended from the arena of commercial secrets to the arena of technological secrets. But there is a shortage of modern authority in the latter field, notwithstanding the fact that *Weld-Blundell* was decided as far back as 1920—over 60 years ago. To fill the lacuna, the Law Commission in its draft Breach of Confidence Bill for the overall statutory regulation of the topic suggested the introduction of specific provision covering negligent disclosure or use (see Appendix).

4.53 Reference may be made finally in this connection to the important 1985 European case of *Adams v. Commission of the European Communities*,[29] in relation to the duty of care owed by a third party recipient of confidential commercial information to his source. The plaintiff here, while still an employee, had furnished to the Commission certain documents concerning alleged anti-competitive practices by his employer, as a result of which the latter had incurred a substantial fine under Article 86 of the Treaty of Rome for abuse of dominant position. The employer naturally sought to ascertain from the Commission the identity of their source; the Commission in turn gave the employer copies of the documents, insufficiently masked (since they were unfamiliar with procedures within the employer's offices for distribution of this kind of document) to prevent an inference as to identity being drawn; they also subsequently confirmed the correctness of the employer's inference. It was held by the European Court of Justice that there was a duty of care on the part of the Commission to keep the informant's identity secret,

28 [1920] A.C. 956.
29 [1986] 2 WLR 367

which had been broken in the circumstances and damages were awarded accordingly.

4.54 With the increasing legal regulation of commercial activities in the United Kingdom in recent times, this decision may well point the way ahead for similar expansion of the law here, quite apart from any statutory intervention.

CHAPTER 5

Unauthorised Use

OCCURRENCE

5.01 Given that the first two elements of the *Coco v. Clark*[1] formula (information of confidential quality + obligation of confidence) are fulfilled, it is usually fairly clear as to whether or not there has been unauthorised use. In the absence of permission from the proprietor of the confidential information (plaintiff), use by the defendant of the confidential information for his own commercial profit (whether by selling, soliciting, consulting or other activity) is naturally likely to rank as unauthorised. Usually the question is, rather, whether or not the defendant can set up a legitimate defence to the complaint of unauthorised use; in other words, what limitations can be put on the proprietor's otherwise unfettered right to authorise (or not to authorise as the case may be) any use of the confidential information. In the broadest sense, these limitations can be grouped under three heads:

(a) those based on expiration of confidence;
(b) those based on the public interest;
(c) those based on remoteness.

EXPIRATION

Entry into public domain

5.02 Expiration can occur once the allegedly confidential information has moved (intentionally or unintentionally) out of the private or secret and into the public domain. There are a multiplicity of possible modes of such entry. But to take a simple example first, current advertisements of certain spirits and liqueurs often refer to the secret combinations of herbs or the like which have been used in their manufacture. Thus, in a 1984 advertisement for a well-known brand of gin it was asserted:

> "Then in the final distillation, juniper berries, angelica root and coriander seeds are combined with a secret selection of herbs. The exact recipe of which is known only to six people. And the result is a gin of extraordinary clarity and brilliance, with a flavour and fragrance all of its own."

1 [1969] R.P.C. 41; [1968] F.S.R. 415.

And in a comparable one for a liqueur of the brand already mentioned in Chapter 2 in connection with the decision in *Lecouterier v. Rey*[2]:

> "Only three people know the secrets of the 130 herbs in Green Chartreuse."

5.03 But suppose that a recalcitrant monk were to depart from the monastery, following some internal dispute, and reveal publicly in the course of a sermon the combination of herbs used in the liqueur; alternatively, suppose that a consulting analytical chemist with a taste for spirits and some spare time available were to be able to deduce with the aid of his modern chromatographic equipment that residues of chemicals A, B, C were to be found in the gin, strongly suggesting that the combination of berries, roots and seeds was D, E, F, and were to publish his results in a scientific journal. It would be difficult in both cases for the original owners of the secrets to take any action against any other manufacturers or members of the public at large who were to take advantage of the information. The substratum of any action against the new users, the confidential information itself, would have vanished. The fact that in no sense could it be said that the original owners had permitted the use would be immaterial.

5.04 This is not to deny the possibility of the abbot suing the monk for the harm caused to the monastery by his default—even though that might well be fruitless in the long run so far as gaining any effective recompense to the monastery for the damage to their sales. As for the analytical chemist, however, the distillery's difficulty would be that it could be argued that by the very act of publicising the secret nature of the ingredients it was presenting the analytical chemist with a challenge—an implied invitation—to exercise his skill and ascertain the secret; hence that there was an implied consent to publication of the secret, once so found out.

5.05 Other modes of entry into the public domain include deliberate voluntary disclosure by the owner of the confidential information (which is self-explanatory); independent voluntary disclosure by a third party who has come across (say in the course of his own research work) the same item of information and has decided to publish it; disclosure in response to statutory requirements (for example, labelling requirements under the Food and Drugs Act 1955[3] or Medicines Act 1968[4]); gradual leaking-out of constituent items of information over the years until eventually a clear picture of the whole can be assembled (as in the gradual

2 27 R.P.C. 268.
3 4 & 5 Eliz. II c. 16.
4 1968 c. 67.

cracking of a scientific problem, say the crystalline structure of DNA, or a spy mystery); and disclosure among too large a proportion of the relevant public. There can of course be others.

Exclusive distribution

5.06 Extreme examples of an over-wide circle of distribution can be seen in some of the cases concerning Letters Patent for inventions. The point arises here because prior-dated documents of confidential (as opposed to publicly available) character are excluded from the corpus of prior art capable of being relied on in an attack on the validity of the patent. Thus, in *Dalrymple's Application*[5] a technical bulletin concerning the manufacture of baking tins with non-stick coatings and marked on its outer cover with the words "CONFIDENTIAL—not to be published" and on its first page with the words "ALL RIGHTS RESERVED—PRIVATE AND CONFIDENTIAL—The Bulletin is issued to you as a member. Its contents are strictly confidential, and must not be disclosed to non-members." had been sent to all 1,079 members of the British Baking Industries Research Association, eight different Government Departments and various other scientific workers and research organisations. It was held (not surprisingly) that the bulletin was incapable of being regarded as *de facto* confidential, notwithstanding the marking; although not distributed to the public at large, yet it had reached a very substantial proportion of the interested public; moreover, the whole point of distributing the bulletin was to enable recipients to make use of the information which it contained. In the earlier case of *Young's Patents,*[6] distribution of a "Private and Confidential" technical report to around 10 only out of 350 members of the British Cast Iron Research Association was held similarly fatal to *de facto* confidentiality.

Public and private subject-matter

5.07 A frequent situation in practice is that, at the relevant time of allegedly unauthorised use, the information is a mixture of public and secret subject-matter. A well-known example is provided by *Seager v. Copydex,*[7] already mentioned in Chapter 1 (at para. 1.02) in relation to the whole foundation of confidential information law.

5.08 The plaintiff in this case was a clockmaker turned inventor. Following an accident in which a neighbour's child had fallen and hurt

5 [1957] R.P.C. 449.
6 60 R.P.C. 51.
7 [1967] R.P.C. 349; [1967] F.S.R. 211; [1967] 1 W.L.R. 923; [1967] 2 All E.R. 415; 2 K.I.R. 828.

herself badly upon a loose carpet, he had invented and sold a carpet grip which he called the "Klent" grip; he had also taken out a patent for the "Klent" grip, and this had been published by the Patent Office; at that point, the information as to the "Klent" grip was open to all the world to see. During the course of some subsequent negotiations with the defendants as to marketing of the "Klent" grip, he also revealed to them an idea for another type of grip. The defendants eventually put on to the market a carpet grip, called the "Invisigrip", which was very similar to the latter. In giving judgment for the plaintiff, Denning M.R. said:

> "The principle is clear enough when the whole of the information is private. The difficulty arises when the information is *in part public and in part private*. As, for instance, in this case. A good deal of the information which Mr. Seager gave to Copydex Limited was available to the public, such as the patent specification in the Patent Office, or the KLENT grip, which he sold to anyone who asked. If that was the only information he gave them, he could not complain. It was further knowledge. But there was a good deal of other information he gave them which was private, such as the difficulties which had to be overcome in making a satisfactory grip; the necessity for a strong sharp tooth; the alternative forms of tooth, and the like. When the information is mixed, being partly public and partly private, then the recipient must *take special care to use only the material which is in the public domain*. He should go to the public source and get it, or at any rate, not be in a better position than if he had gone to the public source. He should not get a start over others by using the information which he received in confidence. At any rate, *he should not get a start without paying for it*." (at 368, emphasis added)

Springboard

5.09 *Seager* thus represents an application of the so-called "headstart" or so-called "springboard", doctrine. This doctrine is not restricted to cases of mixed public+secret information, although it has its main application there; it covers also instances where the information in question was, at the time of communication, wholly secret. The term "springboard" itself derives from the case of *Terrapin v. Builders' Supply*[8] a few years before, where it was said by the Court:

> "As I understand it, the essence of this branch of the law, whatever the origin of it may be, is that a person who has obtained information in confidence is not allowed to use it *as a springboard* for activities detrimental to the person who made the confidential communication, and *springboard it remains even when all the features have been published or can be ascertained by actual inspection by any member of the public*." (at 391, emphasis added)

5.10 The term "springboard" provides a colourful guide in this connection, but is by no means without its own difficulties. For example,

8 [1967] R.P.C. 375

it leaves uncertain the position of the person who has previously received confidential information in relation to a certain topic during the course of negotiations or otherwise, who has subsequently discontinued his relations with the provider of the information and who now quite genuinely wishes to proceed with work in that field of his own accord. On the face of it, he is at a positive disadvantage. As it was put in *Coco* (see para. 5.01 *ante*):

> "Communication thus imposes on him a *unique disability*. He alone of all men must for an uncertain time abjure this field of endeavour, however great his interest." (at 49, emphasis added)

5.11 The approach which has gradually emerged to solve this conundrum is to emphasise that there is a limit to the springboard's bounce. As stated in *Potters-Ballotini v. Weston Baker*[9]:

> "Although a man must not use such information as a springboard to get a start over others, nevertheless the springboard does not last for ever. If he does use it, a time may come when so much has happened that he can no longer be restrained."

5.12 Precisely how soon depends on all the circumstances of the case; in a technological field which is advancing rapidly, with a number of rival concerns actively engaged in competition, the period may well be shorter than in a field which is more static. Conversely, the period may be longer where the recipient of the unauthorised disclosure (assuming him to be a rival manufacturer) is already engaged in the field than where he is not; the relative contribution provided by the information would normally be greater in the former than in the latter case, because the rival manufacturer would already have his business running and therefore be able to take commercial advantage of the information more promptly. It may also be relevant to consider whether the information has been provided by an ex-employee of the plaintiff (original owner of the confidential information) who is now working for the defendant (recipient of the same) or one who has been in limbo since that previous employment. An individual ex-employee defendant (particularly if skilled) may be treated in principle more generously than a corporate defendant; and, conversely, an individual plaintiff may be treated more generously than a corporate plaintiff.

5.13 The mode in which the defendant actually acquired the publicly available part of the information may also be relevant in an instance where the relevant information is—at the time of communication—a mixture of public and private material. The springboard period is likely

9 [1977] R.P.C. 202.

to be longer in the case when the publicly available part (as well as the private part) was acquired via the plaintiff than when it was acquired from the public source; this is because a further duty (in respect of the notionally available but in fact unappreciated information) can then be regarded as arising, quite apart from the recipient's primary duty not to make improper use of the owner's objectively secret information. Where the publicly available part has been adopted by a number of rivals the period may be shorter than where it has been adopted by just a single competitor.

5.14 These various factors are illustrated in the case-law. Thus, in *Harrison v. Project & Design*[10] (home stair lifts) the facts given in the report suggest that a total springboard period of some 4½ years (early 1969 to November 1974), including a period of around 3½ years after publication of the plaintiff's patent (which taught the main idea, although not all the confidential working drawings), was permitted to a plaintiff solo inventor viz-à-viz a defendant manufacturer. In *Fisher-Karpak Industries v. Nichols,*[11] on the other hand, the period was limited to a year in a case of commercial information purloined by ex-employees, who were now engaged in a competing business. The Court commented:

> "I am acutely conscious of the fact that competition should be encouraged and I am acutely conscious of the fact that it must be quite wrong to impose a restraint which is effectively only going to operate to stop a man using his acquired skills rather than to stop him misusing information which he ought never to have taken into use at all."

5.15 In *Cranleigh Precision Engineering v. Bryant,*[12] reliance was placed by the Court upon the point that the defendant Bryant (ex-managing director of the plaintiffs) had originally received the information as to the published patent of Bischoff (a third party) from the plaintiffs' patent agents in his capacity as employee; the Bischoff patent showed a generally similar construction of above-ground swimming pool to that of the plaintiffs, but without their special co-acting clamping strip/overlapping interfit. The information which the defendant was using was accordingly part public (objectively but not subjectively) and part private, and injunctions were granted. Of course if the defendant, having decided to leave and set up as a competing swimming pool manufacturer, had made his own search in the Patent Office library for the latest information on the topic and had thereby found the Bischoff patent specification for the first time as a result of his own efforts, the position could have been very different.

10 [1978] F.S.R. 81.
11 [1982] F.S.R. 351 at 352.
12 [1966] R.P.C. 81; [1964] F.S.R. 111; [1965] 1 W.L.R. 1293; [1964] 3 All E.R. 289.

5.16 The *Cranleigh Precision Engineering* decision was recently considered further in *Speed Seal v. Paddington,*[13] where the public disclosure (of an oil rig coupler design), had been made by the defendant himself following termination of his previous association with the plaintiff. It was pointed out that there were, in principle, three possible situations: (1) disclosure by the owner of the information himself (as in *Mustad v. Dosen*[14] where the plaintiffs had themselves applied for, and consequentially had published by the Patent Office, a patent disclosing the relevant machine for manufacture of fish hooks); (2) disclosure by a stranger (as where the third party finds and publishes independently); and (3) disclosure by a person who was under an obligation of confidence (as in the case of an ex-employee). In situations (2) and (3), but not (1), the Court may intervene to prevent use of the published information, since here there could be an abuse of confidence. In contrast, such abuse was not possible in situation (1) because of the owner's voluntary act in putting the information into the public domain in the first place.

PUBLIC INTEREST

5.17 This defence can be regarded as starting from a vivid phrase used in the early 1856 case of *Gartside v. Outram*[15]:

> "There is no confidence as to the disclosure of an iniquity."

5.18 A number of cases in recent years have drawn attention to its potential width. Thus, in *Initial Services v. Putterill*[16] (1967), it was successfully used in favour of an ex-employee who had given particulars to a newspaper of certain activities of his former employers suggesting a breach of the Restrictive Trade Practices Act 1956. In *Hubbard v. Vosper,*[17] (1971) it was similarly successful (at the interlocutory stage) in respect of information concerning the cult of scientology. *Beloff v. Pressdram*[18] (1972) involved an article in a satirical magazine; its interest lies primarily in the comprehensive definition offered by the Court:

> "The defence of public interest clearly covers . . . disclosure which . . . must be disclosure in the public interest, of matters carried out or contemplated, in breach of the country's security, or in breach of law, including statutory duty, fraud, or otherwise destructive of the country or its people, including matters medically dangerous to the public; and doubtless other misdeeds of similar gravity."

13 [1985] 1 W.L.R. 1327.
14 [1963] R.P.C.41; [1963] 3 All E.R. 416.
15 (1856) 26 L.J. Ch. 113.
16 [1968] 1 Q.B. 396; [1967] 3 W.L.R. 1032; [1967] 3 All E.R. 145.
17 [1972] 2 Q.B. 94; [1972] 2 W.L.R. 389; [1972] 1 All E.R. 1023.
18 [1973] R.P.C. 765 at 783–4; [1973] F.S.R. 33; [1973] 1 All E.R. 241.

5.19 The suggestion that the defence extends to confidential information relating to matters of possible medical danger to the public is of particular significance. It could be argued that this heading is wide enough to cover such areas as nuclear energy, drug trials, and hazardous industrial processes generally notwithstanding the commercial value of the information involved. The definition also makes it clear that the defence is not limited to instances where the defendant has behaved in some disgraceful or criminal-like manner; the law has grown beyond the original Victorian concept of iniquity. As put by Denning M.R. in *Fraser v. Evans*[19] in 1968 (report of public relations consultant to the Greek Government):

> "I do not look upon the word "iniquity" as expressing a principle. It is merely *an* instance of *just cause or excuse* for breaking confidence. There are some things which may be required to be disclosed in the public interest, in which event no confidence can be prayed in aid to keep them secret."

5.20 The extent of the modern expansion of the defence is reflected in a pair of 1984 cases—*Francome v. Mirror Group*[20] and *Lion Laboratories v. Evans*.[21] In *Francome,* publication of eavesdropped telephone conversations of a leading jockey (which allegedly revealed breaches of the rules of racing) was restrained pending trial on the balance of convenience; but what is interesting is the suggestion in the speech of Donaldson M.R. that:

> ". . . there is a countervailing public interest in exposing conduct which involves a breach of the law *or* which is '*antisocial*'."

5.21 "Anti-social" is a term both wide (in overall scope) and vague (as to the precise boundaries of that scope). In *Lion Laboratories*, interlocutory relief was refused in respect of intended newspaper publication of the contents of the plaintiffs' internal documents casting doubt upon the accuracy of the Lion "Intoximeter"; this was a device for gauging alcohol level by breath-testing, statutorily authorised to be used for this purpose so that drink-driving offences might be proved solely by its uncorroborated evidence. Such considerations as the inherent desirability of preserving properly existing confidentiality (the latter a criterion which was clearly met by the documents here) and undesirability of providing a "mole's charter"; the breaches of copyright likely to occur as a result of the publication being unauthorised; judicial reluctance to countenance disloyalty or lend its aid to breach of trust (by the ex-

19 [1969] 1 Q.B. 349 at 362; [1968] 3 W.L.R. 1172; [1969] 1 All E.R. 8.
20 [1984] 1 W.L.R. 895; [1984] 2 All E.R. 408.
21 [1984] 3 W.L.R. 539; [1984] 2 All E.R. 417; [1985] 1 Q.B. 526.

employees who had taken the documents); the general unsuitability of newspaper columns as a forum for trial of complex scientific issues; the need for employees to discuss and argue out problems within the employing company without fear of their words being used to discredit the company subsequently; the advantage that trade competitors would gain from the disclosure; these were all overriden because:

> "The issue raised by the defendants is a serious question concerning a matter which affects the life, and even the liberty, of an unascertainable number of Her Majesty's subjects." (at 554)

(a rather odd turn of phrase since it is usually the life of the innocent pedestrian, rather than that of the driver, which is affected by the latter's consumption of alcohol) and:

> "It would surely be wrong to refuse leave to publish material that may lead to a reappraisal of a machine that has the potential for causing a wrongful conviction of a serious criminal offence." (at 561)

5.22 But the public's prurient curiosity is not enough to found a "public interest" defence. To cite *Lion Laboratories* again:

> ". . . there is a world of difference between what is *in* the public interest and what is *of* interest to the public." (at 562, emphasis added)

REMOTENESS

5.23 This issue arises where the confidential information has fallen into the hands of some third party not directly linked to the original owner of the confidential information. The remoteness is one of party, as distinct from remoteness of time, such as arises in connection with the issue of expiration of confidence.

5.24 A prime example is represented by the instance where a newspaper or the like publishes (or is intending to publish) confidential material relating to other activities "in the public interest"; many of the cases discussed under the preceding section of this chapter were of this kind. Generally, the approach of the court here is to hold that a plaintiff only has standing, that is, *locus* in the first place, if the circumstances are such that it can properly be said that the defendant owes him a duty of good faith. Although the third party may be a stranger, literally speaking, the aura of confidentiality may extend so as to put him within the plaintiff's potential grasp and thereby create a nexus between them.

5.25 In the *Francome* case, for example, the allegedly confidential conversations were those of the plaintiff jockey; and it was reasonably foreseeable (to say the least) that those words, if broadcast generally by the defendant newspaper, might (if authentic) injure his reputation and livelihood. Likewise, in the *Lion Laboratories* case, there was the clear risk of damage to the plaintiff manufacturer. In contrast, the Court in *Fraser* held that the plaintiff failed on that point (quite apart from the "public interest" defence, on which he also failed). The Greek Government (for whom the report had been prepared) would have had standing to sue the newspaper but the plaintiff journalist himself did not; the latter's confidential aura extended only so far as the Greek Government, who had commissioned and paid for the report; it was the Greek Government who were entitled either to circulate freely the report and hence publish its contents, or alternatively to keep it secret, as they so wished. To quote from Denning M.R.:

> ". . . The jurisdiction is based not so much on property or on contract as on the duty to be of good faith. No person is permitted to divulge to the world information which he has received in confidence, unless he has just cause or excuse for doing so. . . . But the *party complaining must be the person who is entitled to the confidence* and to have it respected. He must be a person *to whom the duty of good faith is owed.* It is at this point that I think Mr. Fraser's claim breaks down." (at 361, emphasis added)

5.26 Instances where the confidential information is of the conventional trade secrets kind tend to present a different type of situation; the defendant is normally anxious here in any event to maintain confidentiality of the subject-matter acquired; that is, to conceal rather than reveal, since revelation would be likely to render his acquisition commercially valueless. Three types of situation at least can be envisaged, in general terms:

(1) where an employee offers to sell or otherwise deal in the secret to a third party, on the explicit basis that it was one of his employer's present or ex-secrets (and hence correspondingly valuable);

(2) where he offers to sell or otherwise deal in the secret to a third party in such circumstances that the third party ought reasonably to appreciate that what he was being offered was another's secret—say where an unskilled person offers to sell details of a manufacturing formula of a kind which in the normal course of circumstances he could not possibly be expected to be familiar with, and the third party refrains from asking for his source of knowledge;

(3) where the third party acquires the secret in good faith and for value without notice; this could be the case where, for example, a manufacturing company purchases from a professional designer a series of drawings showing a new type of flip-top lid for a shampoo bottle, wholly ignorant of the fact that the latter had originally acquired them

improperly—say by stealing the drawings from another client, or copying from another client's pending product.

In situations of type (1) the Court would almost certainly intervene; the chain of confidence, and hence the duty, is there. But situations of types (2) and (3) present greater problems.

5.27 It can be argued that in type (3) situations, in particular, the loss should fall upon the original proprietor of the confidential information rather than on the innocent third party purchaser, on the general equitable principle of providing relief to a *bona fide* purchaser for value without notice; the whole action for breach of confidence can be regarded as rooted in equity, and hence equitable principles generally should apply. Moreover, the original proprietor always has his potential remedy against the defaulting intermediate party as an alternative; the counter-argument to this, of course, is that the intermediate party may be wholly incapable in reality of meeting the claim for damages of the level which might be involved in a case of trade secrets of manufacturing importance.

5.28 Dicta can be found pointing either way, in the reported cases. Referring, for example, to cases already mentioned in this or earlier Chapters:

Morison v. Moat[22]

> "It *might* be different, if the Defendant was a purchaser for value of the secret without notice of any obligation affecting it; . . ." (at 263)

Stevenson Jordan & Harrison v. Macdonald & Evans (Court of first instance)[23]

> "Counsel for the Plaintiffs *expressly disclaimed* any suggestion that at the date of the execution of D.10 the Defendants were (or should have been) aware that Mr. Hemming was acting in breach of his duty to the Plaintiffs. Does this circumstance frank their avowed intention to consummate Mr. Hemming's wrongdoing? The original and independent jurisdiction of this Court to prevent, by the grant of an injunction, any person availing himself of a title *which arises out of a violation of a right or a breach of confidence*, is so well established as a cardinal principle that only a binding authority to the contrary should prevent its application by this Court." (at 195)

The *Morison* decision was distinguished on the basis that in the Vice-Chancellor's view:

> "It is not inconsistent with the power of the Court to prevent disclosure by injunction *if proceedings are commenced in time.*" (at 195, emphasis added)

22 (1851) 9 Hare 241.
23 (1951) 68 R.P.C. 190.

In other words, the Court may be more willing to give relief against a third party at *quia timet* stage (as in *Stevenson Jordan*, where publication of the book containing the assertedly confidential information had not yet occurred) than at a later stage by which time the third party had already commercially utilised the information (as in *Morison*, where the defendant had already begun to make and sell his competitive medicine).

Fraser v. Evans[24]

> "Even if he comes by it innocently, nevertheless *once he gets to know* that it was originally given in confidence, he can be restrained from breaking that confidence." (at 361, emphasis added)

5.29 This latter dictum suggests that an originally innocent and hence unimpeachable third party purchaser can subsequently become a guilty, and hence impeachable one. Such a change in status would again appear to be contrary to normal equitable principles and also provides certain practical contradictions; for example, if the third party purchaser has gone onto the market with articles made by the assertedly confidential process of the plaintiff, is he to be liable for damages only in respect of articles produced subsequent to the writ (or letter before action)? It should be remembered that *Fraser* again was an application for a *quia timet* interlocutory injunction. And suppose that he has invested substantial capital in building a plant for operating the secret process. Is this all to be wasted once he finds out that the information concerning the secret process was bought illicitly? There is a lack of clear modern binding authority on the point, derived from a case fought fully at trial. This absence may well be due to the fact that it is rare for the Court to find that the purchaser was entirely innocent in the kind of circumstances normally present in trade secrets cases.

5.30 The rather commoner situation is that of type (2)—that is, where the third party purchaser was being naive, to say the least, in assuming that he was dealing with a *bona fide* seller. The Court may find it conceptually easier, here, to act against the purchaser on the basis of an imputed duty of good faith; in other words, that the purchaser was under a duty, given the nature of the person offering him the confidential material, to make reasonable enquiries before purchasing so as to satisfy himself as to the seller's title.

24 [1969] 1 Q.B. 349.

CHAPTER 6

Confidential Information in Relation to Intellectual Property Generally

6.01 It will be appreciated from the foregoing chapters that rights in confidential information can be closely associated with other kinds of intellectual property right. Where the confidential information is of a technological character, the relationship with patent rights may be particularly important; copyright considerations may also enter if, as in the leading case of *Saltman Engineering v. Campbell Engineering*[1], the information is partly embodied in engineering drawings or the like. Outside the technological sphere, copyright tends to become more significant. Unauthorised publication by a newspaper of the contents of a "leaked" business or political memorandum would normally be actionable both as breach of confidential information and breach of copyright. The impact of confidential information on the remaining two main heads of intellectual property—registered designs and trade marks—is, generally speaking, rather less.

PATENTS

General Nature

6.02 Patent law is a statutory subject; in contrast to the position with confidential information, the law is codified, the present statute being the Patents Act 1977.[2] This Act preserves part of the previous statute, the Patents Act 1949,[3] for so-called existing patents (that is, patents dated before the 1977 Act). The 1949 Act is itself a successor to major Patents Acts in 1907,[4] 1883[5] and 1852,[6] with various supplementary legislation in between; between 1852 and 1624, when the original Statute of Monopolies[7] was passed, development was essentially under the aegis of the common law.

1 65 R.P.C. 203.
2 1977 c. 37.
3 12, 13 & 14 Geo. VI, c. 87.
4 7 Edw. VII, c. 29.
5 46 &47 Vict. c. 57.
6 15 & 16 Vict. c. 83.
7 21 Jac. I, c. 3.

6.03 The basic *modus operandi* of the patent system is that in return for a limited (in time) monopoly the inventor discloses his invention to the public, so that on expiration of the monopoly the invention enters the public domain and all are free to use it; the current maximum monopoly period is 20 years. There is therefore a fundamental antithesis between protection of new technology by means of the common law of confidential information and the statute law of patents; the former is concerned with keeping the new technology secret, the latter with ensuring that it is disclosed. Nevertheless the two modes of protection do at times march—sometimes uneasily—hand in hand.

Choice of route

6.04 An inventor (or his employer) may eschew the patent route for various reasons, and decide to rely on confidentiality alone. These reasons include:

(1) the expense of taking out patents, and litigating to enforce them against infringers;
(2) the potentially shorter life of the patent protection (assuming that confidentiality can be maintained);
(3) the desire to keep competitors guessing;
(4) a lack of patentable quality in the invention or technology.

The first three of these reasons are self-explanatory, but the fourth requires some amplification.

6.05 Lack of patentable quality itself divides in turn into the two limbs of inherent unpatentability, and unpatentability in face of the art. Inherent unpatentability arises from the prohibition in the 1977 Act (which followed, broadly speaking, earlier law in this respect) as to patenting of inventions in certain fields; the most important prohibited categories are:

(a) discoveries, scientific theories and mathematical methods;
(b) computer programs;
(c) varieties of animals, plants and any essentially biological (as distinct from microbiological) processes for the production of the same;
(d) medical treatment of humans or animals.

The wide scope of these prohibitions, particularly in relation to present-day computer technology and genetic engineering, is clear. Unpatentability in face of the art arises when the new item of technology is—although perhaps practically important and valuable—not sufficiently different from the prior art to rank as truly inventive. Minor adjustments to automatic machinery, or the operating conditions of a chemical process, may fall into this category. Of course there is also unpatentability if the subject-matter has been already disclosed *in toto* in the prior art, for then there is a lack of novelty.

6.06 Conversely, the inventor (or his employer) may opt for protection via patents on account of expected difficulty in maintaining confidentiality; elaborate precautions over a lengthy period may have to be pursued. Patent protection also has the advantage of being a monopoly in the objective sense. The patentee can stop other parties using the subject-matter of the patent (whilst still in force) even if they have independently evolved it. The owner of confidential information, on the other hand, has to show that the other party obtained the information improperly from him in the first place, directly or indirectly; a causal link has to be established.

Subsequent patenting

6.07 What the law has traditionally frowned on, however, is the practice of first using the information secretly for commercial profit and then subsequently, when for example it is feared that the information is about to leak out, applying for a patent. Such reluctance can be traced back to the early 19th century. In the leading case of *Wood v. Zimmer*[8] in the year 1815 a patent directed to a new method of making verdigris (a pigment) of a brighter green than heretofore was upset by reason of prior sale by the patentee over a few months period before taking out the patent. No question seems to have arisen as to the possibility of ascertaining from the product the particular chemical method employed; it is hardly conceivable that suitable analytical techniques for this purpose were contemporaneously available. It was argued by Counsel for the Plaintiffs that:

> "Though Zinck sold the article before, that is to say, in August 1811, and that patent was not obtained till January 1812 he did not thereby forfeit his privilege in the invention. He might still obtain a patent; the invention is still his; and the secret locked in his own breast. Though sold, in a few instances, the property was not rendered common *whilst he kept the secret.* The secret was not disclosed till the patent was obtained." (emphasis added)

Yet Gibbs C. J., in his instrucitons to the jury, roundly declared:

> ". . . Some things are obvious as soon as they are made public. Of others the scientific world may possess itself by analysis. Some inventions almost baffle discovery. But to entitle a man to a patent, the invention must be new to the world. The public sale of that, which is afterwards made the subject

8 Holt N.P. 58.

of a patent, *though sold by the inventor only*, makes the patent void." (emphasis added)

In the Patents and Designs Act 1932[9] (which first formally codified grounds for invalidity of a patent), the objection was expressed as:

> "(o) that prior to the date of the patent the invention was secretly worked on a commercial scale and not merely by way of reasonable trial or experiment . . ."[10]

and maintained (with the reasonable trial or experiment exception) in the Patents Act 1949 as:

> "(l) that the invention, so far as claimed in any claim of the complete specification, was secretly used in the United Kingdom, otherwise than as mentioned in sub-section (2) of this section, before the priority date of that claim."[11]

6.08 The new 1977 Act no longer draws any distinction between prior use and prior secret use; reference is made instead to:

> "**2.** (1) An invention shall be taken to be new if it does not form part of the state of the art.
>
> (2) The state of the art in the case of an invention shall be taken to comprise all matter (whether a product, a process, information about either, or anything else) which has at any time before the priority date of that invention been *made available to the public* (whether in the United Kingdom or elsewhere) by written or oral description, by *use* or in any other way." (emphasis added)

The change in statutory wording was necessary because of the United Kingdom's adherence in the interim to the European Patent Convention. Although it is too soon as yet to be sure, it would seem doubtful whether any major change in the law has been effected; the *Wood v. Zimmer* principle is strongly entrenched, and prior sale of a product made by an undetectable process does still literally make that product available to the public, in the sense that they may benefit from it.

6.09 What the new Act does give the prior secret user, however, is the right to continue his use in face of a third party's subsequent patent even if the secret use does not rank as a "making available" sufficient to invalidate the patent;[12] in other words, a shop-right in favour of the earlier secret user has been established in any event.

Parallel protection

6.10 But joint patent and confidential information protection can, as

9 22 & 23 Geo. V, c. 36.
10 S. 3, introducing new s. 25(2)(o) of 1907 Act.
11 S. 32(1)(l).
12 S. 64.

already mentioned, be usefully deployed in certain circumstances. The most common is that of an important "break-through" type of invention followed by a series of improvements by the same workers (or different workers in the same company), so that there is common ownership.

6.11 The so-called "float" process for making sheet glass may be taken as an example. This involved flowing out the molten glass over a bath of molten tin; in its day (1953) it was a revolutionary process. The original patent—although it no doubt provided the best information which the inventors had at the time—was naturally quite inadequate so far as detailed manufacturing instructions were concerned. That role had to be fulfilled by improvement patents (where the detail was sufficiently distinctive to be further patentable in its own right) and/or associated confidential information; the whole was successfully licenced out by the owners (Pilkington Brothers plc) on a world-wide basis over many years.

6.12 Another well-known example was provided by the discovery (in 1959) of the 6–APA nucleus of penicillins, which provided the key to the development of the whole new class of semi-synthetic penicillins for use as antibiotics. The relevant patents were directed to 6–APA and certain classes of penicillins derived therefrom, as new chemical compounds; essentially laboratory-scale only preparative procedures for the new products were described. The relevant licence agreement extracted in the report of *Beecham Group v. Bristol Laboratories*[13] (already discussed in Chapter 4) provided not only a licence under the patents but also a licence in respect of:

> ". . . all such particulars and information . . . concerning secret processes, secret methods, secret formulae, cultures, strains, enzymes and other confidential know-how and materials . . . relating to the Subject-Matter . . ."

either already owned by Beecham (licensor) or to be developed thereafter (up to a given cut-off date). Under the confidential information aspect of the agreement, the licensor would accordingly have to hand over, *inter alia*, all information relative to the commercial production of the new penicillins as well. This could be valuable, since a commercially feasible process is not necessarily merely a scaled-up version of the original process successful in the laboratory and disclosed in the patent. The question of process yield, in particular, may be of great importance and necessitate modification of the original process.

6.13 The potential significance of confidential information in this context is reflected also in Recommendation 14 of the Nicholson Report

13 [1978] R.P.C. 521 at 576.

(*Intellectual Property Rights and Innovation*, December 1983)[14]. This suggests that the compulsory patent licence provisions of the 1977 Act be strengthened by enabling the licence to call also for ". . . the transfer of *associated know-how*, in cases of anticompetitive or monopoly abuse" (emphasis added).

Licensing considerations

6.14 Actual drafting of the licence agreement, in cases of combined patent and confidential information protection, is a matter requiring particular care—although somewhat beyond the scope of this book. The position of possible further (post-agreement) improvements made by the licensee should be dealt with in the licence agreement, as well as further improvements by the licensor; also the position which arises when the patent licence comes to an end (through effluxion of time, revocation of patent or other case). *Regina Glass Fibre v. Schuller*[15] (already mentioned in Chapter 4 at paras. 4.12 ff) illustrates the difficulty which can arise with an agreement which fails to deal explicitly with the point. The impact of certain statutory termination provisions is dealt with later.

6.15 Care may also need to be taken to preclude restrictive conditions such as are rendered void by section 44 of the 1977 Act (tying-in clauses as to supply, and the like). For patent pools—that is, where a number of patentees (three or more) combine together to license out their patents and associated confidential information as a whole—the Restrictive Trade Practices Act 1976[16] may impinge also. For agreements having a European dimension, the Regulations of the Commission of the European Communities concerning the application of Article 85(3) of the Treaty of Rome and jurisprudence concerning Articles 85(1) and 86 may apply. The current block exemption (in relation to Article 85(3)) makes it quite clear that patent and confidential information agreements are liable to be treated in similar fashion as pure patent licences. Article 1(1) of the Regulation No. 2349/84[17] introducing the exemption provides:

> "Pursuant to Article 85(3) of the Treaty and subject to the provisions of this Regulation, it is hereby declared that Article 85(1) of the Treaty shall not apply to patent licencing agreements, and *agreements combining the licensing of patents and the communication of know-how*, to which only two undertakings are party and which include one or more [specified] obligations: . . ." (emphasis added)

14 Cmnd. 9117, para. 6.7.
15 [1972] R.P.C. 229; [1972] F.S.R. 141.
16 1976 c. 34.
17 1984 O.J. L219/15.

For research and development agreements (which may both employ existing confidential information and lead to possible new confidential information and/or patentable inventions), the impact of associated block exemption in Regulation No. 418/85[17a] has also to be borne in mind.

6.16 The interplay between confidential information and patents can be seen elsewhere in the provisions of the 1977 Act concerning (i) premature disclosure of an invention; (ii) employee rights in inventions; and (iii) termination of licences. These are now considered in turn.

Premature disclosure

6.17 The point as to premature disclosure arises from the requirement of patent law that an invention be novel; the relevant section 2(1) of the 1977 Act has already been quoted. The requirement of novelty of course does not mean that an inventor can never risk divulging his invention at all prior to applying for a patent; it would be absurd, for example, if he were unable to approach an outside contractor with a view to making an experimental model of his invention. The general approach taken here by the law is that, provided that he can prove that the communication was made in confidence, then the information was not thereby made available to the "public" in the first place at all.

6.18 To alleviate the harshness of the statutory requirement for novelty, in the case of prior disclosures flowing from a breach of confidence (whether by the outside contractor in the case just given, or otherwise) section 2(4) continues by providing a grace period within certain limits of time (six months) and relationship (between the person who makes the improper disclosure and its original source). A like grace period is allowed in respect of non-confidential disclosure (inevitably so) of the invention at duly certified international exhibitions.

Employee rights

6.19 The point as to employee rights derives from the new statutory provisions of the 1977 Act on the subject of employee inventions. Henceforth, inventions made by scientific-type employees (where inventions might reasonably be expected in normal performance of their duties) and managerial-type employees (who had a special obligation to further the interests of the employer's undertaking) are to belong to the

17a 1985 O.J. L53/5.

employer; the employee's rights are restricted to compensation, provided that certain conditions, e.g. that the invention was of "outstanding benefit"[18] to the employer, are met. All other kinds of employee inventions are, however, to belong to the employee.

6.20 To prevent an employer from forcing employees to waive their statutory rights in such circumstances, section 42(2) provides generally that any term(s) which diminish an employee's rights in this respect shall—to the extent of the diminution—be unenforceable. Section 42(3) continues, however, by providing:

> "(3) Subsection (2) above shall not be construed as derogating from any *duty of confidentiality* owed to his employer by an employee by virtue of any rule of law or otherwise." (emphasis added)

Precisely what the ambit of that duty is remains unspecified here: the reference to "any rule of law" means that the boundary has to be determined instead by the common-law and/or statutory rules along the lines already discussed. It is likely, however, that the overall duty of confidentiality will be held as embracing at least the constituent duties of (i) requiring all employees (whether of scientific, managerial or shopfloor grades) to disclose to their employer in the first instance that they have made a potentially patentable invention, and (ii) refraining from disclosing the invention outside until the employer has had a reasonable time to assess whether it belongs to him or not.

Termination of licences

6.21 There are two noteworthy provisions in this respect, statutorily provided for in section 45 of the 1977 Act. The first, contained in section 45(1) and a continuation of a similar provision in the earlier 1949 Act, is to the effect that a licence can be determined as of right on three months' notice once the relevant patent(s) has expired. This has the undoubtedly desirable result of preventing a licensor, in the case of an ordinary combined patent and confidential licence, from extracting out of a licensee continued royalties on both the patented subject-matter and the associated confidential information at a future time when only the confidential information limb remains alive as intellectual property. The licensee can, as it were, cancel the patent limb at this time and reduce his royalty accordingly.

6.22 If, with a view to blunting the impact of section 45(1), the licensor has included in the licence agreement a term calling for payment of the

18 S. 40(1).

same royalty irrespective of whether or not the patent is in force, then section 45(3) may come into play on the licensee's behalf. This second provision gives the Court power to vary the terms of a licence agreement of its own accord, on application of either party, once the patent has expired, if satisfied that it would be "unjust" for the applicant to continue to comply with all terms and conditions. The power is not merely one of declaring the licence void (and hence unenforceable) but one of amendment at judicial intervention. Potentially, the power is far-reaching; but it is not yet clear as to how it will be applied in practice. The provision is new in the 1977 Act, in contrast to the provision of section 45(1).

Infringement

6.23 Reference may be made finally to the question of infringement of patents. In cases where the infringer has evolved the alleged infringement (say, a spaghetti-manufacturing machine which the plaintiff contends falls within the terms of his patent claims) quite independently, or where he has just copied the plaintiff's own patented model as marketed, there is unlikely to be any additional ground for complaint as regards confidential information; in the first case, there is no causal link, and in the second the patentee's own marketing has destroyed the secrecy. But if the infringer has suborned an employee of the patentee and obtained details from him as, for example, to the patentee's technique for making the machine on a robot-controlled production line, then the rival machine may also effectively embody subject-matter obtained by breach of confidence. The patentee could therefore sue the alleged infringer for both patent infringement and breach of confidential information (by way of inducing the ex-employee to reveal the same and/or subsequently using the same), and sue the ex-employee separately for making the revelation.

COPYRIGHT

6.24 Copyright law is again a statutory subject, being governed by the Copyright Act 1956[19] (itself a successor to a string of prior statutes dating back to the first limited Statute of Queen Anne in 1709[20]) as amended by subsequent legislation. The rights given to copyright owners are defined in extensive terms; likewise the definition of what constitutes an infringement (which in turn depends upon the type of copyright involved—literary, dramatic, musical or artistic—and the commercial dealings present).

19 4 & 5 Eliz. II, c. 68.
20 8 Anne, c. 21.

Proviso of confidence

6.25 For present purposes, the essential point is that by section 46(4) of the 1956 Act:

> "(4) Nothing in this Act shall affect the operation of any rule of equity relating to *breaches of trust or confidence*." (emphasis added)

The impact of this proviso can be marked.

6.26 Firstly, it may enable the "author" (in the widest sense, not restricted just to literary works) to obtain relief in circumstances where he may have been unfairly dealt with but nevertheless cannot bring his case strictly within the four corners of the 1956 Act. Suppose that he is a literary author, and that his agent improperly orally reads over the synopsis of his latest novel to a rival author, thereby enabling the latter to start work immediately upon a similar work and hence cream off some of his eventual sales. The oral disclosure may fail to rank as an infringing act within the scope of section 2(5) of the 1956 Act. Yet there has undoubtedly been a breach of confidence, and the proviso makes it clear that he can still proceed against the agent under this head in respect of the damage which he has incurred.

6.27 Another example is provided by the non-expert eye test of section 9(8) in relation to three-dimensional objects made from two-dimensional drawings:

> "(8) The making of an object of any description which is in three dimensions shall not be taken to infringe the copyright in an artistic work in two dimensions if the object would not appear, to persons who are not experts in relation to objects of that description, to be a reproduction of the aristic work."

An unscrupulous competitor may, for example, corrupt an employee surreptitiously to photograph drawings showing the cross-sections of a mould suitable for manufacturing a new kind of plastics riding hat, and from those make his own mould producing an identical hat. Owing to the complexity of the mould drawings (the mould being made up in parts, containing numerous inlet and outlet ports and the like) it is almost impossible for the non-expert layman (as opposed to the expert professional moulder) to recognise the final shape of hat in the cross-sectional views; the section 9(8) test cannot be met. Yet the competitor may still be caught for breach of confidence. Of course the corrupted employee would in any case be similarly caught but if he is indigent the only party in a position to pay for the harm done may be the competitor; hence it is much more important to be able to sue him rather than the employee.

6.28 Secondly, and conversely, it enables a plaintiff who may be unsure of the strength of his case when couched in terms of breach of confidence—say perhaps there is some doubt as to the confidential quality of the material transmitted—to combine this plea with one of copyright infringement. The copyright complaint provides another arrow for the plaintiff's quiver. No formal election as between causes of action is necessary at the pleading or trail stage, although naturally the Court, if prepared to find in his favour on one head, may decline to decide the other; and even if it does decide both issues, it is unlikely to give duplicate relief (see Chapter 16). Of course, the possibility of copyright complaint only arises where the material is in the first place of a kind which attracts copyright protection; the formal definitions in sections 2 and 3 of the 1956 Act, particularly the expanded meaning of "artistic work" provided by section 3(1), apply here.

Examples

6.29 Many of the decisions discussed in earlier chapters illustrate the successful reliance by the plaintiff upon such combined causes. In *Saltman Engineering v. Campbell Engineering* (see para. 2.16) no less than four separate causes of action were put forward—breach of confidential information, breach of copyright, breach of contract and conversion—but success on the first was enough to dispose of the matter.

6.30 Other instances (Chapter 5) are provided by *Hubbard v. Vosper*[21] (disclosures concerning the cult of scientology) and *Fraser v. Evans*[22] (disclosure of public relations report for Greek Government; claim for libel included also), although in both cases the defendants were able, in interlocutory proceedings, to stave off the copyright infringement complaint on the basis of the "fair dealing" defence in section 6(2) of the 1956 Act. In *Lion Laboratories v. Evans*[23] (documents concerning the manufacture and calibration of the Lion "Intoximeter") the Court considered the heads of complaint as equivalent for purposes of interlocutory proceedings. A much earlier (1849) and equally famous case in the same line was that of *Prince Albert v. Strange*[24] (paras 2.07f).

Computer software

6.31 Computer software represents an area in which the prospect of combined copyright and confidential information protection may prove

21 [1972] 2 Q.B. 84; [1972] 2 W.L.R. 389; [1972] 1 All E.R. 1023.
22 [1969] 1 Q.B. 349; [1968] 3 W.L.R. 1172; [1969] 1 All E.R. 8.
23 [1984] 3 W.L.R. 539; [1984] 2 All E.R. 417.
24 1 Mac, & G. 25.

to be of increasing significance in future. Computer programs as such are excluded from protection under the Patents Act 1977[25] and it is as yet uncertain as to how far this prohibition can be circumvented, in the case of computer-related inventions, by suitable dressing-up of the invention in alternative clothes.

6.32 The position of computer programs under copyright law is quite different. Following an earlier period in which protection was given at the interlocutory level, as exemplified in the cases of *Sega Enterprises v. Richards*[26] and *Thrustcode v. W. W. Computing*,[27] but no final conclusion reached as to applicability of the Copyright Act 1956, the Copyright (Computer Software) Amendment Act 1985[28] was passed. This came into force on 17 September 1985 and makes it clear that, irrespective of whatever might have been the position under the parent Act, computer programs were henceforth to be protected as literary works.

6.33 There are consequential provisions as to what constitutes "adaptation" and "reproduction in a material form" in relation to computer programs, these being two of the more important potential infringing acts in relation to literary works. For the former, conversion of the program into or out of a computer language or code, or into a different computer language or code, is stated to be embraced. For the latter, it is stated that storage of the work in a computer is included.

6.34 It follows, therefore, that there may be prospects of taking action for breach of copyright and breach of confidential information in respect of computer subject-matter just as much as there is for other more conventional types of copyright works. So far as employee problems are concerned, if a dishonest employee steals, say, the program of his employer's video game (or any analogous computer data form), then there may be breach of confidential information by the employee, and breach of both confidential information and copyright by the rival competitor to whom he sells the programme; the position is analogous to that which arises in respect of patented subject-matter. More complex kinds of tortfeasance are of course possible, bearing in mind the overall bundle of rights given to a copyright owner under the 1956 Act.

6.35 The separate question of the confidentiality of computer-held data is discussed later (particularly in Chapters 9 and 10).

25 S. 1(2)(c).
26 [1983] F.S.R. 73.
27 [1983] F.S.R. 502.
28 1985 c. 41

DESIGNS

6.36 Registered designs occupy another corner of the intellectual property scene. The applicable statute is the Registered Designs Act 1949.[29] Designs can be registered provided that they are new or original and relate to:

> ". . . features of shape, configuration, pattern or ornament applied to any article by any industrial process or means, being features which in the finished article appeal to and are judged solely by the eye." (Section 1(3))

and do not include:

> "a method or principle of construction or features of shape or configuration which are dictated solely by the function which the article to be made in that shape or configuration has to perform." (*ibid*)

6.37 Generally, confidential information and registered designs hang together to a considerably lesser extent than do confidential information and patents. Bearing in mind the intrinsic purpose of design registration—namely, to protect the eye, i.e. visible, appeal of an article—there is inevitably less scope for any associated confidentiality in relation thereto. The article the subject of a design registration necessarily has to proclaim itself in a manner that a patented article does not. The patented aricle may have been produced with the aid of a secret process, or provide problems of analysis as regards the features of its composition.

6.38 Perhaps the most important aspect for present purposes lies in the protective provisions included in the Registered Designs Act in respect of improper disclosures made prior to filing of the application for protection in the Design Registry, which might otherwise deprive the registration of novelty or originality and hence invalidate it. The provisions are more generous than those in the Patents Act 1977 inasmuch as there is no chronological time limit; they provide (in Section 6(1)) that no design registration should be invalidated (or refused registration in the first place) by reason only of:

> "(a) The disclosure of the design by the proprietor to any other person in such circumstances as would make it *contrary to good faith* for that other person to use or publish the design;
> (b) the disclosure of the design *in breach of good faith* by any person other than the proprietor of the design." (emphasis added)

6.39 Both points are illustrated in the case of *Chudzikowski v. Sowak*.[30] The plaintiff here, a Pole, had thought of a new design of table or bedside

29 12, 13 & 14 Geo. VI, c. 88.
30 [1957] R.P.C. 111.

lamp characterised by a foul anchor, from one of the arms of which was suspended a light in the form of a cabin lamp. He had the design made up and put into physical form by a fellow Pole, a handicraftsman, who worked on premises belonging to the defendant. The handicraftsman had been told quite explicitly by the plaintiff not to give out any information concerning the design: nevertheless the defendant coaxed him into handing over the model for money. This all occurred prior to the plaintiff's application for design protection being filed. It was held that the disclosure by the handicraftsman to the defendant did not in the circumstances invalidate protection by virtue of sub-section (b), the handicraftsman realising that he was doing wrong at the time in handing over the model; the plaintiff's original disclosure of the idea to the handicraftsman was also protected, having been made explicitly on a confidential basis for the purpose of making up the model, so bringing (although the point was not contested in the case) sub-section (a) into play.

6.40 Protection is also given (without chronological limit) by section 6(1)(c) for the "first and confidential" order for goods bearing a textile design and (up to six months) by section 6(2) in respect of prior display of the design at certified international exhibitions. This last provision is comparable to that allowed in the case of patents, as already mentioned.

TRADE MARKS

6.41 There are no provisions in the relevant Statute, the Trade Marks Act 1938,[31] corresponding generally to section 2(4) of the Patents Act 1977, section 46(4) of the Copyright Act 1956 or section 6(1) of the Registered Designs Act. So far as patents and registered designs are concerned, this may well be due to the fact that prior disclosure or use does not invalidate a subsequent registered mark. Indeed, prior use may on the contrary be essential in order to enable a necessary reputation in the mark, to make it distinctive in fact, to be built up.

6.42 But ideas and plans for future marks can represent valuable confidential information. It is clearly valuable intelligence for, say, a major motor car manufacturer to know that over the course of the next decade a rival is intending to introduce a new series of, say, "Z" marks for his range of saloons—say Zebedee, Zebra, Zongo and Zanzibar. The employee in the manufacturer's advertising agency who discloses this

31 1 & 2 Geo. VI, c. 22.

improperly to a rival can thus be sued in standard fashion for breach of confidential information just as much as if the information was of a technological or other commercial nature.

6.43 Apart from situations of this kind, association of trade marks with confidential information normally arises only where the product being sold under the trade mark is itself the subject of some secret formula or preparative process. Some examples of such association have already been given in Table 1 (Chapter 2, para. 2.10), involving the "Yorkshire Relish" (*Powell v. Birmingham Vinegar Brewery*[32]) and "Chartreuse" (*Lecouterier v. Rey*[33]) marks. Although these cases arose in different contexts, *Powell* being a passing-off dispute (that is, in respect of an unregistered trade mark) and *Lecouterier* a dispute as to ownership of registered marks, both illustrate the point that in cases of products of secret formulae the sale by a third party ignorant of the formula of a similar product under a similar name is liable to deceive the public; this in turn may justify judicial intervention.

32 14 R.P.C. 720; [1897] A.C. 710; 66 L.J. Ch. 763; 76 L.J. 792.
33 27 R.P.C. 268; [1910] A.C. 262; 79 L.J. Ch. 394; 102 L.J. 293; 26 T.L.R. 368.

CHAPTER 7

Confidentiality in the Course of Legal Proceedings—Part I

INTRODUCTION

7.01 The corollary to the principle that "justice must not only be done, but also seen to be done" is of course that legal proceedings should be conducted in open court. And, although it has been suggested that the Courts were not open as of right in earlier times such as the days of Edward I (1272–1307), a 1766 writer was able to declare flatly:

> "In the modern sense of an open Court the Legislature could never have allowed any fees to be taken for admittance."[1]

7.02 The landmark case in this century is perhaps *Scott v. Scott*[2] in 1913, where the question arose as to whether or not the Court had power to order a nullity suit to be heard *in camera* in the interest of public decency. The female petitioner had sued for nullity and led medical evidence to the effect that she was still a virgin some eleven years from the date of marriage; following a hearing *in camera,* and pronouncement of decrees nisi and absolute, the petitioner had obtained transcripts of the proceedings and sent them to certain persons, including relatives of her former husband; the petitioner had apparently been anxious to acquaint them with her side of the story as to the alleged non-consummation, in case the former husband had given an inaccurate account. The former husband responded by applying to commit her for contempt of Court. In holding that the Court should never have ordered an *in camera* hearing in the first place, the point was put by Viscount Haldane in the following terms:

> "While the broad principle is that the Courts of this country must, as between parties, administer justice in public, this principle is subject to apparent exceptions, such as those to which I have referred. But the exceptions are themselves the outcome of a yet more fundamental principle that the chief object of Courts of justice must be to secure that justice is done."[3]

The fact that the medical evidence in question was of an unsavoury

1 Barrington, *Observations on Statutes* (1796 Ed) p. 144.
2 [1913] A.C. 417.
3 At 437.

character (according to the mores of the day) was not enough to justify an exception under the then contemporary practice of the Court; the position today in non-consummation cases is different, as mentioned later.

7.03 The "exceptions" referred to in the quoted extract represent the cases where there may, as it were, be confidentiality in the actual conduct of Court proceedings—in other words, secrecy at trial. Such exceptions do not represent the only application of confidentiality in the course of legal proceedings, or subsequent thereto. There are pre-trial aspects, also, particularly in relation to the discovery of documents; these are considered mainly in the next chapter, Chapter 8.

HEARINGS IN CAMERA

7.04 "Camera" is an old word for "chamber" (as in *camera stellata*—the Star Chamber of Tudor days), and over the years the expression "in camera" has come to be used in law to denote proceedings which are heard privately (literally—in the judge's chamber) as opposed to being heard in open Court.

7.05 In 1913, when *Scott v. Scott* was decided, the principal exceptions in the civil field to the general rule of an open hearing were:

(1) litigation concerning secret processes;
(2) litigation concerning wards of Court and of lunatics (to use the contemporary phraseology).

7.06 The reason for the first exception is largely self-evident. To quote Viscount Haldane again:

> "The other case referred to, that of litigation as to a secret process, where the effect of publicity would be to destroy the subject-matter, illustrates a class which stands on a different footing. There it may well be that justice *could not be done at all* if it had to be done in public."[4] (emphasis added)

Yates Circuit Foil v. Electrofoils,[5] referred to at para. 3.12 *ante* in connection with confidential quality, represents a modern instance where the Court permitted an entire hearing to be held *in camera* for this reason.

7.07 The reason for the second exception is different. It was expressed by Viscount Haldane to be:

4 *Scott v. Scott* [1913] A.C. 417 at 437.
5 [1976] F.S.R. 345.

> ". . . the Court is really sitting primarily to guard the interests of the ward or lunatic. Its jurisdiction is in this respect parental and administrative, and the *disposal of controverted questions is an incident only* in the jurisdiction."[6] (emphasis added)

7.08 Since *Scott v. Scott* the exceptions have, to speak generally, become appreciably enlarged. Two distinct threads can be seen in the modern law.

Statutory power

7.09 Firstly, there are a number of variegated circumstances in which the Court is empowered by statute or statutory rules to exclude the public and sit *in camera*. Examples here are:

(1) domestic proceedings in magistrates' courts;[7]
(2) adoption proceedings;[8] and
(3) evidence on questions of sexual capacity in nullity proceedings (thus overruling the actual decision in *Scott v. Scott*).[9]

In the criminal sphere, comparable statutory restrictions can be found, for example, in:

(4) evidence given by children in cases involving offences contrary to decency or morality;[10] and
(5) proceedings under the Official Secrets Act 1920.[11]

The provision in the latter, itself a subject of current controversy, is couched in wide terms, as:

> ". . . if . . . application is made by the prosecution, on the ground that the publication of any evidence to be given or of any statement to be made in the course of the proceedings would be prejudicial to the national safety, that all or any portion of the public shall be excluded during any part of hearing, the Court may make an order to that effect, . . ."

Like controversy surrounds the quasi *in camera* restrictions represented by:

(6) the provisions in the Sexual Offences (Amendment) Act 1976 for anonymity of defendants[11a] and complainants in prosecution of rape charges.

6 *Ibid*, at 437.
7 Magistrates' Courts Act 1980, s. 69(2), (4).
8 Adoption Act 1976, s. 64.
9 Matrimonial Causes Act 1973, s. 48(2).
10 Children and Young Persons Act 1933, s. 37(1).
11 S. 8(4).
11a 1976 c. 82.

Inherent power

7.10 Secondly, there is, quite apart from and superimposed on the exceptions, a general principle that the Court always has an inherent jurisdiction to sit partly or wholly *in camera* where the ends of justice so demand it. In *Attorney-General v. Leveller Magazine,* concerning the direction of a magistrates' court to conceal the identity of a certain "Colonel B" who had given evidence in committal proceedings under the Official Secrets Acts, the principle was expressed as:

> "Apart from statutory exceptions, however, where a Court, in the exercise of its inherent power to control the conduct of proceedings before it, departs in any way from the general rule, the departure is justified to the extent and to no more than the extent it reasonably believes it to be necessary *in order to serve the ends of justice.*"[12] (emphasis added)

The "ends of justice" reason is of course a similar fount to that relied on many decades before by Viscount Haldane for the then more limited exception (under inherent power) of cases involving wards and/or lunatics. What has happened in the interim is really the judicial recognition that the reason provides a flexible instrument whereby *in camera* protection can be ordered, if desirable, for each new set of circumstances that comes along.

7.11 The overall impact of the Court's general power is reflected also in the later provisions of the Magistrates' Court Act 1980 already cited (Footnote 7) in relation to domestic proceedings in such Courts. Section 69(2), (4) first gave the Court certain statutory powers to limit public access and ensure privacy. Section 69(5) then continues by providing that:

> "(5) The powers conferred on a magistrates' court by this section shall be *in addition to* and *without prejudice to any other powers* of the court to hear proceedings in camera." (emphasis added)

7.12 It is under the general principle, again, that trade secrets cases continue (if the circumstances warrant) to be heard *in camera* to the extent necessary; they are treated more fully in a later separate section of this Chapter (paras. 7.31ff). Another kind of example under this head arises where the Court considers that witnesses might be deterred from giving evidence at all if the hearing were to be in public. Thus in *R v. Governor of Lewes Prison ex parte Doyle,*[13] following a conviction before a closed field general court martial in relation to acts arising from the Easter rising in Dublin in 1916, it was stated:

> ". . . if there had been a trial in open court—that is, with the public admitted—in the existing local conditions it would have been unsafe; and in

12 [1979] A.C. 440 at 450.
13 [1917] 2 K.B. 254.

> my judgement if it is *unsafe* for justice to be administered it is equivalent to saying that justice *could not in those circumstances be properly administered.*"[14] (emphasis added)

7.13 A striking recent example was provided by the case of *R v. Chief Registrar of Friendly Societies ex parte New Cross Building Society*. The Chief Registrar had made orders under the House Purchase and Housing Act 1959[15] and Building Societies Act 1962,[16] which effectively prevented the Society from accepting investment money and hence gravely interfered with its activities, on account of his concern as to the Society's management. The Society took proceedings for judicial review of these orders. The whole of the hearing, before both High Court and Court of Appeal, was permitted to be held *in camera* since:

> "If the society had to publicize the chief registrar's action in the process of getting the orders quashed, the loss of public confidence in the society would be such that whether or not the orders were quashed, the society would be forced to close. In other words, a public hearing would effectively have *deprived the society of the relief* to which in law and justice it was or might be entitled."[17]

Trial within a trial

7.14 Another rather more common example is provided by that of the so-called "trial within a trial" situation in a criminal case; the admissibility of an alleged confession by the accused, or other possibly prejudicial evidence, may have to be determined. To argue that point, the jury are sent out (in order that their minds may not be influenced by the facts of the confession in case the confession is held to be inadmissible in law) while the public can remain. There is in effect a partial denial of access.

Subsequent publication

7.15 The question of publication in the public press or other news medium outside the Court of happenings inside the Court is to be distinguished from the question of public access in the first place—although both are concerned generally with what might be termed the confidentiality of the proceedings.

7.16 In the case of "a trial within a trial" during the course of a criminal prosecution, for example, the press (as well as other members of the

14 At 272.
15 7 & 8 Eliz. II c. 33.
16 10 & 11 Eliz. II c. 37.
17 [1984] Q.B. 227 at 235.

public) would normally be permitted to remain in Court to hear the arguments for and against the admissibility of the confession or other evidence. But if a newspaper were to print a report of those arguments prior to conclusion of the main trial and pronouncement of a verdict, it might well be committing a contempt. By such publication the whole purpose of sending the jury out while admissibility was being determined would have been negated; members of the jury could buy and read the newspaper just as any other member of the public could. But once a verdict has been pronounced, the purpose has ended; the jury cannot subsequently claw back its verdict. It follows that publication would then be quite proper.

7.17 Domestic proceedings in magistrates' courts again provide another example. Under Section 69(2) of the Magistrates' Courts Act 1980,[18] the public in general is denied access but an exception is made for:

"(c) representatives of newspapers or news agencies".

Such representatives may therefore be in a position to hear the entire case. Yet, although they may have heard it all, subsequential publication of content of the evidence led may still be restricted. By Section 71(1) of the same Act, the particulars which may be published are limited to:

(a) the names, addresses and occupations of the parties and witnesses;
(b) the grounds of the application, and a concise statement of the charges, defences and counter-charges in support of which evidence has been given;
(c) submissions on any point of law arising in the course of the proceedings and the decision of the court on the submissions;
(d) the decision of the court, and any observations made by the court in giving it."

HEARINGS IN CHAMBERS

7.18 Conceptually different from, although in practice similar to, a Court hearing *in camera* (partly or fully) is a hearing in chambers. A Court hearing is, intrinsically, one of open character; the restrictions as to access which may be grafted onto it have been discussed above. A hearing in chambers on the other hand is, intrinsically, one of private character.

7.19 It is beyond the scope of this book to discuss the question of exactly what constitutes Court work and what constitutes chambers work; the precise dividing line is hard to determine. The definition

18 1980 c. 43.

contained in section 67 of the Supreme Court Act 1981[19] is itself couched in somewhat elastic terms:

> "Business in the High Court shall be heard and disposed of in court except insofar as it may, under this or any other Act, under rules of court or *in accordance with the practice of the court,* be dealt with in chambers." (emphasis added)

The commentary in the "White Book" to Order 32 of the Rules of the Supreme Court nevertheless provides extensive lists of matters which are conventionally dealt with in chambers before a Judge or Master, for Queen's Bench/Family and Chancery Divisions.

7.20 In the broadest sense, however, it may be said that chambers matters are generally of (i) administrative or (ii) interim procedural kind. An administrative matter is represented, for example, by the appointment of guardians of minors' estates (in the Chancery Division). An interim procedural matter is represented, for example, by an application for leave to serve a writ out of the jurisdiction or an *ex parte* application for an interlocutory injunction. Much of the chamber's jurisdiction can therefore be exerted by the master (an official of the Court) in place of the judge himself.

CONTEMPT

7.21 The topic of contempt of Court has been mentioned earlier in this Chapter in connection with hearings *in camera.* It is closely associated with the question of access but is strictly to be distinguished therefrom. Punishment for contempt of Court represents, in effect, the sanction for breach of any ruling including one that proceedings be *in camera;* it is the procedural handmaid to the substantive law in this respect. At its widest, of course, contempt covers a much greater territory; shouting insults at the judge or causing a disturbance in the court room, for example by waving of political banners, might well rank as contempt even though no question of the proceedings being *in camera* arises. As stated in *Attorney General v. Leveller Magazine:*

> ". . . although criminal contempts of court may take a variety of forms they all share a common characteristic; they involve an *interference* with the due administration of justice either in a particular case or more generally as a continuing process. It is *justice itself that is flouted* by contempt of court, not the individual court or judge who is attempting to administer it."[20] (emphasis added)

19 1981 c. 54.
20 [1979] A.C. 440 at 449.

For present purposes, the main rules are contained in the statutory provisions of the Administration of Justice Act 1960[21] (section 12) and the Contempt of Court Act 1981[22] (sections 8, 10 and 11).

7.22 Section 12(1) of the 1960 Act provides generally that the publication of information relating to proceedings before any court sitting in private shall not rank as contempt except in cases involving:

(1) wardship, adoption, guardianship, custody and the like of infants;
(2) property and affairs of mental patients;
(3) national security (as a result of which the Court has sat in private);
(4) secret processes, discoveries or inventions; and
(5) any other case where the Court, given that it has intrinsic power to do so, has expressly prohibited the publication of information concerning the proceedings.

"Sitting in private" is stated to include both Courts sitting *in camera* and in chambers (illustrating the considerable equivalence between the two); "Court" is stated to include tribunals also, so rendering the provision applicable to the considerable number of administrative tribunals extant today.

7.23 The format of the provision is also to be noted. By providing that publication shall not rank as contempt except in the cases enumerated, it follows that a third party who improperly gains access to some proceedings *in camera* of another type, for example an application for an interlocutory order of the Anton Piller type, and subsequently publishes a report of the same, is not liable under the Act.

7.24 Section 8 of the 1981 Act is a general provision making it a contempt to breach the confidentiality of the jury room; in the statutory language of sub-section (1):

> ". . . it is a contempt of court to obtain, disclose or solicit any particulars of statements made, opinions expressed, arguments advanced or votes cast by members of a jury in the course of their deliberations in any legal proceedings."

7.25 This provision essentially made new law. There had traditionally been a convention that jury room deliberations were to be secret. But there was no comprehensive common law rule to that effect; and in *Attorney General v. New Statesman*,[23] a case involving publication of a

21 8 & 9 Eliz. II c. 65.
22 1981 c. 49.
23 [1981] Q.B. 1.

juror's comments in relation to the acquittal of a well-known politician and others on serious charges, it had been held that such rule as there was had limited scope. Disclosure of jury secrets was only contempt if it tended or would tend to imperil the finality of jury verdicts or to affect adversely the attitude of future jurors and the quality of their deliberations—a test not met in the circumstances of that case. The juror involved had honestly thought that certain aspects of the case ought to be made public, and was not seeking any reward for his disclosures. The new provision effectively blocks that exception and enunciates a much wider rule.

7.26 Section 10 of the 1981 Act represents a controversial provision. It reads as follows:

> "No court may require a person to disclose, nor is any person guilty of contempt of court for refusing to disclose, the source of information contained in a publication for which he is responsible, unless it be established to the satisfaction of the court that disclosure is necessary *in the interests of justice or national security or for the prevention of disorder or crime.*" (emphasis added)

7.27 The provision may be regarded as a statutory affirmation, so far as the printed word is concerned, of the common-law principle that a journalist does not have total immunity from disclosing the sources of his information; all depends upon the exact circumstances—see *British Steel v. Granada Television.*[24] The subject of journalist and mole is discussed more fully later, in Chapter 14. The next Chapter 8 considers also to some extent the position of other types of confidant. But the present work is not intended to be comprehensive on the overall topic of compellability of witnesses; that is to be found in works on the law of evidence.

7.28 Section 11 provides as follows:

> "In any case where a court (having power to do so) allows a name or other matter to be withheld from the public in proceedings before the court, the court may give such directions prohibiting the publication of that name or matter in connection with the proceedings *as appear to the court to be necessary for the purpose for which it was so withheld.*" (emphasis added)

7.29 The provision thus overlaps with those of Section 12(1) of the Administration of Justice Act 1960, particularly since the final limb of Section 12(1) is couched in general terms; it is only the earlier limbs of Section 12(1) which are restricted to certain specified kinds of proceedings (wardship *et seq*). There would appear to be no precise dividing line

24 [1981] A.C. 1096.

between the two. But it is clear that Section 11 is directed primarily at preventing the subsequent disclosure of witnesses' identities and the like, in cases where the Court deems fit—in other words, to put on a formal statutory basis the kind of prohibition ordered in the "Colonel B" case *(Attorney General v. Leveller Magazine)*, para. 7.11 *supra*.

7.30 For purposes of the Contempt of Court Act 1981, "Court" is again defined as including tribunals.

TRADE SECRETS CASES

7.31 Mention has been made above of the powers of the Court to hold hearings of trade secrets cases *in camera*, and to prohibit subsequent publication to the world at large of information concerning the secrets. A further complication arises in cases of this kind—namely, that of keeping the subject-matter of the process or the like secret from the other party to the action as well.

7.32 Consider the case of a patent infringement action in which the defendant sets up the plea that he is making his product by means of a secret process. If that process, although secret, falls within the terms of the patent, then he is no doubt liable as an infringer. Conversely, however, the defendant may justifiably be most unwilling to inform the plaintiff patentee of his secret process. If the defendant's secret version of the patented process is superior to the plaintiff's version (say, the defendant has found better reaction conditions in a chemical case), then the latter may well be tempted to adopt the former's version; alternatively, he may use the knowledge acquired from the former's version as a springboard for further development work of his own. Strictly, such adoption or development might rank as a breach of confidence in its own right (on the basis that use of information disclosed compulsorily in the course of Court proceedings would rank as unauthorised use). But policing of such breach could be difficult; and the plaintiff, although entitled to be compensated for the defendant's tort, should not strictly be permitted to gain positively from its commission.

7.33 To overcome this kind of difficulty the Court has evolved over the years the practice of allowing limited inspection only of the defendant's process. Cases in this line of authority include:

(1) *British Thomson-Houston v. Duram (No. 2)*[25] (1920) manufacture of tungsten filaments for electric lamps): An order was granted that not

25 37 R.P.C. 121.

more than two experts be allowed to take samples of the defendants' product in various stages of its manufacture and to report to the Court upon the facts disclosed by the inspection and the experts' opinion founded thereon. The experts were to be put on terms not to disclose anything appearing on the inspection to constitute part of the alleged secret process, without permission of the Court; however, they were to be allowed to report to the plaintiffs, but without disclosing any details, their opinion as to whether the defendant's process infringed.

(2) *Coloured Asphalte v. British Asphalt & Bitumen*[26] (1935) (manufacture of asphaltic bitumen): similar order granted to permit inspection by the plaintiffs' counsel, solicitor and expert.

(3) *British Celanese v. Courtaulds*[27] (1932) (manufacture of artificial silk): order granted to permit inspection by plaintiffs' counsel, solicitor and experts, with proviso:

> "And that neither the Plaintiffs' Counsel experts nor solicitor shall disclose to the Plaintiffs or any other person any facts in relation to the Defendants' business, works or processes *which they may observe which are immaterial to the questions in the action* and, in particular in relation to the design dimensions and layout of the dry spinning machines and the devices used on or in connection therewith which do not form the subject of any claim of which infringement is alleged." (emphasis added)

7.34 The point may also arise, albeit under a new guise, at the stage of discovery of documents in the action. Whereas at one time, the vital details may have been confined just to the heads of a few key personnel—production manager, works foreman and the like—it is now increasingly common for details of the process (although still secret) to have been written down as well. Alternatively, it may be that the relevant information can be conveyed more accurately by means of written documents than personal view; inspection of the assembly of pipes, gauges, reactors, vessels and the like of a modern chemical plant is unlikely in itself to provide a complete picture of the process even to the most skilled chemist. Knowledge is necessary also of what is being fed in, and where, and what is emerging.

7.35 It now seems clear from the recent decision in *Warner-Lambert v. Glaxo Laboratories*[28] (manufacture of therapeutic steroids) that similar principles apply to such written information. It is also noteworthy that the Court here was prepared (after reviewing all the earlier authorities) to expand the scope of disclosure to all of the plaintiffs' (i) counsel, (ii) solicitor, (iii) patent agent, (iv) expert and (v) company chairman (the

26 53 R.P.C. 89.
27 50 R.P.C. 63.
28 [1975] R.P.C. 354.

plaintiff was a United States Corporation), although not to (vi) the plaintiffs' general United States house counsel, (vii) the plaintiffs' United States patent counsel nor (viii) an expert employed by the plaintiffs in Italy. As for the potential embarrassment which might arise for the chairman if, coincidentally, one of his own employees comes to him with a suggestion to use a similar technique as that actually employed by the defendants in their secret process:

> "This is a difficulty which he must resolve as an honourable man: he must be poker-faced, just as he must if quizzed by members of his Board."[29]

The emphasis upon the need for honour in this aspect of the law of confidential information echoes, once again, the equitable and moral origins of the jurisdiction generally.

29 At 363.

CHAPTER 8

Confidentiality in the Course of Legal Proceedings—Part II

INTRODUCTION

8.01 Chapter 7 was concerned primarily with the question of confidentiality in the actual conduct of a trial and in its subsequent reporting. This chapter, in contrast, considers confidentiality in respect of chronologically earlier matters; it is concerned primarily with the question of the extent to which confidential matter nascent pre-trial can nevertheless be subsequently exposed at trial to the searchlight of the judicial process.

8.02 This is a complicated skein to unravel. It can of course be easy to assert that a previous record, document or communication in the possession of one of the parties or of a potential witness and now realised to be relevant to an issue arising at trial was, in a general lay sense, "confidential". It can be much more difficult to decide as to what, if any, head of protection against disclosure is available in law. The cry of "confidentiality" may have been raised parrot-wise, simply as a screen to try and cover up material which is embarrassing to a party's case.

8.03 The subject as a whole shades into that of the law of evidence generally—which it is not the purpose of this book to expound. Different considerations may apply according to the format of the item desired to be kept secret (oral or written); the nature of the trial (civil or criminal); the nature of the item (a record made unilaterally by one person as distinct from a communication passing bilaterally from one to another); the nexus between the person(s) involved at the time and those now a party to the trial; this list is not exhaustive. Emphasis will accordingly be placed in this chapter upon the kinds of situation which are most prominant in practice—particularly those which tend to occur in civil proceedings, the whole concept of confidence being one of equity and hence one for the civil courts to administer.

8.04 Mention may also be made of the nomenclature in this area of the law of confidence. Matter which the law permits to be kept secret from the eyes of the other party to the proceedings, i.e. kept confidential, is often referred to as "privileged"; the noun "privilege" is correspondingly used to denote the right of the party involved to keep secret the "privileged" matter. But usage is not always consistent. And it is essential to remember that the mere fact that matter is confidential in character—say an expert's report headed "Confidential" or a memorandum summarising conversations held with another in clandestine circumstances—is not decisive as to the existence of privilege. As stated unambiguously in *Alfred Crompton Amusement Machines v. Customs & Excise*:[1]

> " 'Confidentiality' is not a separate head of privilege . . ."

although it may naturally be a very pertinent consideration so far as the existence of certain kinds of privilege is concerned. Confidentiality may accordingly be a condition precedent, but not a condition controlling.

ORAL COMMUNICATIONS (PRIVILEGED)

8.05 Issues concerning allegedly privileged prior oral communications normally arise in the context of giving evidence at trial; is a witness inherently competent to give evidence of such a kind, and then if he is competent, can he be compelled to do so? Not all witnesses are willing; a subpoena may have had to be obtained. Issues concerning allegedly privileged prior written communications, on the other hand, tend to surface at the earlier stage of discovery of documents—at least in civil proceedings. Although there is a considerable area of overlap between the two—both as regards the substantive law applicable and because a communication which was originally made orally may have been reduced to writing by one of the parties to it—nevertheless the procedural difference renders it convenient to split them here.

8.06 The main classes of prior oral communications which require consideration are:

(i) communications made in professional confidence;
(ii) marital communications;

which will now be considered in turn.

Professional

8.07 Concerning professional communications, the most important kind is that of communications with a legal adviser. The general rule here

1 [1974] A.C. 405 at 433.

is that oral communications between a party and his legal adviser are privileged—provided of course that the communications can be fairly regarded as deriving from a lawyer/client relationship and are not directed to the furtherance of some illegal object, say a fraud or a crime. Thus, a disclosure made by a client to his solicitor over lunch concerning his next year's crop-sowing plans, following a formal morning interview to discuss his forthcoming appearance in the local magistrates' court on a motoring offence, is liable not to be privileged. Nor is advice given by a solicitor as to how best to organise and run a spurious charity.

8.08 The classical justification for the rule is contained in the remarks of Jessel M. R. in 1876 in *Anderson v. Bank of British Columbia:*[2]

> "The object and meaning of the rule is this: that as, by reason of the complexity and difficulty of our law, litigation can only be properly conducted by professional men, it is absolutely necessary that a man, in order to prosecute his rights or to defend himself from an improper claim, should have recourse to the assistance of professional lawyers, and it being so absolutely necessary, it is equally necessary, to use a vulgar phrase, that he should be able to *make a clean breast of it* to the gentleman whom he consults with a view to the prosecution of his claim, or the substantiating his defence against the claim of others; that he should be able to place unrestricted and unbounded confidence in the professional agent, and that the communications he so makes to him should be kept secret, unless with his consent (for it is *his privilege, and not the privilege of the confidential agent*), that he should be enabled properly to conduct his litigation." (emphasis added)

8.09 When the communication is between the legal adviser of his client and a third party, the privilege is more limited in extent. Not merely must there be a proper professional lawyer-client relationship extant, but also there must be litigation in contemplation or existence and the communication must have been made for purposes relevant to that litigation—say, for obtaining expert advice or collecting evidence. It should be mentioned, however, that legal professional privilege is always—as the word "privilege" inherently implies—an option open to the client for his advantage if he so chooses rather than a bar. The client (although not the legal adviser) can always waive the privilege. If he does, then either the adviser or client can give evidence as to the oral communication which passed between them; the same naturally applies to written communications.

8.10 Outside the field of legal advice, communications do not in general attract privilege; a special statutory exception is made under the Patents

2 2 Ch. D. 644 at 649.

Act 1977[3] in respect of communications with patent agents concerning pending or contemplated patent proceedings (as opposed to communications for the purpose of drafting patent specifications, and the like). The fact that the communication is made to a person who might otherwise be regarded as of professional status—say, a teacher, chartered surveyor, optician, chartered accountant, actuary or veterinary surgeon—does not help. Accordingly, a lay person seeking advice on a specialist matter (outside the ordinary ken of a lawyer) which runs the chance of being litigious may well be better advised to obtain that advice through his lawyer rather than directly, if he wishes its contents to remain confidential.

8.11 In respect of certain kinds of adviser and the like, the refusal to accord privilege has attracted controversy. This is particularly so in respect of communications to doctors, spiritual advisers and journalists. The landmark case in this connection is that of *Wheeler v. Le Marchant*, where it was said in 1881 by Jessel M.R.:[4]

> "In the first place, the principle protecting confidential communications is of a very limited character. It does not protect all confidential communications which a man must necessarily make in order to obtain advice, even when needed for the protection of his life, or of his honour, or of his fortune. There are many communications which, though absolutely necessary because without them the ordinary business of life cannot be carried on, still are not privileged. The communications made to a *medical man* whose advice is sought by a patient with respect to the probable origin of the disease as to which he is consulted, and which must necessarily be made in order to enable the medical man to advise or to prescribe for the patient, *are not protected*. Communications made to a *priest* in the confessional on matters perhaps considered by the penitent to be more important even than his life or his fortune, *are not protected*. Communications made to a friend with respect to matters of the most delicate nature, on which advice is sought with respect to a man's honour or reputation, are not protected. Therefore it *must not be supposed that there is any principle which says that every confidential communication which it is necessary to make in order to carry on the ordinary business of life is protected.*" (emphasis added)

8.12 The exclusion of communications to priests may reflect the relatively minor importance of the confessional in the forms of worship of the Church of England, the established church in the United Kingdom. As pointed out in the *Anderson* case,[5] *supra*:

> "Again, in foreign counties where the Roman Catholic faith prevails, it is considered that the same principles ought to be extended to the

3 1977 c. 37 (s. 104)
4 17 Ch. D. 675 at 681.
5 At 651; see para. 8.08.

> confessional, and that it is desirable that a man should not be hampered in going to confession by the thought that either he or his priest may be compelled to disclose in a Court of Justice the substance of what passed in such communication. This, again, *whether it is rational or irrational, is not recognised by our law.*" (emphasis added)

And in view of the increasing secularisation of modern society, it may be doubted whether any change as regards spiritual advisers is likely in future.

8.13 The modern position may be regarded as summarised by the speech of Lord Edmund Davies in *D v. NSPCC*,[6] a case concerning a mother's attempt to obtain from the NSPCC the name of an informant who had telephoned them concerning a feared ill-treatment of her infant child. Although in this case the defendant was allowed to maintain secrecy upon the "public interest" exception (discussed later in this chapter), the holding is still quite unequivocal on the central issue–

> "(1) In civil proceedings a judge has *no discretion*, simply because what is contemplated is the disclosure of information which has passed between persons in a confidential relationship (other than that of lawyer and client), to direct a party to that relationship that he need not disclose that information even though its disclosure is (a) relevant to and (b) necessary for the attainment of justice in the particular case. If (a) and (b) are established, the *doctor or the priest must be directed to answer* if, despite the strong dissuasion of the judge, the advocate persists in seeking disclosure. This is also true of all other confidential relationships in the absence of a special statutory provision, such as the Civil Evidence Act 1968, regarding communications between patent agents and their clients." (emphasis added)

Chapter 13, *post*, explores further the difficulties presented to doctors and journalists under the present state of the law.

Marital

8.14 The position as regards marital communications can be dealt with more briefly. At one time, when the concern of the law in upholding the sanctity of the marriage bond was perhaps rather stronger than it is today, all communications between spouses were protected. The Evidence Amendment Act 1853,[7] section 3 laid down quite clearly:

> "No husband shall be compellable to disclose any communication made to him by his wife during the marriage, and no wife shall be compellable to disclose any communication made to her by her husband during the marriage".

with similar provision in the Criminal Evidence Act 1898,[7a] section 1(d).

6 [1978] A.C. 171 at 245.
7 16 & 17 Vict. c. 83.
7a 61 & 62 Vict. c. 36.

8.15 But the exclusion was limited by the Civil Evidence Act 1968,[8] section 16(3) to criminal proceedings only, so leaving a spouse generally compellable in respect of prior communications when it comes to civil proceedings. It is not directly material whether the communication was made explicitly on confidential terms (indeed, that might be somewhat unlikely in the circumstances), or whether the communication was of oral or written kind.

8.16 For the precise contemporary position as to compellability of a spouse in criminal proceedings in respect of communications previously passing between them, reference should be made to works on criminal evidence. There can be limited instances, involving the person or liberty of the spouse, where there is compellability at common law; and conversely, there are certain specific statutory areas, for example in the social security field, where immunity from being so compelled is explicitly preserved. The provisions of the Police and Criminal Evidence Act 1984 may apply.

WRITTEN COMMUNICATIONS (PRIVILEGED)

8.17 Reference has already been made in a number of places above to the general equivalence of the substantive law as regards categories of privilege, for prior oral and written communications. But there are important practical differences according to whether the communication is one of an oral or written kind. If the communication sought to be adduced in evidence was one of oral kind, and a claim of privilege is refused, the other party is unlikely to know of the precise contents of the communication until trial and oral evidence is given of that oral communication; indeed, the party who has compelled—say the doctor—to give evidence of the patient's communication to him in the surgery may find that the evidence is not in fact at all helpful to his own case and come to regret having forced the answers in the first place. But if the communication was one of a written kind, and still extant, it would normally be expected to be produced at the discovery stage pre-trial. This gives the party who forced production of the communication the opportunity of considering the document in advance. If he finds it unhelpful to his case, he may decide not to rely upon it at all at trial; the mere fact that he has compelled its production does not mean that he is subsequently compelled in turn to use it. Alternatively, it may serve to set him off down some new track in the litigation, or to prepare some expert counter-evidence of his own. Questions may also arise as to what, if any,

8 1968 c. 64.

subsequent use he may make of the document. Another question which may arise is when the claim of privilege is successful, but nevertheless the party seeking to adduce the privileged document obtains a copy of it by other means.

8.18 The main classes of documents which can be withheld from disclosure are:

(i) documents attracting professional privilege;
(ii) documents tending to incriminate;
(iii) documents privileged on grounds of public interest;

and these will now be considered in turn.

Professional documents

8.19 The documents attracting professional privilege are essentially restricted by considerations similar to those already discussed for oral communications; that is, to ones attracting legal professional privilege (which in turn means that the document must either be directly between lawyer/client or, in the case of lawyer/third party communications, have been prepared in contemplation of legal proceedings) and not excluded as being directed to the furtherance of illegality. The case of communications to doctors, priests and the like is naturally in any event of much less significance here, since patients or supplicants normally convey their information orally rather than in writing—although the doctor, at least, may well have made a subsequent written note of his conversation with the patient. The fact that the document may unequivocally have been regarded by the parties at the time as confidential—say the document is a surveyor's report headed "Confidential" on page 1—is not decisive. It either does or does not attract legal professional privilege on the objective criteria previously discussed.

8.20 Examples of documents which normally would be privileged are therefore letters to a solicitor requesting legal advice, and his reply to the same; cases for Counsel and Counsel's subsequent opinion; communications with a foreign lawyer; internal communications between an employer and his in-house salaried legal adviser; drafts of agreements, conveyances and the like.

8.21 But not all written communications from a client to a solicitor are protected. In *Smith-Bird v. Blower*,[9] a letter saying:

9 [1939] 2 All E.R. 406.

> "In reply to yours of the 22nd instant, I beg to confirm that I gave Mr. Harry Brown a note of authority to convey the above property to him for £510. I further note that you will let me know when you wish me to come over to complete."

was held not to be privileged since it was written by the defendant in the case not for the purpose of obtaining legal advice from his solicitors, but in answer to an inquiry by them to inform them of the fact that he had agreed to sell the property in question to a Mr Brown. In *Jones v. Great Central Railway*[10] letters between a dismissed employee and officials of his union containing information about the dispute which led to his dismissal, which had to be provided before the union would sanction the engagement of a solicitor to act on his behalf, were likewise refused privilege. The executive committee and/or the general secretary of the union could not be regarded as the *alter ego* of the solicitor, since they had to consider the information and come to a decision of their own before approaching the solicitor at all. As shown by these examples, difficult border-line cases may arise and works on the law of evidence should be consulted for a fuller picture. The privilege may of course be waived, at the client's option, just as in the case of oral communications with a legal adviser.

8.22 An interesting recent case involving the illegality exception is *Gamlen Chemical v. Rochem*,[11] where certain senior ex-employees of the plaintiffs had left to set up in competition, in the business of selling chemicals for cleaning ships. Allegations of conspiracy to injure, breach of duty of fidelity and breach of confidence had been made. Amongst the documents on which discovery was requested were ones relating to the instructions given by the ex-employees to a solicitor co-defendant in connection with the formation of the defendant companies and generally for setting-up the corporate and commercial structure within which the new business was to operate. Discovery was ordered, notwithstanding the absence of the actual word "fraud" in the statement of claim, on the basis that this was clearly a case where fraud (in the sense of the term as used by those in commerce) and dishonesty was involved. As for the argument that the Court should be slow to extend the exception to the privilege of legal professional communications:

> ". . . which is essential to the fair working of our system of justice and the proper protection of individual interests . . ."

the answer was:

> "That is very true, but it is equally important, in my judgment, not to

10 [1910] A.C. 4.
11 [1983] R.P.C. 1.

whittle down the existing protection given to victims of fraud, otherwise in many cases there would be no hope of an injured plaintiff ever obtaining the necessary material for defining and proving the wrong that he has suffered by secret and dishonest combinations."[12]

Incriminating documents

8.23 As for documents tending to incriminate or expose to a penalty, the general principle is that a party so affected may object to producing them, although he may not be able to object to making the initial list so as to acquaint the other party with the fact of their existence. Hence in *Waterhouse v. Barker*,[13] a female defendant who had assertedly fraudulently obtained a large sum of money from the plaintiff's deceased husband following alleged acts of adultery was able to resist an application under the Bankers' Books Evidence Act 1879[14] for leave to inspect her bank account records. But this principle has been eroded at times, in certain areas, by statutory derogation. Under the Exchange Control Act 1947,[15] for example, the Treasury could compel a person to produce such books, accounts, or other documents as may be required by the Treasury for the purpose of securing compliance with or detecting evasion of the Act. Other examples exist in the fields of bankruptcy, land registration, libel and elsewhere. By section 14(1)(a) of the Civil Evidence Act 1968,[16] the crimination or penalty must arise (so far as resisting discovery in civil proceedings is concerned) under United Kingdom law.

"Public interest" documents

8.24 As for documents privileged on grounds of public interest, this is a plant having deep historical roots. What has been controversial in more recent times, culminating in a whole sheaf of cases in the House of Lords in the past decade or so, is the extent of the privilege; how luxuriant is the sheltering foliage of the plant over the legal soil beneath? The controversy reflects the contemporary increase both in the interventionary powers of the state in the affairs of private citizens and in the demand for justice (as distinct from law). This head of privilege thus stands in contrast to the head of legal professional privilege where—although successive decisions may continually adjust its precise periphery—the general scope of the privilege is clear and its justifiability largely unchallenged. The head is sometimes referred to as Crown privilege, but this is really a misnomer;

12 At 7.
13 [1924] 2 K.B. 759.
14 42 & 43 Vict. c. 11.
15 10 & 11 Geo. VI c. 14 (Schedule 5, Part I, Para. 1(1)).
16 1968 c. 64.

although a Minister of the Crown may, in the circumstances of a particular case, be the most appropriate person to asert the privilege, the privilege is by no means restricted to cases where a department of State or other organ of government is a party.

8.25 In broad terms, the law is to be seen as having gradually retreated from the high point (as regards scope of the privilege) of *Duncan v. Cammell Laird*[17] in 1942. The *Duncan* case itself involved an attempt to obtain discovery of documents relating to the construction of a submarine, the *Thetis*, which had sunk in 1939 just prior to the outbreak of World War II, with great loss of life; the suit was a private one, as between representatives of the deceased and the builders of the submarine, but the plans, specifications and the like of the submarine were clearly—particularly in a time of hostilities—matters relevant to national defence. Discovery was, not surprisingly in the circumstances, refused. But Viscount Simon, speaking unanimously for the House of Lords, chose to give his reasons expressed in wider language than necessitated by the facts. The dicta which gave rise to controversy, when subsequently sought to be relied on by governmental or the like bodies in situations far removed on their facts from *Duncan,* were principally:

> ". . . the objection is sometimes based upon the view that the public interest requires a particular class of communications with, or within, a public department to be protected from production on the ground that the *candour and completeness of such communications might be prejudiced if they were ever liable to be disclosed in subsequent litigation* rather than on the contents of the particular document itself."[18] (emphasis added)

> "The principle to be applied in every case is that documents otherwise relevant and liable to production must not be produced if the public interest requires that they should be withheld. This test may be found to be satisfied either (a) by having regard to the contents of the particular document, or (b) by the fact that the document belongs to a class which, on grounds of public interest must as a class be withheld from production."[19]

8.26 The leading cases since include:

(1) *Conway v. Rimmer*[20] (1968)—Reports made by superintendent to chief constable concerning a probationary police constable held not privileged.

(2) *R v. Lewes Justices ex parte Home Secretary*[21] (1972)—Correspondence between assistant chief constable and Gaming Board,

17 [1942] A.C. 624.
18 At 635.
19 At 636.
20 [1968] A.C. 910.
21 [1973] A.C. 388.

concerning suitability of an applicant for a gaming licence, held privileged.

(3) *Norwich Pharmacal v. Customs & Excise*[22] (1973)—Customs & Excise documents showing names and addresses of importers of a drug allegedly infringing a patent held not privileged.

(4) *Alfred Crompton Amusement Machines v. Customs & Excise*[23] (1973)—Internal documents and memoranda (which contained information obtained from third parties) of Customs & Excise in connection with the assessment of purchase tax held privileged.

(5) *Burmah Oil v. Bank of England*[24] (1979)—Documents relating to the governmentally directed rescue of an oil company from grave financial difficulties arising out of an international oil crisis held privileged.

(6) *Lonrho v. Shell Petroleum*[25] (1980)—Documents and transcripts of evidence presented to private governmental inquiry concerning possible breach of oil sanctions held privileged.

(7) *Campbell v. Tameside Council*[26] (1982)—Reports of teachers, psychologists and psychiatrists to local education authority concerning a pupil of alleged violent disposition held not privileged.

8.27 The position now is essentially that the Court must perform a balancing act in deciding whether or not to order discovery. As stated in *Campbell, supra,* by Ackner L. J:

> "The proper approach where there is a question of public interest immunity is a *weighing*, on balance of the two public interests, that of the nation or the public service in non-disclosure and that of justice in the production of the documents." [27] (emphasis added)

8.28 The striking of the balance, in any given case, must depend upon its own facts. The "class of documents" approach of *Duncan, supra*, is now discredited; nor is the fear of future lack of candour controlling. The Court may itself inspect the documents, to assist in carrying out the balancing operation. Whilst no exhaustive list of relevant factors can be drawn up, in *D v. NSPCC* (para. 8.13 *supra*) it was pointed out that:

> "The categories of public interest are not closed, and must *alter from time to time* whether by restriction or extension as social conditions and social legislation develop"[28] (emphasis added)

22 [1974] A.C. 133.
23 [1974] A.C. 405.
24 [1980] A.C. 1090.
25 [1980] 1 W.L.R. 627.
26 [1982] 2 Q.B. 1065.
27 At 1076.
28 [1978] A.C. 171 at 230.

8.29 It is undoubtedly correct to say that the significance of the documents to the proceedings in issue is normally highly material. If the Court, after its own inspection of the same, concludes that they are of only low or marginal significance, and hence not strictly necessary for fairly disposing of the matter, then naturally it may be slow to bar the claim to privilege. But, conversely, high or even extreme significance is not necessarily enough to exclude the claim. In *D v. NSPCC*, for example, the Society's written record of the informant's name was essential to the action which the mother wished to initiate against the informant (as well as the action against the Society); without the name, she did not know whom to sue. Yet the Society's privilege in the document on public interest grounds (quite apart from its confidential nature) was upheld.

RESTRICTIONS ON USE

8.30 The inherent difference between a prior confidential oral communication and a prior confidential written commucication, in the context of their possible subsequent deployment at trial, has already been mentioned. The permanence and/or copiability of the latter as opposed to the transitoriness of the former (unless of course simultaneously recorded on a tape or like medium) gives rise to opportunities for other use. Likewise, the contents of the one are certain, whereas the contents of the other are uncertain; two separate persons may have widely differing recollections of their conversation but the written words are in themselves fixed; the fact that the meaning of the words as written may be open to argument, or that they may represent an inaccurate record of an oral conversation, represents different issues.

8.31 The Court has accordingly developed the broad rule that where a prior written communication (or other record) of confidential nature has had to be disclosed in the course of legal proceedings—either under normal discovery or following an unsuccessful claim of privilege (legal professional or otherwise)—then that disclosure is limited to the purposes of those proceedings only. In other words, the person forced to provide the disclosure can (except for any part of the matter actually revealed in open Court at trial and independently noted there by third party attendees), retain confidentiality of the material so far as the world at large is concerned; there is, in short, a loss of confidentiality only so far as the other party to the proceedings is concerned. The disparity between the quantum of material produced at discovery and that actually deployed at trial can of course be very considerable, in view of the wide wording of O.24 r.1(1) of the Rules of the Supreme Court 1965:[29]

> ". . . there shall be . . . discovery by the parties to the action of the documents . . . relating to matters in question in the action."

taken with the classic exegesis of that definition in *Compagnie Financière du Pacifique v. Peruvian Guano* in 1882 to the effect that there must be disclosed any document which:

> ". . . may—not which must—either directly or indirectly enable the party . . . either to advance his own case or to damage the case of his adversary." [30]

and a document may so advance or damage

> ". . . if it is a document which may *fairly lead him to a train of inquiry*, which may have either of these two consequences." [31]

8.32 *Distillers v. Times Newspapers* [32] involved a situation where there had been misuse of documents produced on discovery. The matter sprang originally from the teratogenic effects of the drug Thalidomide. In previous actions brought by and/or on behalf of the handicapped children Distillers had produced, on discovery, a very considerable volume of documents concerning the drug; many of these had been given in turn to an expert retained on the children's behalf; he in turn had sold the documents to a national newspaper, which in turn (following settlement of the children's action) was concerned to publish articles based on the contents of the documents. Interlocutory relief was granted to Distillers. *Riddick v. Thames Board Mills* [33] again involved documents produced on discovery in a settled action, by an ex-employee against the company for alleged wrongful arrest and false imprisonment arising in the course of his dismissal. The employee was held not to be entitled to use a report prepared by a member of the company's personnel department, which had been produced on discovery in the settled action, in a subsequent action for defamation based on the report.

8.33 In *Home Office v. Harman*,[34] the rule reached perhaps its highwater mark. Documents had been disclosed to the solicitor for a plaintiff in respect of an action against the Home Office for alleged unlawful confinement in the "control unit" of a prison, following an unsuccessful claim of public interest privilege. Apparently "all material parts" of the

29 S.I. 1965 No. 1776.
30 11 Q.B.D. 55 at 63.
31 At 63.
32 [1975] Q.B. 613.
33 [1977] Q.B. 881.
34 [1983] A.C. 280.

documents had been read out in Court at the trial. Shortly afterwards, the solicitor gave inspection of the documents to a journalist who subsequently wrote a newspaper article relying on their contents. It was held by the House of Lords that this act of the solicitor was a contempt of Court.

8.34 Another instance, less controversial in nature but still showing the tightness of the Court's rein over use of discovered documents, is provided by the patent case of *Halcon International v. Shell Transport and Trading*.[35] Here, the plaintiffs were refused permission to make use of research documents obtained from the defendants on discovery for corresponding litigation abroad. On the other hand, in *Sony Corporation v. Anand*[36] it was held that information obtained as a result of an Anton Piller order for discovery could be used for bringing subsequent actions elsewhere against other parties (the suppliers in Hong Kong and Taiwan of the infringing cassette tapes), bearing in mind the different fundamental purpose of the Anton Piller type of order (discussed more fully in Chapter 15).

INDIRECT OBTENTION

8.35 Another side of the effect of permanence (of a written document) as contrasted to transitoriness (of an oral communication) is shown in the line of cases concerning the instance when one party does nevertheless—by chance or by trick—obtain copies of the other party's properly privileged document. The leading case here is *Calcraft v. Guest* [37] in 1898. The substantive question was as to the upper boundary of a fishery, the action being in trespass. Subsequent to trial, some records of a case over a century before (in 1787) involving the same point (in the context of an action for assault) were found. These included proofs of witnesses, and rough notes of evidence used in the defence. The documents themselves were privileged from production, on the basis that they had originally attracted legal professional privilege in the normal way and

> "I take it that, as a general rule, one may say once privileged always privileged." [38] (Lindley M.R.)

They could thus not be used as primary evidence. But it was held nevertheless that the appellant, having come into possession of the documents in a legitimate fashion (the respondent's solicitor had found in

35 [1979] R.P.C. 97.
36 [1981] F.S.R. 398.
37 [1898] 1 Q.B. 759.
38 At 761.

a coach-house some old papers belonging to his grandfather's firm, who had handled the 1787 case, and had of his own volition advised the appellant's solicitor of their existence and had permitted inspection) could give secondary evidence as to their contents. The difference in evidential quality as between primary evidence and secondary evidence of the contents of a document is a matter of the law of evidence; but in practice it may not amount to very much, and the privilege may therefore effectively be defeated.

8.36 If the documents were obtained by a trick, as opposed to chance or accident, the position is different. The Court may be prepared on equitable grounds to restrain their subsequent use either wholly, as in *Lord Ashburton v. Pape,*[39] or at least partly to the extent that their contents have not yet been given in evidence, as in *ITC Film Distributors v. Video Exchange.*[40]

39 [1913] 2 Ch. 469.
40 [1982] Ch. 431

CHAPTER 9

Consumer Credit Act

INTRODUCTION

9.01 Although confidentiality in relation to consumer credit occupies only a niche in the law of confidentiality generally, and in the Consumer Credit Act 1974[1] itself, it has practical implications for a very considerable proportion of the populace. For reasons which need not be developed here, credit transactions are increasingly gaining favour at the expense of cash transactions, so far as the ordinary consumer is concerned. The Consumer Credit Act 1974 is a comprehensive statute regulating the entire field of consumer credit; it was passed in 1974 following the reports of the Crowther Committee on Consumer Credit[2] (1971) and (particularly so far as concerns questions of confidentiality) the Younger Committee on Privacy[3] (1972). The recent Data Protection Act 1984[4] (discussed more fully in Chapter 10) has its own separate impact in relation to consumer credit data falling within the definition of "data" in that Act—essentially, data recorded by automatic, mechanical or computer retrieval means as opposed to hand-written index cards.

CREDIT-REFERENCE AGENCIES

9.02 The Younger Committee had reported that there was a degree of public concern as to the operation of credit rating agencies. The agency might divulge confidential information concerning a given individual's credit-worthiness to a person not entitled to receive it—say a nosy neighbour as opposed to a High Street trader asked to supply a new refrigerator on hire purchase terms. Perhaps more importantly, it might divulge (even to a properly entitled person) information which was inaccurate. This was not to suggest, however, that the establishment and operation of such agencies was in any way an activity inherently contrary to public policy. They were undoubtedly of substantial value to traders

1 1974 c. 39.
2 Cmnd. 4596.
3 Cmnd. 5102.
4 1984 c. 35.

selling on hire-purchase, credit-sale and like terms, inasmuch that they discouraged traders from entering into such arrangements with consumers who had little prospect of meeting the resulting financial obligations; likewise, such consumers could be discouraged from over-extending themselves by reason of difficulty in obtaining credit in any event. Rather, it was a case of the bad reputation of the few sullying the good reputation of the many.

9.03 The relevant provisions of the 1974 Act for credit-reference agencies (to employ the phraseology used in the Act) are principally contained in sections 157–160 (in Part X of the Act, "Ancillary Credit Businesses"). The relevant regulations made under the Act are contained, at present, in The Consumer Credit (Credit Reference Agency) Regulations 1977[5] and The Consumer Credit (Conduct of Business) (Credit References) Regulations 1977.[6]

9.04 The present position as regards such agencies can be summarised as follows:

(1) any credit reference agency must be licensed in the first place by the Director-General of Fair Trading (sections 21 taken with 145(1)(e) and 147(1));

(2) any debtor or hirer (prospective or actual) can require the creditor, owner or negotiator (prospective or actual) as the case may be to disclose the name and address of any credit reference agency to whom application has been made for information as to the former's credit-worthiness (section 157(1));

(3) any individual consumer can require a credit reference agency to furnish particulars of their file on him or her (section 158);

(4) any individual consumer can correct the particulars on such file, if inaccurate (section 159).

In short, the consumer now has the triple-barrelled right to know which credit reference agency has been applied to, to inspect his file at that agency, and to correct it if the particulars in the file are wrong.

9.05 The credit reference agency may be granted an exemption (partial or whole) from the inspection provisions, and consequentially from the correction provisions, in respect of business consumers; application has to be made to the Director-General of Fair Trading under section 160. The purpose of such exemption is to protect the agency's sources of information; since the business consumer's file might well indicate those

5 S.I. 1977/329.
6 S.I. 1977/330.

sources, commercial pressures could be brought to bear against the sources which would render them in turn unwilling to provide any further confidential credit information in future.

DISSEMINATION OF INFORMATION

9.06 Apart from the provisions specific to credit reference agencies, the Act contains also a general prohibition against dissemination (in the absence of consent) of information obtained under the Act about any individual or person. Sections 174(1) and (2) are drafted in wide terms:

> "(1) No information obtained under or by virtue of this Act about any individual shall be disclosed without his consent.
>
> (2) No information obtained under or by virtue of this Act about any business shall be disclosed except, so long as the business continues to be carried on, with the consent of the person for the time being carrying it on."

Certain limited exceptions (for example in relation to functions under the Trade Descriptions Act 1968,[7] Competition Act 1980,[8] investigation of any criminal offence, or proceedings under the Fair Trading Act 1973[9]) are provided for in sub-sections (3) and (4).

9.07 The overall effect therefore is that information obtained under operation of any Part of the Act (not merely but including information arising under the credit-reference agency provision) is in principle to be treated as confidential. To take a specific example outside the credit-reference agency sphere, personal information as to health or earnings provided by a mortgagor to a mortgagee during negotiations for a land mortgage (other than ordinary building society or local authority mortgages) would rank as confidential in the latter's hands. Within the credit-reference agency sphere, an example of breach would be where the agency permitted unauthorised publication in a local newspaper of a particular individual's credit history.

LIABILITY

9.08 Contravention of any of the provisions of the Act relating to credit-reference agencies or to disclosure of information obtained under the Act is expressed to be an offence; this is in keeping with the *modus*

7 1968 c. 29
8 1980 c. 21.
9 1973 c. 41.

operandi of the Act generally, to create criminal liability. The duty of enforcement is cast therefore upon the Director-General of Fair Trading and/or local weights and measures authorities, following section 161(1). Section 170 goes on to add:

> "(1) A breach of any requirement . . . by or under this Act shall incur no civil or criminal sanction as being such a breach, except to the extent (if any) expressly provided by or under this Act.
>
> . . .
>
> (3) Subsection (1) does not prevent the grant of an injunction or the making of an order for certiorari, mandamus or prohibition . . ."

9.09 The precise effect of these provisions on the right of the individual to take civil proceedings in respect of contraventions of the Act is as yet unsettled. On general legal principles, it would seem that an individual could certainly apply for *quia timet* relief against threatened unauthorised disclosure of confidential credit information by a third party. By definition he has the requisite special interest; he might suffer damage personal to him if the disclosure were made. The principle re-affirmed in *Gouriet v. Union of Post Office Workers,*[10] for example in Lord Fraser's speech, by:

> "The general rule is that a private person is only entitled to sue in respect of interference with a public right if either there is also interference with a private right of his or the interference with the public right will inflict special damage on him—" (at 518)

would seem to apply.

10 [1978] A.C. 435; [1977] 3 All E.R. 70.

CHAPTER 10

Data Protection Act

INTRODUCTION

10.01 The Data Protection Act 1984[1] provides another statutory incursion into the law of confidentiality, whereby protection for the individual is intended to be enhanced. The Act is based upon the Report of the Committee on Data Protection[2] (1978). This Report, known shortly as the Lindop Report, can be regarded as a continuation, within the data-processing field, of the Younger Report (Report of the Committee on Privacy,[3] 1972) mentioned in the preceding chapter on the Consumer Credit Act 1974. Similar thinking underpins both Acts so far as confidentiality is concerned; in relation to the credit-reference agency provisions of the latter there is indeed some specific overlap, as discussed later in this chapter.

10.02 The Data Protection Act sets up a comprehensive statutory scheme in relation to the use of modern techniques for handling of personal data by third parties. The preamble to the Act describes it as:

> "An Act to regulate the use of automatically processed information relating to individuals and the provision of services in respect of such information."

It is not the purpose of this chapter to provide a complete exposition of the Act; rather, it is to focus upon the confidentiality provisions. Some preliminary discussion of the main structure of the Act is requisite, however, for this purpose.

STATUTORY SCOPE AND DEFINITIONS

10.03 The Act commences (section 1) by providing formal definitions of certain terms which might be expected otherwise to possess ordinary English meanings. These terms recur throughout the Act and hence control its precise compass in those respects. This is not to suggest that

1 1984 c. 35.
2 Cmnd. 7341.
3 Cmnd. 5102.

the formal definitions positively distort the ordinary meanings of the words; but they do provide certain limitations at times. The following terms are so defined: "Data"; "Personal data"; "Data subject"; "Data user"; "Computer Bureau" (carrying on thereof); "Processing" (in relation to data); "Disclosing" (again in relation to data). Some of the definitions merit further exegesis here.

10.04 "Data" is defined as meaning:

> "information recorded in a form in which it can be processed by equipment operating automatically in response to instructions given for that purpose."

This denotes essentially (as already mentioned in Chapter 9) data recorded in automatic, mechanical or computer retrieval means. Information recorded in a form intended to be processed by non-automatic means is excluded. Any hand-written records of a traditional kind—say index cards in a doctor or tailor's filing system—are hence likely to be excluded, since the handwriting probably renders the records inherently unsuitable for machine or electronic reading; this is particularly so if different handwriting is present in different parts of the card, as entered periodically over the passage of time. Records in typescript are not as such bound to be included; the typescript and card (or other substratum) must be such as to enable processing of the recorded information by automatic means. The main thrust of the definition is undoubtedly, however, to data recorded on modern forms of substratum—microfilm, magnetic tape, computer discs and the like.

10.05 "Personal data" is defined as meaning:

> "data consisting of information which relates to a living individual who can be identified from that information in the possession of the data user), including any expression of opinion about the individual but not any indication of the intentions of the data user in respect of that individual."

Identifiability is the key point here; if the data is of such a kind as to be inherently incapable of pointing to a particular person (say the result of a statistical survey of travellers alighting at King's Cross railway station as to their reaction to train catering facilities) or inadequate in fact so to point (say where names but not addresses are included in the data), then it fails to rank as "personal data", even though it is "data". But recordal of an individual's data under a code-name, or number (say a bank account or credit-card number) would count if the data user has a separate cross-reference index from which actual identification can be made.

10.06 The inclusion of "any expression of opinion" widens the scope of personal data quite considerably, however; the term is hence not limited just to concrete facts about the individual concerned. As regards the types of factual data which are included (assuming identifiability), it is clear that all the standard parameters, e.g. personal physical characteristics, age, marital data, school records, medical records, employment records, financial data, at least, are in principle embraced. The important question of exemption of certain types of personal data from the subject-access and non-disclosure provisions of the Act is dealt with separately below.

10.07 "Data subject" is self-explanatory; it just denotes the individual who is the subject of the personal data involved. "Data user" means essentially the person who holds data (personal data or otherwise). Carrying-on of a "computer bureau" and "processing" are defined in terms largely as might be anticipated (although these definitions, and also of "data user", are all expressed in quite long and exhaustive terms, in accordance with conventional practice of the Parliamentary draftsman). A given person can be both a "data user" and a carrier-on of a "computer bureau" simultaneously. "Disclosing" is specified to include the disclosure of information "extracted from" the data; the inference is that such information is to be distinguished from the raw input data recorded as such. For example, if the building society's computer records show all the actual dates on which the house-purchaser has defaulted on the monthly payments due, advice that he defaulted "more than 20 times" might rank as extracted information. But in instances where cross-reference is needed to complete the identification there is no disclosure until both are provided.

DATA PROTECTION PRINCIPLES

10.08 The Act continues (Section 2 and Schedule 1, Part I) by enunciating the eight data protection principles, to which many of the subsequent specific provisions are keyed. These principles are:

"*Personal data held by data users* (italicised in Act)

1. The information to be contained in personal data shall be obtained, and personal data shall be processed, fairly and lawfully.
2. Personal data shall be held only for one or more specified and lawful purposes.
3. Personal data held for any purpose or purposes shall not be used or disclosed in any manner incompatible with that purpose or those purposes.
4. Personal data held for any purpose or purposes shall be adequate, relevant and not excessive in relation to that purpose or those purposes.
5. Personal data shall be accurate and, where necessary, kept up to date.

6. Personal data held for any purpose or purposes shall not be kept for longer than is necessary for that purpose or those purposes.

7. An individual shall be entitled—

(a) at reasonable intervals and without undue delay or expense—
   (i) to be informed by any data user whether he holds personal data of which that individual is the subject; and
   (ii) to access to any such data held by a data user; and

(b) where appropriate, to have such data corrected or erased.

Personal data held by data users or in respect of which services are provided by persons carrying on computer bureaux (italicised in Act)

8. Appropriate measures shall be taken against unauthorised access to, or alteration, disclosure or destruction of, personal data and against accidental loss or destruction of personal data."

Principle no. 8 applies both to regular data users and also to persons carrying on computer bureaux.

10.09 Statutory exegesis of some of these principles is provided in Schedule 1, Part II. As regards principle no. 1 (fair and lawful obtention of data) it is precribed that, supply under statutory authorisation or the like apart:

". . . in determining whether information was obtained fairly regard shall be had to the method by which it was obtained, including in particular whether any person from whom it was obtained was deceived or misled as to the purpose or purposes for which it is to be held, used or disclosed."

As regards principle no. 3, (no incompatible use or disclosure of data), for example, it is prescribed that:

"Personal data shall not be treated as used or disclosed in contravention of this principle unless—

(a) used otherwise than for a purpose of a description registered under this Act in relation to the data; or

(b) disclosed otherwise than to a person of a description so registered."

As regards principle no. 8 (maintenance of security of data) it is prescribed that:

"Regard shall be had—

(a) to the nature of the personal data and the harm that would result from such access, alteration, disclosure, loss or destruction as are mentioned in this principle; and

(b) to the place where the personal data are stored, to security measures programmed into the relevant equipment and to measures taken for ensuring the reliability of staff having access to the data."

10.10 Principles nos. 1, 3 and 8 can be regarded as those most directly relevant to the general issue of confidentiality in relation to the data involved. The analogies between these principles and their associated statutory interpretation and general law of confidence are clear. The requirement for initial lawful obtention of the data can, for example, be regarded as a mirror-image reflection of the principle of obligation of confidence (Chapter 4); for if there is an obligation of confidence as regards the data, then its release by a first party to a second party results in an obtention by the latter which is unlawful. The prohibition against use or disclosure beyond the purpose for which the data is held reflects directly the principle of unauthorised use (Chapter 5); use is authorised only when within such purposes.

STATUTORY EDIFICE

10.11 On the basis provided by the statutory definitions and the data protection principles, the statutory edifice erected by the Act is essentially one of:

(a) registration and supervision of data users and computer bureaux before the Data Protection Registrar (sections 4–12);
(b) provision of statutory rights to data subjects (sections 21–25);
(c) exemption provisions (sections 26–35)

There are in addition, of course, numerous miscellaneous and supplementary general and appeal provisions (to the Data Protection Tribunal from the Data Protection Registrar). It is important to note that contravention of any of the data protection principles nos. 1–8 can, in the ultimate, constitute a criminal offence. It is these criminal sanctions which provide the Data Protection Registrar with his teeth. Criminal prosecution is not to be undertaken, however, in general until an initial "enforcement notice" stage has proved unsuccessful.

10.12 Full details of the registration systems are beyond the scope of this book; attention will be focussed in the following treatment primarily on the rights of individual data subjects, since it is upon them that questions of data confidentiality impinge most sharply, and (in outline) the exemption provisions.

RIGHTS OF DATA SUBJECTS

10.13 The primary rights of a data subject are those of entitlement:

(1) to be *informed* by the data user as to whether the latter holds personal data relating to him; and if so

(2) to be *supplied* with a copy of that data (section 21(1)(a) and (b), emphasis added).

The data subject has naturally to satisfy the data user of his identity in the first place, and pay the appropriate fee. If the data user holds the personal data in coded form, then he in turn naturally has to provide a suitable explanation of such code.

10.14 One important qualification arises when full disclosure of the personal data would involve in turn disclosure of information relating to another third party—for example, the name of the original informant who may, quite fairly and lawfully, have provided the recorded data. In such instance (a) the third party must consent but (b) the data user must in any event provide such part of the data as can be given without revealing the third party's identity.

10.15 Ancillary to these rights are the rights of the data subject:

(3) to be compensated for any damage or distress suffered by reason of *inaccuracy* of the recorded personal data (section 22(1));

(4) to be compensated likewise for any damage or distress suffered by reason of *loss or unauthorised disclosure* of the data (section 23(1));

(5) to apply for *rectification or erasure* as regards inaccurate data (section 24(1)) (emphasis added).

10.16 In short, the data subject has the bundle of rights to know+inspect+recoup+correct in respect of the personal data held by the data user concerning him. A data user who errs or misuses data is thus at the risk of both civil action, by the data subject involved, and also ultimate criminal action, by the Registrar, once the latter becomes aware of the contravention and has issued an enforcement notice which has been disobeyed by the data user.

10.17 There are, again, certain qualifications as to the ancillary rights.

10.18 As regards inaccurate data, the data user has a defence if he can prove due care; he also has a defence if he has already included in the data any pre-existing complaint by the data subject as to inaccuracy. Inaccuracy in this context means that the data must be incorrect or misleading as to any matter of fact; hence a data user has no redress as regards any expression of opinion in the personal data involved, even if he contests its accuracy.

10.19 As regards loss or unauthorised disclosure, there is again a defence of due care available to the data user, or person carrying on a computer bureau, as the case may be. It is also provided that disclosure to any description of persons cited in the data user's (or carrier-on of a bureau's) original entry in the Register is proper; under section 4(3)(d):

> "a description of any person or persons to whom he intends or may wish to disclose the data"

has to be included. In other words, a data subject cannot assert that a disclosure was unauthorised just because he would have been unwilling to have had his data disclosed to a particular party, had he known at the time that such disclosure was in the offing. The reason for this restriction is clear; if data subjects could object in such arbitrary fashion, data users (and persons carryings on computer bureaux) would be liable to be hamstrung in the conduct of their legitimate business.

10.20 Applications for rectification or erasure require the Court to be satisfied in the first place that there is existing inaccuracy within the meaning of section 22 (in relation to the rectification limb) or existing unauthorised disclosure within the meaning of section 23 (in relation to the erasure limb); the Court also has to be satisfied, so far as erasure is concerned, that there is a substantial risk of further unauthorised disclosure unless the erasure is made.

10.21 There is as yet no case-law in respect of these statutory protective provisions for the data subject.

ASSOCIATED PROVISIONS

10.22 Associated with the rights to data subjects by the group of statutory provisions in sections 21–25 just discussed are the direct prohibitions against unauthorised disclosure contained in sections 4, 5 and 15.

10.23 These overlap with the provisions as to rights of data subjects; a given unauthorised disclosure may, for example, both constitute a breach of section 5(2)(d) and also give rise to a claim for compensation under section 23(1). The essential difference is that the Registrar can take action under the associated provisions himself without any intervention by the data subject who has been injured. In the broadest sense, section 23 can be regarded as providing the personal particular benefit (to a given injured data subject) of the general public interest (in preventing unauthorised discosure) reflected in the Registrar's duty in ensuring that the provisions of sections 4, 5 and 15 are fulfilled and/or punished in breach.

10.24 Specifically, section 4(3)(d) requires (as already mentioned) that a data user applying for entry in the Registrar must, *inter alia,* provide in the first place a description of the persons to whom he may wish subsequently to disclose the data collected; inevitably, this description is likely to be drafted in terms of a class of persons, rather than a specific individual person. Section 5 mirrors this requirement, once data has obtained registration; by sub-section (2)(d), a registered data user shall not:

> "disclose such data held by him to any person who is *not* described in the entry."

Section 15(1) adds to this, in respect of persons registered to carry on a computer bureau, by specifying that:

> "Personal data in respect of which services are provided by a person carrying on a computer bureau shall not be disclosed by him without the prior authority of the person for whom those services are provided."

10.25 Comparable associated provisions are present also as regards the original collection of the personal data. Prior to registration, a data user must give a description of the source(s) which he may intend or wish to use in order to collect the personal data (section 4(3)(c)); and once registered, he must not actually obtain data from any other source(s) (section 5(2)(c)).

10.26 Again, there is as yet no case law under these associated provisions.

EXEMPTIONS

10.27 Much of the Act is devoted to enumerating the exemptions (partial or total) from its rigours. In categorising the partial exemptions an important distinction is drawn as between so-called "subject access provisions" (primarily those of section 21) and "non-disclosure provisions" (primarily those of sections 5(2)(d) and 15). A complete analysis is beyond the scope of this book but the main heads of exemption are treated below.

10.28 Personal data can be exempted from the provisions of the Act as a whole in the cases listed in the following Table 3:

Table 3

*Exemption No.**	*Instance*	*Section*
1	Where exemption is required for the purpose of safeguarding national security	27(1)
2	When data is held for purposes of remuneration, pensions or accounts	32(1)
3	When data is held by an individual and concerned only with the management of that individual's personal, family or household affairs or held by him only for recreational purposes	33(1)
4	When data is held by an unincorporated members' club and relating only to the members of the club	32(2)(a)
5	When data is held by a data user for distribution purposes and consisting only of names and addresses	33(2)(b)
6	When data is held by a person who is under a statutory duty to make the data available to the public in any event	34(1)

*(see note to Table 5.)

10.29 Personal data can be exempted from the subject-access provisions in the following cases (Table 4):

Table 4

Exemption No.	*Instance*	*Section*
7	When held for the prevention or detection of crime	28(1)(a)
8	When held for the apprehension or prosecution of offenders	28(1)(b)
9	When held for the assessment or collection of any tax or duty	28(1)(c)
10	When consisting of information as to the physical or mental health of the data subject	29(1)
11	When held for, or acquired in the course of, the carrying out of social work by government departments, local authorities, voluntary organisations and the like	29(2)

Table 4 (cont.)

Exemption No.	*Instance*	*Section*
12	When held for the purpose of regulating banking, insurance, investment or other financial services	30(1)
13	When held for purposes of making judicial appointments	31(1)
14	When protected by legal professional privilege	31(2)
15	When held only for preparing statistics or carrying out research	33(6)
16	When access to the data is already prohibited or restricted by other statutory enactments	34(2)
17	When a data subject is already entitled to see his data under the provisions of section 158 of the Consumer Credit Act 1974 (credit-reference agencies)	34(3)
18	When the data is kept only for purposes of replacing lost, destroyed or impaired data	34(4)
19	When compliance with a request for subject-access would render the data user liable for prosecution for an offence under another enactment	34(9)

10.30 Personal data can be exempted from the non-disclosure provisions in the following cases (Table 5):

Table 5

*Exemption No.**	*Instance*	*Section*
20	When disclosure of the data is required for the purpose of safeguarding national security, and the data is not already wholly exempt	27(3)
21	When disclosure is for the purpose of the prevention or detection of crime; the apprehension or prosecution of offenders; or the assessment or collection of any tax or duty	28(3)
22	When disclosure is required by or under any enactment, rule of law or Court Order	34(5)(a)

Table 5 (cont.)

*Exemption No.**	*Instance*	*Section*
23	When disclosure is made for the purpose of obtaining legal advice or during legal proceedings	34(5)(b)
24	When disclosure is made to the data subject or his representative	34(6)(a)
25	When the data subject or his representative has consented to the disclosure	34(6)(b)
26	When the disclosure is made to the servant or agent of the data user, or person carrying on a computer bureau, for purposes of enabling the same to perform their functions	34(6)(c)

*(Exemptions are numbered for reference purposes only; there is no corresponding numbering in the Act.)

10.31 It should be noted that exemptions as outlined above are not necessarily granted automatically in blanket-like fashion. The grant may be hedged about. For example, grant of exemption no. 1 (national security) may require the furnishing of a certificate signed by a Minister of the Crown certifying that it is required. For exemption no. 4 (unincorporated member's club), the individual data subject (member) must be asked if he objects to the exemption being accorded so far as he is concerned. Grant of exemption nos. 10 and 11 (physical or mental health, social work) is at the discretion of the Secretary of State; the strict statutory language is that the Secretary of State "... *may* by order exempt from the subject access provisions, or modify those provisions...". Exemption nos. 7, 8 and 9 (prevention or detection of crime, etc) are expressed to be subject to the preliminary requirement that subject access would be likely to prejudice those functions. Exemptions nos. 24–26 (disclosure to data subject himself, etc) on the other hand are stated to apply both where the given circumstances positively exist and also where the data user has reasonable grounds for believing that the circumstances exist; the data user has in effect a wider degree of protection. The exemptions just mentioned are referred to only for illustrative purposes; the full statutory language needs to be consulted before coming to a conclusion in any case arising in practice on a special exemption.

10.32 An additional exemption, from data protection principle no. 1 (fair and lawful obtention of the personal data), is provided by section 28(2)(4) in respect of personal data of the kinds enumerated in sections

28(1)(a), (b) and (c) (prevention or detection of crime; apprehension or prosecution of offenders; assessment or collection of any tax or duty); this data may already be exempt from the subject-access provisions (see exemptions nos. 7, 8 and 9 in Table 4 above). The additional exemption means that there is no contravention of the basic data protection principles (and hence no ground for issuing of any enforcement notice by the Registrar and/or eventual prosecution) where personal data of these kinds has been obtained in the first place by means which might be regarded as deceitful or otherwise generally unlawful; details of possible douceurs and the like to criminal informants can thus continue to be shielded from view. Undoubtedly it is the public interest in these areas which led Parliament to make the special additional exception.

10.33 Although most of the exemptions are reasonably clear, the examples in the following Table 6 may assist appreciation.

Table 6

Exemption No.	*Example*
1	MI 5 operatives
2	Payroll data
3	Record of personal darts, snooker scores
4	Tennis club members' list
5	Publisher's magazine circulation list
6	Share register
7, 8, 9,	Informants' reports
10	Medical records
11	NSPCC records
12	Data held by Chief Registrar of Friendly Societies
13	Data held by Department of Trade and Industry as to scientific attainments of members of the Patent Bar
14	Remarks about a witness's credibility made by client to his solicitor once legal proceedings have commenced
15	Gallup or MORI poll data
16	Data restricted under the Adoption Act 1958 [4]
17	Credit history
18	Duplicate (back-up) records
19	Agent's records of concert party performances which might infringe section 21(5) of the Copyright Act 1956 [5]
20	Membership list of political protest campaign
21	See examples under exemption nos. 7, 8, 9
22	Names and addresses of company directors
23	Microfilm records of clients' visits to Citizen's Advice Bureaux
24, 25, 26,	Self-explanatory

4 7 & 8 Eliz. II c. 5.
5 4 & 5 Eliz. II c. 74.

POSTSCRIPT

10.34 At this stage it is speculative to comment as to how influential the Data Protection Act will in practice eventually prove to be. But in instances where data is inherently of the kind specified in the Act (that is, recorded in a form processable by equipment operating automatically in response to instructions) and personal (in the sense defined in the Act), it is clear that the Act will control at the expense of conventional umbrella labellings. A drug user's advice bureau may, for example, pronounce generally that all its dealings with clients are "confidential"; if its case notes are hand-written and arranged in a manual card index, that may well be so, other considerations apart. But if the case load grows so much that the notes are computerised, it is the impact of the Act which will have to be borne in mind.

CHAPTER 11

Rehabilitation of Offenders Act

INTRODUCTION

11.01 The Rehabilitation of Offenders Act 1974[1] represents a still further statutory excursion into the law of confidentiality. The no doubt laudable purpose of the Act is to enable those convicted of lesser offences (to use a generalisation) to be free, after lapse of a suitable period of time, of the shackles provided by their possible regurgitation. In other words, the convicted person is to be allowed to start again with a clean slate; he is to be set free from the fear that his social standing, or employment prospects, are forever liable to be diminished at a moment's notice by revelation of some blot in his past. In the picturesque, although perhaps rather over-simplified language of Lord Denning M.R. in *Reynolds v. Phoenix Assurance*:

> "The effect of this Act is that a spent conviction is to be wiped out altogether from the knowledge of anyone. Even police officers or Court officers cannot disclose it to anyone. If they do they may be liable for a punishment themselves. . . . So you can see how strong this Act is in wiping everything out." [2]

SPENT CONVICTIONS AND REHABILITATION

11.02 The primary enabling provision is contained in section 1(1) of the Act which reads, in essentials, as follows:

> "(1) . . . where an individual has been *convicted*, whether before or after the commencement of this Act, of any offence or offences *and the following conditions are satisfied*, that is to say—
>
> (a) he did not have imposed on him in respect of that conviction a sentence which is *excluded from rehabilitation* under this Act; and
>
> (b) he has not had imposed on him in respect of a *subsequent* conviction during the rehabilitation period . . . a sentence *excluded from rehabilitation* under this Act;
>
> then, *after the end* of the rehabilitation period so applicable . . . that individual shall for the purposes of this Act be treated as a

1 1974 c. 53.
2 [1978] 2 Lloyds' Rep 22 at 24.

> *rehabilitated person* in respect of the first-mentioned conviction and that conviction shall for those purposes be treated as *spent*." (emphasis added)

This provision introduces the statutory phraseology in terms of which much of the Act is couched—namely, that a previous conviction becomes "spent" after completion of the "rehabilitation" period so that the individual in question then becomes a "rehabilitated" person.

11.03 The division between convictions that can be rendered spent and those that cannot is drawn primarily in terms of length of the sentence of imprisonment for the conviction: the line is set at 30 months.[3] For sentences of 30 months or below, spending of the conviction is possible after a rehabilitation period which may itself depend on the exact length of sentence, but which in no case exceeds 10 years; the rehabilitation periods themselves can be reduced by half for those aged under 17 at the date of conviction.[4] Above 30 months, spending of a conviction is not possible, although rights under the Royal Prerogative for granting of free pardons, quashing convictions or sentence or commutation of sentence are not affected.[5] It is also specifically provided that there shall be no spending of a sentence of imprisonment for life.[6]

11.04 It should be noted that the possible spending of a conviction does not depend upon the nature of the offence involved. This can lead to consequences which might, on general grounds of public policy, be thought undesirable. For example, the man who kills *in flagrante delicto* his wife's paramour and is convicted of murder can never have his conviction spent even though it be most unlikely that he would ever do the same again. A person convicted of company fraud or offences concerning children may on the other hand be able to do so, notwithstanding that there may be a significant risk of repetition. And it is in respect of the latter, rather than the former, that publicity as to his past may be useful to the public at large. The Act provides sweepingly in section 4(1) that:

> ". . . a person who has become a rehabilitated person . . . in respect of a conviction *shall be treated for all purposes in law* as a person who has not committed or been charged with or prosecuted for or convicted of or sentenced for the offence or offences which were the subject of that conviction;" (emphasis added)

11.05 The wide wording of section 4(1) means also that a revelation as

3 S. 5(1)(b).
4 S. 5(2)(a).
5 S. 7(1)(a).
6 S. 5(1)(a).

to a given person having been charged with an offence, and/or committed for trial in connection therewith, may be caught by the Act even though no reference is made to conviction. This is not unreasonable. In a middle-class suburb, one may have as much pejorative effect as the other on a local pillar of the community.

ADDITIONAL RIGHTS

11.06 To render this general provision more effective, the Act confers additional specific rights upon the rehabilitated person in the areas of:

(1) admission of evidence
(2) disclosure in extra-judicial contexts
(3) actions for defamation
(4) official records

These will now be considered in turn.

Admission of evidence

11.07 Section 4(1)(a) enunciates quite flatly that:

> "... *no evidence shall be admissible* in any proceedings before a judicial authority ... to prove that any such person has committed or been charged with or prosecuted for or convicted of or sentenced for any offence which was the subject of a spent conviction." (emphasis added)

and supplements this in sub-section (b) by correspondingly restricting the posing in the first place of questions concerning the spent conviction:

> "(b) a person shall *not*, in any such proceedings, *be asked*, and, if asked, shall *not be required to answer*, any question relating to his past which cannot be answered without acknowledging or referring to a spent conviction or spent convictions or any circumstances ancillary thereto." (emphasis added)

11.08 The apparent scope of these sub-sections is, however, sharply eroded by the subsequent exceptions of sections 7(2)–(4). Briefly, these provide that the rule against admission does not apply in criminal proceedings, and certain other specific types of proceedings including, in particular, service disciplinary proceedings and domestic proceedings relating to adoption, wardship, marriage, custody of minors and the like (sub-section (2)); not in instances where the judicial authority is satisfied that justice cannot be done in the case except by admitting the evidence as to a spent conviction(s) (sub-section (3)); nor in instances where the proceedings are otherwise of a kind specified by an order of the Secretary of State (sub-section (4)), for example proceedings before the Gaming Board for Great Britain or before the disciplinary tribunals of various professions.[7] So far as criminal proceedings are concerned, the evidence may of course be relevant in a number of contexts; the most usual are where the character of a witness (or the accused) is under attack, and where the evidence shows system.

11.09 The broad result, therefore, is that the rule against admissibility of evidence is limited to proceedings in the civil field only, and even within that field there are additional restrictions.

Disclosure in extra-judicial contexts

11.10 Section 4(2) provides limitations, which can in the general sense be regarded as comparable to those in section 4(1), in relation to the asking of questions (and hence the provision of evidence by the answers thereto) as to a spent conviction(s):

> "... *otherwise* than in proceedings before a judicial authority-"

In such instance, the question is to be treated by the person asked as not relating to any spent conviction, and the answer may be framed accordingly (sub-section 2(a)); and the person asked is not to be subject to any liability or be otherwise prejudiced in law by reason of such framing of his answer (sub-section 2(b)). It should be noted that this protection is extended both to the rehabilitated person (if it be he who is asked the question) and third persons generally.

11.11 As to what is meant by "judicial authority", which represents the dividing-line between the kinds of proceedings covered by sections 4(1) and 4(2), section 4(6) provides a formal definition. This is couched in wide terms; much more than just the ordinary courts of law are comprehended. It reads:

> " 'proceedings before a judicial authority' includes, in addition to proceedings before any of the ordinary courts of law, proceedings before any tribunal, body or person having power—
>
> (a) by virtue of any enactment, law, custom or practice;
> (b) under the rules governing any association, institution, profession, occupation or employment; or
> (c) under any provision of an agreement providing for arbitration with respect to questions arising thereunder;
>
> To determine any question affecting the rights, privileges, obligations or liabilities of any person, or to receive evidence affecting the determination of any such question."

7 1975 S.I. No. 1023.

On the face of the words, even an interview between a candidate member and the admissions committee of the local golf club might rank as such proceedings; the club could be regarded as an association; there would be rules governing its constitution; the privilege involved is that of playing on the golf course involved. Likewise, for any expulsion proceedings of an existing member (rehabilitated within the meaning of the 1974 Act) initiated consequent to the exposure in the local press of his criminal past. Whether Parliament really intended to cast the net so widely may be doubted; but the size of its trawl should be kept in mind.

11.12 Quite separate from the question of evidence in proceedings (whether before a judicial authority or otherwise), section 4(3) provides a rehabilitated person with substantial protection against what might be regarded as the usual consequences of failure to disclose a previous conviction.

11.13 By sub-section 3(a):

> "any obligation imposed on any person by any rule of law or by the provisions of any agreement or arrangement to disclose any matters to any other person shall not extend to requiring him to disclose a spent conviction or any circumstances ancillary to a spent conviction (whether the conviction is his own or another's);"

Some examples may illustrate the scope of this exemption. A doctor in private practice as an obstetrician wishing to sell the goodwill of his practice to a successor at a price formula dependent on future profits may naturally have included in the sale agreement a term requiring his successor to warrant that he had provided full information as to previous career and character; in view of the personal nature of the doctor/patient relationship, the obstetrician might naturally wish to be satisfied that his successor would prove acceptable to his existing patients, and these matters would be relevant to the same. Yet the exemption might well enable a successor who had a spent conviction for indecently assaulting a female patient justifiably to conceal the fact, notwithstanding its potentially disastrous effect on the practice if it were ever subsequently revealed. As for obligations imposed by rule of law, as opposed to private agreement, reference may be made, for example, to the obligation of *uberrima fides* between insured and insurer which normally arises in insurance law.

11.14 Sub-section 3(b) discharges the normal obligations of disclosure, likewise, so far as employment and the like of the rehabilitated person is concerned. The statutory wording is:

"a conviction which has become spent or any circumstances ancillary thereto, or any failure to disclose a spent conviction or any such circumstances, shall not be a proper ground for dismissing or excluding a person from any office, profession, occupation or employment, or for prejudicing him in any way in any occupation or employment."

All three stages of (i) initial rejection of the candidate employee (or the like), (ii) refusal to promote, or the like, once employed, and (iii) subsequent dismissal are accordingly protected.

11.15 It should be noted finally that the Secretary of State has a general power to control by order the precise application of sections 4(2) and (3); this power, given by section 4(4), is analogous to his power (under section 7(4)) to control the precise application of section 4(1). Offices and employments so regulated include such as judicial appointments, constables, teachers, probation officers and traffic wardens; regulated occupations include those of firearms dealer, director or manager of an insurance company, dealer in securities, occupier of explosives premises, and manager of a place approved under the Abortion Act 1967 [8] for the termination of pregnancy. These examples, just as with the examples already given of excluded proceedings under section 7(4), are not intended to provide a comprehensive list, and may in any event vary from time to time.

Actions for defamation

11.16 This area can be reviewed more briefly. The Act needs, for sake of completeness, to deal with the position which arises when a rehabilitated person sues another for defamation in respect of the latter's actual but improper disclosure of the former's spent conviction. Disclosure of the conviction prior to effluxion of the rehabilitation period is of course unaffected; the conviction does not become formally spent until that period is expired.

11.17 The solution adopted by the Act is, shortly, as follows:

(1) The defences of justification, fair comment and privilege (absolute or qualified) are in principle retained; but

(2) The defence of justification can be rebutted on proof that publication of the spent conviction has been made with malice (sections 8(3) to (5));

(3) The defence that the publication constituted a fair and accurate report of judicial proceedings is not available where the publication refers

8 1967 c. 87.

to evidence which is inadmissible by virtue of section 4(1) (discussed above); an exception (that is, the defence is still available) arises where the judicial report is contained in any *bona fide* series of law reports or account of judicial proceedings published for *bona fide* educational, scientific or professional purposes.

11.18 As for (1) and (2), the meanings of justification, fair comment, privilege and malice in the law of defamation generally have to be kept in mind, although it may be noted that in *Herbage v. Pressdram* [9] the Court of Appeal stated (in interlocutory proceedings) that "malice" in section 8(5) meant:

"... published with some irrelevant, spiteful or improper motive."

11.19 As for (3), it would seem clear that the intention of Parliament was to preclude the defendant from relying on newspaper reports and the like of the spent conviction and previous trial; the possibly more sensational tone of these (as compared to the drier text of a formal law report and the like) might prejudice the rehabilitated plaintiff in the eyes of the defamation jury; also, the proceedings might well have never been reported in the latter type of report in the first place.

Official records

11.20 The final limb of the specific protection afforded by the Act to the rehabilitated person is represented by the provisions prohibiting disclosure of official records relating to any spent conviction. These are contained in section 9. The main provision is that of sub-section (2), under which any person having custody of or access to records of a spent conviction shall be guilty of an offence if, knowing or having reasonable cause to suspect that information he has obtained in the course of his duties relates to the same, he:

"discloses it, otherwise than in the course of those duties, to another person."

11.21 Disclosure at the request (actual or reasonably believed) of the rehabilitated person is of course unobjectionable (sub-section (3)); any person who obtains such information from an official record by means of fraud, dishonesty or bribe is also guilty of an offence (that is, both the person seeking the leak and the leaker himself can be prosecuted) (sub-section (4)); there is again a power vested in the Secretary of State to control by order the precise scope of the section (by excepting certain disclosures or classes of disclosure).[10]

9 [1984] 1 W.L.R. 1160 at 1164.
10 S. 9(5).

CASE LAW

11.22 Case law under the Act has so far been relatively sparse, due in part probably to its recent enactment and in part to its overall fairly narrow and quite precisely defined scope; the quantitative limitation of potentially spendable convictions to those of 30 months of imprisonment or less effects a substantial diminution in the numbers of those who might otherwise be the most concerned not to have their past exposed. Two decisions will, however, be discussed.

11.23 *Reynolds v. Phoenix Assurance* in 1978, mentioned already at the beginning of this chapter, concerned correlation of the section 7(3) exemption (the needs of justice) with the broad section 4(1) rule rendering evidence of previous spent conviction inadmissible. A claim under insurance contract was involved. Shortly before trial, the defendant insurers applied to amend their pleadings so as to allege non-disclosure of a previous conviction (now spent) of the plaintiff some 12 years prior to the date of the contract. It was argued that this was a material matter which the plaintiff should have disclosed at the time, on the basis of settled insurance law; had they known of the conviction, the defendant insurers might either have declined the risk entirely, or varied the premium charged.

11.24 It was held by the Court of Appeal that amendment of the pleadings was permissible. But they would not go so far as to direct positively that evidence of the spent conviction was admissible at trial; this was a matter for the trial judge, at the hearing itself. The trial judge, the relevant "judicial authority", would have to be satisfied that the needs of justice, as the case unfolded before him, required its admission. The decision thus underlines the discretionary nature of the "needs of justice" jurisdiction.

11.25 *X v. Commissioner of Police of the Metropolis*[11] concerned the scope of the term "official duties" in section 9(2) (unauthorised disclosure of official records). It was held here that transmission of information by the Metropolitan Police to the Paris Office of the International Criminal Police Organisation (Interpol) concerning X (suspected by the Paris Office of planning swindles in Andorra) came within its official duties. It was shown that there was a long-standing practice of supplying such information to Interpol, at their request; and that information was never given without adequate reason being provided. In the circumstances of contemporary society, the police could properly be said to have duties in

11 [1985] 1 W.L.R. 420.

connection with the combatting of international crime (even if their duties in earlier times had been more localised in nature). Hence although the transmission abroad might possibly give rise to subsequent dissemination of the information (the Police Commissioner inevitably losing control over the information once it had left the country), it was proper to accord a wider meaning to the exemption provision.

CHAPTER 12

Official Secrets Acts and the like

INTRODUCTION

12.01 Chapters 9, 10, and 11 have considered areas wherein the State has ventured statutorily with a view to regulating confidentiality in the interests of individuals—the customer (in relation to his credit worthiness), the data subject and the criminal, under the Consumer Credit Act 1974,[1] Data Protection Act 1984[2] and Rehabilitation of Offenders Act 1974[3] respectively.

12.02 This chapter is concerned, in contrast, with the statutory attempts made by the State itself to regulate confidentiality in its own interests. The principal provisions in this connection are of course those which have been enacted from time to time in the various Official Secrets Acts. But those Acts do not constitute the only course. Provisions directed to preventing the unauthorised disclosure of information of potential or actual significance to the State may be found in a wide variety of other statutes appurtenant to the functioning of direct (e.g. Departments of State) or indirect (e.g. statutory authorities) organs of the State; an exhaustive treatment is not possible within the compass of this book, although some representative illustrations will be considered later in this chapter. Both civil and/or criminal liabilities may be created, depending on the circumstances of the case and the statute(s) involved.

12.03 In a somewhat different category are those statutory provisions which affect the confidentiality of information belonging to individuals or concerns for the purpose of statutory regulation of some business or professional activity. It can of course be argued that these provisions relate indirectly also to the interests of the State, in the sense that any legislation (primary or delegated) was presumably made in the first instance for some purpose of the State. But it can often be hard to suggest seriously, in many of these instances, that disclosure of the information in question would lead to positive damage to the State; often, there is no

1 1974 c. 39.
2 1984 c. 35.
3 1974 c. 53.

possible overtone of national security or defence arising; even to the individuals or concerns providing the information in the first place the potential damage in the event of a breach of confidentiality may be minimal, although this is not always the case.

12.04 Typical examples include, for example, the restrictions on dissemination of information provided by farmers under the Agricultural Statistics Act 1979[4] (section 3); by registered medical practitioners under the Abortion Act 1967[5] (section 2(1)); and information obtained by enforcement authorities, upon entry to premises, under the Medicines Act 1968[6] (section 118(2)). Both Crown servants, strictly so called, and other persons may be liable for breach of any such confidentiality provision. Again, the precise circumstances and the statutory context control.

12.05 The total number of such ancillary statutory provisions is very considerable. The Franks Committee (discussed more fully later) was in 1972 able to locate no less than seventy-one such provisions; their number has probably increased since. It is beyond the scope of this book even to attempt to deal with them fully. What matters is a general awareness of the fact that any statute of regulatory kind may well include provisions affecting the confidentiality of information obtained or arising in pursuance of the regulatory activity involved.

OFFICIAL SECRETS ACTS

Statutory history

12.06 The first legislation in this area was the Official Secrets Act 1889. Unauthorized disclosure of official information—in modern parlance, "leaks"—represented, however, a practice having much earlier roots. The 1972 Report[7] of the Departmental Committee on section 2 of the Official Secrets Act 1911[8] (the Franks Committee) records some of the controversial instances, including those of publication of Lord Wellesley's dispatches from Spain in 1809 and Lord Castlereagh's correspondence at the Congress of Vienna in 1815. And in 1873 the Permanent Secretary to the Treasury wrote:

> "The unauthorized use of official information is the worst fault a civil servant can commit. It is on the same footing as cowardice by a soldier."

4 1979 c. 13.
5 1967 c. 87.
6 1968 c. 67.
7 Cmnd. 5104.
8 1 & 2 Geo. V c. 28.

12.07 Other instances around this time were those of premature disclosure to the press of a secret Anglo-Russian treaty concerning the Congress of Berlin (where a temporary copying clerk in the Foreign Office was unsuccessfully prosecuted under the Larceny Act 1861[9]) in 1878; and of General Gordon's proclamation (the Franks Committee does not specify its contents) in 1884. The immediate spur to legislation was apparently provided by two cases in 1887; the first was that of publication of instructions to the Intelligence Department of the Royal Navy, and the second involved the sale by a dockyard draughtsman to a third party (possibly a foreign power) of confidential tracings and designs of warships. Although the draughtsman could be (and apparently was) dismissed for breach of trust, no further criminal sanction could be applied against him under the law as it then stood.

12.08 The 1889 Act[10] accordingly provided for there to be offences of spying and/or sabotage (to use a generic expression) and also "breach of official trust"; the latter was punishable, in certain instances, by penal servitude for life; criminal liability was firmly established. The 1889 Act was repealed in 1911, and the Official Secrets Act 1911 (as subsequently revised by the amending Acts of 1920,[11] and 1939[12]) constitutes the statute currently in force. The 1911 Act preserves the general line of demarcation found in the 1889 Act, although the precise wording in the definitions of the offences has changed. There are therefore, in practice, two distinct limbs to the Act, directed respectively to:

(1) spying and/or sabotage; and
(2) unauthorised communication of official information in general.

Section 1

12.09 The first limb is mainly a matter of substantive criminal law, and is covered by section 1. This provides as follows:

"**1.**—(1) If any person for any *purpose prejudicial* to the *safety or interests* of the State—

(a) approaches, inspects, passes over or is in the neighbourhood of, or enters *any prohibited place* within the meaning of this Act; or
(b) makes any sketch, plan, model or note which is calculated to be or might be or is intended to be directly or indirectly useful to an *enemy*; or

9 24 & 25 Vict. c. 96.
10 52 & 53 Vict. c. 52.
11 10 & 11 Geo. V c. 75.
12 2 & 3 Geo. VI. c. 121.

(c) obtains, collects, records, or publishes, or communicates to any other person any secret official code word, or pass word, or any sketch, plan, model, article or note, or other document or information which is calculated to be or might be or is intended to be directly or indirectly useful to an *enemy*;

he shall be guilty of . . ." (emphasis added)

Further statutory definition is provided elsewhere in the Act of such terms as "prohibited place", "sketch", "model" and "document" used here.

12.10 It can be seen at once that this provision is apt to cover what might be regarded as the conventional activities of secret agents of hostile nature, whether of foreign or domestic nationality; this is particularly so during a time of war, when the requirement for safety or interests of the State is obviously heightened. A given act may have, in time of war, a quality of prejudicial purpose in this connection which it would lack completely in time of peace.

Section 2

12.11 It is the second limb, covered by section 2, that is generally more germane in the present context. There can of course be some overlap of the two sections, for example in the case where the "foreign power" (of section 2(1A)) is also an "enemy" within the meaning of section 1. The decision in *R v. Parrott*[13] holds that a potential enemy can also rank as an enemy, so that the overlap is perhaps somewhat greater than might be thought at first blush.

12.12 The striking feature of section 2 as a whole is its great width, on the literal meaning of the words employed. It is set out in full below. The words in italics have been selected so as to illustrate in particular the potential scope of the section.

"**2.**–(1) If any person having in his *possession* or control any secret *official* code word, or pass word, or any sketch, plan, model, article, *note, document, or information* which relates to or is used in a prohibited place or anything in such a place, or which has been made or obtained in contravention of this Act, or under His Majesty *or which he has obtained or to which he has had access owing to his position as a person who holds or has held office under His Majesty*, or as a person who holds or has held a contract made on behalf of His Majesty, or as a person who is or has been employed under a person who holds or has held such an office or contract,—

13 (1913) 8 Cr.App.R 186.

(a) communicates the code word, pass word, sketch, plan, model, article, note, document, or information to any person *other than* a person to whom he is *authorised* to communicate it, or a person to whom it is *in the interest of the State his duty to communicate* it, or,

(aa) *Uses* the information in his possession for the benefit of any foreign power or in any other manner *prejudicial to the safety or interests of the State;*

(b) *retains* the sketch, plan, model, article, note, or document in his possession or control when he has no right to retain it or when it is contrary to his duty to retain it or fails to comply with all directions issued by lawful authority with regard to the return or disposal thereof or

(c) fails to *take reasonable care* of, or so conducts himself as to endanger the safety of the sketch, plan, model, article, note, document, secret official code or pass word or information:

that person shall be guilty of a misdemeanour.

(1A) If any person having in his possession or control any sketch, plan, model, article, note, document, or *information which relates to munitions of war*, communicates it directly or indirectly to any foreign power, or in any other manner prejudicial to the safety or interests of the State, that person shall be guilty of a misdemeanour;

(2) If any person *receives* any secret *official* code word, or pass word, or sketch, plan, model, aricle, note, document, or information, *knowing, or having reasonable ground to believe*, at the time when he receives it, that the code word, pass word, sketch, plan, model, article, note, document, or information is *communicated to him in contravention* of this Act, he shall be guilty of a misdemeanour, unless he proves that the communication to him of the code word, pass word, sketch, plan, model, article, note, document, or information was contrary to his desire." (emphasis added)

12.13 It is of course necessary, in any given instance, for the Crown to prove the triple correspondence of person, subject-matter and act. In other words, the Crown has to show that a person (as defined) has performed a prohibited act (as defined) in respect of subject-matter (as defined). What is prohibited, in any given instance, may depend upon the precise nature of the person and the subject-matter involved. There is an interplay between the three basic ingredients of the possible offence. Proof of performance of the prohibited act may, in particular, provide a formidable hurdle for the Crown to surmount in the case of communication and the like of the restricted subject-matter (in the absence of admissible confession by the accused); this is because corroboratory evidence by the communicatee as to the occurrence of communication may naturally be impossible to obtain; the relevant diplomatic representative of the foreign power may claim diplomatic immunity, or alternatively be sent back home as soon as the accused is charged. Similar considerations apply in this respect of course in cases of prosecution under section 1 of the Act; and the general difficulty presented by reliance on confession evidence has recently been amply illustrated by the Cyprus airmen case.[14]

12.14 Significantly, it is not only Crown servants who are within the ambit of section 2. Also affected, as the Franks Committee emphasised, are the following further categories of person:

(a) Government contractors and their employees;
(b) persons to whom official information has been entrusted in confidence by a Crown servant;
(c) persons in possession of official information as a result of earlier contravention of the Act; in other words, those further down the leakage chain (for example the editor who hears from the journalist who originally persuaded the civil servant's secretary) can be caught as well;
(d) persons who have come into possession (by whatever means) of secret official code or pass words, or information relevant to munitions of war;
(e) recipients of official information, provided that they know or had reasonable ground to believe that the information communicated to them was of this kind; an exception is made for receipt contrary to desire (since it may well be impossible for a communicatee to prevent an oral communicator speaking to him or a writing communicator from sending a letter to him).

"Munitions of war" information

12.15 The group of persons (d) is—notionally at least—particularly wide in the sphere of technology and industry generally. This is because of the breadth of the formal statutory definition (in the subsequent section 12) of "munitions of war," under section 2(1A); those in possession of secret official codes and the like (the other branch of group (d), under section 2(2) are obviously very few. The definition is:

> "The expression 'munitions of war' includes the whole or any part of any ship, submarine, aircraft, tank or similar engine, arms and ammunition, torpedo, or mine, intended or adapted for use in war, *and any other article*, material, or device, whether actual or proposed, intended for such use." (emphasis added)

12.16 Apart from conventional armaments, the catch-all inclusion of "any other article intended for use in war" is arguably capable of rendering section 2(1A) applicable to persons having information on such

14 New Law Journal Vol. 135, 1173.

diverse items as field bandages, heavy boots and portable cooking equipment—certainly so if developed in response to military orders, although that is not a pre-requisite, since section 2(1A) lacks (in contrast to the position under section 2(1)) any qualification as to the information being "official". The fact that the articles might have widespread civilian utility also—for ambulance-men at sports arenas, ramblers and campers respectively—would be secondary.

12.17 An alternative view is that the phrase should be construed *ejusdem generis* with the previous list of articles "ship, submarine . . . mine". On this approach, articles of the kinds referred to above would come outside section 2 (which would appear to be a sensible conclusion). But an *ejusdem generis* construction would by the same token serve also to exclude articles of a kind highly significant to modern warfare but unknown—in practical terms—in 1920 when the definition was first created. Radar and like tracking systems, nerve gases, biological warfare generally might fall outside, although it could be argued that inter-continental ballistic missiles fall inside (on the basis that a rocket is analogous to a torpedo, both being launched from afar against a given target with the only difference being that one moves through the air and the other through the sea; for missiles launched from submerged submarines the initial section of the trajectory will indeed be in the sea and the analogy becomes even closer). Such a result would provide an argument against the *ejusdem generis* construction. Separate provisions (discussed later in this chapter) apply in any event to atomic devices and plants.

12.18 The present position in short is that the precise scope of section 2(1A) as regards the type of information potentially embraced is uncertain; consequentially, there is uncertainty as to precisely who is affected by this part of the Act, since liability is in principle controlled by possession of information of the relevant kind. But it is clear that section 2(1A) may well be wider than is generally supposed.

"Official" information

12.19 Ascertainment of the types of information, and hence types of persons, subject to sections 2(1) and 2(2) of the Act provides fewer difficulties on account of the "official" qualification in the preambles of both. It goes without saying that a civil servant normally obtains his official information on account of his holding an office under the Crown. Again, if an engineering drawing is headed "Property of the Ministry of Defence" it is virtually self-evident that it ranks as an official document and hence that any person handling the drawing improperly is liable to be prosecuted; likewise if a contractor building an extension to a naval dockyard is shown on the site a plan of the existing works. The whole point of the difference between the two, section 2(1A) on the one hand and sections 2(1) and 2(2) on the other, is that section 2(1A) extends beyond the official information sector into the purely private information sector as well.

Proscribed acts

12.20 The proscribed acts are defined separately in each of sections 2(1) (unauthorised disclosure of official information generally), 2(1A) (communication of information relating to munitions of war) and 2(2) (unlawful receipt of official information). Some comment as to their scope has been given already, in describing the classes of persons subject to section 2 of the 1911 Act generally, but these merit further expansion. The more detailed position is:

Section 2(1)—covers communication and/or use and/or retention and/or failure to take reasonable care of the respective subject-matters and in the fashions as defined in sub-paragraphs (a) through (c);

Section 2(1A)—covers only communication of the subject-matter in the fashion defined;

Section 2(2)—covers only receipt of the subject-matter and in the fashion defined.

12.21 The range of acts embraced by section 2(1) is therefore in principle substantially wider than those of sections 2(1A) and 2(2).

Mens rea

12.22 There is no statutorily expressed requirement for *mens rea* as regards offences under sections 2(1) and 2(1A) (communication and the like). This suggests that the offences are ones of absolute nature; and the case law, for example *R v. Crisp and Homewood*,[15] supports this view. In contrast, there is an express *mens rea* requirement for offences under section 2(2) (receipt of information).

Interests of the State

12.23 Application of the "safety or interests of the State" requirement of sections 2(1)(a), 2(1)(aa) and 2(1A) has engendered considerable controversy. The position is usually more clear-cut in cases under section 1(1), where the requirement is also present. The words as they stand are capable of extending far beyond matters of national defence, the prevention and detection of crime, and the like, as to which there is

15 (1919) 83 J.P. 121.

probably a general consensus on the desirability of secrecy. If it goes as wide as the policy of the Government of the day, then it can be argued that there is both uncertainty (since policy will naturally change with the political complexion of the Government) and conflict with the principle that citizens should be free to acquaint themselves with the working of their Government.

12.24 The leading case on the topic is that of *Chandler v. Director of Public Prosecutions.*[16] The decision is, unfortunately, not one of pellucid character (five separate judgements being given in the House of Lords) and arose in any event not under section 2 but section 1 instead. Section 1 involves (as already indicated) defence of the realm (*Chandler* in fact involving a proposed anti-nuclear demonstration at Wethersfield RAF Station) rather than mere unauthorised leakage of embarrassing information. The dicta most favourable to a wider view of interests of the State, and hence a wider restriction, are probably those of Lords Devlin and Pearce which are respectively:

> ". . . the statute is not concerned with what the interests of the state might be or ought to be but with *what they actually are* at the time of the alleged offence." (at 807, emphasis added)
>
> ". . . the interests of the state must in my judgment mean the interests of the state according to the *policies laid down for it by its recognised organs of government* and authority, the policies of the state *as they are, not as they ought, in the opinion of a jury,* to be. Anything which prejudices those policies is within the meaning of the Act 'prejudicial to the interests of the state'." (at 813, emphasis added)

12.25 But it is sometimes overlooked that these remarks were made in a particular context, namely that of current defence precautions (Wethersfield air base being occupied by combat-ready squadrons of the USAF on constant alert and assigned to the Supreme Commander Allied Forces Europe). Hence it is perhaps not wholly surprising that in the more recent case of *R v. Ponting*[17] a jury refused to convict, in face of a direction as to law based upon the speeches of Lords Devlin and Pearce, in an instance of a candid admission by a high-ranking civil servant as to deliberate unauthorised leakage of a document awkward to the Government of the day.

12.26 The Franks Committee (mentioned above) proposed substantial amendments to the present law, to be put into force by a new Official Information Act, but legislation is lacking so far.

16 [1964] A.C. 763.
17 11 February 1985.

"Munitions of War" communications

12.27 The wide scope of section 2(1A) as regards information relating to "munitions of war" has already been mentioned. This information is not restricted to matter of official origin; information of non-official origin (that is, of ordinary private industrial or commercial origin) is covered as well, provided of course that it comes under the "munitions of war" head.

12.28 The uncertainty as to the exact meaning of "munitions of war" can pose awkward dilemmas for the purely private person or organisation. They may have to come to a decision of their own accord as to whether or not the information is so classifiable; the Act fails to provide any clearance procedure. Further problems can arise as regards the extent of the prohibition on dissemination; either direct or indirect communication (to a foreign power) is specifically restricted. Straightforward handing-over of relevant documents in furtive circumstances to representatives present in the United Kingdom of a foreign power would be an obvious instance of direct communication. But indirect communication can arise in a variety of more subtle ways. Possible examples are the advance sending of the written script of a lecture to be given at a forthcoming international conference sponsored and organised by an agency of a foreign Government, or the sending of a patent application to a foreign patent agent for filing in the foreign Patent Office in question; a patent application normally has to be accompanied by a Specification, which provides a comprehensive technical description (usually complete with drawings in an engineering case or specific examples in a chemical case) of the invention involved. It is suggested that this is a further area of present law in which clarifying amending legislation would be highly desirable.

Civil actions

12.29 The Official Secrets Act 1911 (as amended) creates criminal liability on the part of those who contravene its provisions, and therein lies its teeth. But it does not supplant the ordinary civil law concerning breach of confidentiality; the civil law operates in tandem with the criminal law and may well serve to provide additional safeguards for the maintenance of official secrets in specific cases. Two aspects in particular of the ordinary civil law may be important in this context, namely:

(i) Under normal considerations of employment law, it may well be proper to dismiss an employee who breaches his duty of confidentiality towards his employer; thus the civil servant who leaks the politically embarrassing document is still liable to lose his job even if not his liberty;

and the prospect of such disciplinary action may naturally reduce his propensity to leak in the first place.

(2) Impending revelations, for example an asserted exposé by a former agent in his forthcoming memoirs as to inefficiency in counter-intelligence operations on which he was previously engaged, may be restrained by interlocutory injunction (with the consequential prospect of proceedings for contempt if the injunction is broken by going ahead with publication).

PATENTS ACT 1977

12.30 Further regulation of the position in respect of technological subject-matter contained in patent applications is provided by sections 22 and 23 of the Patents Act 1977.[18] Section 22 enables the Patent Office to give directions:

> ". . . prohibiting or restricting the publication of that information or its communication to any specified person or description of persons."

wherever it appears that the patent application:

> ". . . contains information of a description notified . . . by the Secretary of State as being information the publication of which might be prejudicial to the defence of the realm,"

12.31 If such directions are given, the patent application is then subsequently handled by a special procedure, details of which can be found in textbooks of patent law. The secrecy direction can be (and in practice often is) subsequently lifted, as defence interests change or information concerning the invention reaches the public domain by some other means. Nevertheless, section 22 has quite a wide application in practice. As well as instances of inventions of self-evident defence interest—for example, in the fields of atomic bombs, radar or biological warfare—a secrecy order may also be given where the defence application of the invention is merely one out of a number of such applications—for example, a new synthetic lubricant having valuable low-temperature properties making it useful for, *inter alia*, preventing the jamming of machine guns in Arctic conditions.

12.32 Section 23 buttresses this broad power of the Patent Office to order secrecy, by requiring—to speak generally—that any corresponding foreign patent applications should not be filed (or caused to be filed) until a domestic patent application has been filed and a six-week period from such filing has elapsed without any secrecy direction being given; if

18 1977 c. 37.

special written authority is obtained from the Patent Office, however, this holding period can be circumvented. This section can give rise to considerable problems in connection with the first filing of patent applications on inventions made in the laboratories of multi-national concerns, since it is not restricted to inventions originating in the first place within the United Kingdom. It begins to bite once information concerning the invention has reached the United Kingdom, say in an invention report to the Patent Department of the United Kingdom head office from the Luxembourg laboratories of an affiliate or subsidiary. Filing a foreign patent application in circumstances proscribed by section 23 of the Patents Act 1977 can also of course give rise to contravention of the Official Secrets Acts—particularly of section 2(1A) of the 1911 Act. The proscriptions of the two are in principle quite separate, although they can overlap.

ATOMIC ENERGY AND ALLIED ACTS

12.33 Atomic energy constitutes a particular technological field in which special measures have been enacted in order to protect secrecy. The subject is one of some complexity, and only an outline of the main points is provided here. These are:

(1) Membership of or any office or employment under the Atomic Energy Authority is deemed to be an office under the Crown and any contract with the Authority shall be deemed under the Atomic Energy Authority Act 1954 to be a contract with the Crown.[19] By such deeming, the provisions of section 2(1) of the Official Secrets Act 1911 are effectively extended to such employees and contractors.

(2) Unauthorised communication to third parties of any information concerning any atomic energy plant or process to be operated therein is an offence under the Atomic Energy Act 1946.[20] Information already put into the public domain, otherwise than by contravention of the statutory provisions, is excluded.[21] It follows therefore, that information elicited for example at public inquiries (other than evidence given *in camera*) as to the siting and construction of an AGR (advanced gas-cooled reactor) or PWR (pressurized water reactor)-type nuclear power station can be freely disseminated further.

(3) A nuclear site licensed under the provisions of the Nuclear Installations Act 1965[22] is deemed[23] to rank as a "prohibited place" for purposes of the Official Secrets Act 1911.

19 2 & 3 Eliz. II c. 34; Sch. 3
20 9 & 10 Geo. VI, c. 80 at s. 11(1).
21 S. 11(4).
22 1965 c. 37.
23 Sch. 1, para. 3(1).

(4) Unauthorised disclosure of information concerning any manufacturing process or trade secret obtained by persons having powers of entry and inspection under the Radioactive Substances Acts 1948[24] and 1960[25] to premises in which handling and the like of radioactive materials is carried out, is an offence.[26]

(5) The Minister has powers under the Nuclear Installations Act 1965 to give directions to bodies corporate having nuclear site licences under the Act for the purpose of safeguarding information in the interests of national security.[27]

24 11 & 12 Geo. VI c. 37.
25 8 & 9 Eliz. II c. 34.
26 S. 7(5) 1948 Act and s. 13(3) 1960 Act.
27 Sch. 1, para. 5(1).

CHAPTER 13

Personal and Domestic Confidences

GENERAL

13.01 It is common in everyday parlance to speak of confidentiality in relation to certain general kinds of circumstances of a private character. A doctor may, for example, assure his patient that the consultation will be confidential; a banker may assure his customer that his affairs will be kept confidential; the Inland Revenue may assure a taxpayer that his tax return is confidential; a husband may implicitly assume that his wife will keep to herself remarks made over the breakfast table which he would not—if he had been asked—have cared to reveal to the world at large, and vice-versa; a mother may make the same assumption when speaking to her child's teacher. Somewhat more uncommon situations may also arise—say, as between reader and "agony column" journalist, client and professional bereavement counsellor; or patient and optician.

13.02 But does an assertion or assumption of confidentiality in such circumstances really mean what it appears to suggest? It is the aim of this chapter to examine some of the most common kinds of personal and domestic confidences in this light.

13.03 This separate examination should not be taken to mean that the law in this area as a whole is a totally different creature to that encountered in the more purely commercial area, say the duty of confidence which an employee owes to his employer in respect of the employer's secret process or customer lists. Similar common law principles can be perceived; again, statute may intervene over and above the common law so as to affect the practical application of those principles. But it is convenient to categorise.

TAXPAYER AND INSPECTOR

13.04 The Inland Revenue may proclaim loudly, in its leaflets designed to explain the tax system to the man in the street, that all dealings between taxpayer and Revenue are confidential. Expressions of similar grandiloquence can be found in the case law, for example that of Lord Templeman in *R. v. I.R.C. ex parte Preston:*[1]

> "The Commissioners are inhibited from presenting full reasons to the Court for their decisions because of the *duty of confidentiality* owed by the Commissioners to each and every taxpayer." (at 850, emphasis added)

13.05 Of course the assertion is—in a general sense—justified. The Inland Revenue in the United Kingdom does not have the practice, subsisting elsewhere, of laying taxpayers' returns and/or correspondence relating thereto open to public inspection. Hearings before the General and Special Commissioners for the purpose of assessing and determining tax liabilities are held *in camera,* unless both parties to the appeal request a public hearing. Moreover, section 6 of the Taxes Management Act 1970[2] requires officers of the Inland Revenue to make, on appointment, a declaration imposing obligation of secrecy. The form prescribed[3] for inspectors, collectors and the like reads as follows:

> "I, *A.B.*, do solemnly declare that I will not disclose any information received by me in the execution of the duties which may from time to time be assigned to me by the Board of Inland Revenue except for the purposes of my duties, or to the Board of Inland Revenue or in accordance with their instructions, or for the purposes of any prosecution for an offence relating to Inland Revenue, or in such other cases as may be required by law."

13.06 It can be seen at once from this declaration that the obligation of secrecy is not absolute but partial only. There are two heads of exception as regards disclosure beyond the confines of the Inland Revenue itself, namely (i) where revenue offences are involved and (ii) in other cases "as may be required by law."

13.07 Head (i) is of narrow scope and can be regarded as not unreasonable. A Court hearing a tax offence case will not normally go *in camera* once details of the accused's taxes start to be presented; possible embarrassment to the accused is hardly likely to provide sufficient justification for such a step. In principle, any member of the public can attend the Court and learn those details, as spoken of in Court, for himself.

13.08 Head (ii) represents the joker in the pack. "Law" for this purpose naturally includes both the statute law and common law. There have been relatively few relevant statutory exceptions enacted and they tend to be limited to specialised aspects, for example disclosure under section 31(8)

1 [1985] 2 W.L.R. 836.
2 1970 c. 9.
3 Sch. 1, Part III.

of the Finance Act 1966[4] in certain cases to authorised officers of foreign Governments having double taxation agreements with the United Kingdom. But the generality of the common law means that the obligation is liable to be lifted also in circumstances which would hardly occur to the mind of average taxpayer, although to the lawyer they might.

13.09 One example only will be taken. *In R. v. I.R.C. ex parte National Federation of Self-Employed and Small Businesses*[5] the Federation objected to the grant of an amnesty to some 6,000 casual Fleet Street printing workers in respect of past tax evasion in return for proper accounting in future. The Federation sought to contrast the behaviour of the Inland Revenue in this matter with that normally exhibited to their own members. On application for judicial review for relief by way of declaration (that the Inland Revenue acted unlawfully in granting the amnesty) and *mandamus* (that the Inland Revenue should assess and collect back income-tax due from the casual workers), it was held that the Federation had no sufficient interest and the application accordingly failed. But what is relevant in the present context are the remarks of Lord Scarman concerning the Revenue's duty of confidence:

> "Lastly, I wish to comment shortly upon the *duty of confidence* owed by the Revenue to every taxpayer and the *right to discovery*. The duty of confidence can co-exist with the duty of fairness owed to the general body of taxpayers. It is, however, of great importance when discovery is sought by an applicant, as happened in this case. Upon general principles, discovery should not be ordered unless and until the court is satisfied that the evidence reveals reasonable grounds for believing that there has been a breach of public duty: and it should be limited strictly to documents relevant to the issue which emerges from the affidavits. The Revenue in any event will have the right in respect of certain classes of document to plead "public interest immunity," of which in a proper case the court will be the arbiter: *Burmah Oil Co. Ltd. v. Governor and Company of the Bank of England* [1980] A.C. 1090. In the present case, had the Federation shown a sufficient interest, *I doubt whether any legitimate objection could have been taken* to discovery of documents relevant to the making of the special arrangement." (emphasis added)

13.10 The result accordingly, had the Federation been regarded as having adequate interest in the matter, would have been that the contents of documents relating to the grant of the amnesty would have been revealed to a third party. In other words, the duty of confidence would have represented a mere broken shield. To a lawyer, accustomed to the concept of conflicting duties or familiar with Hohfeldian concepts as to

4 1966 c. 18.
5 [1982] A.C. 617.
6 At 654.

the jural association between rights and duties, that may appear an unexceptionable result. But a lay person may think of duty in mere black and white terms—either it does or does not exist, with no grey area in between.

13.11 Here it may be legitimately speculated that such a possible result was hardly envisaged by the actual parties to the amnesty when originally negotiating the same. There might naturally be restrictions as to the use (if any) which the Federation could subsequently make of that information for other purposes, owing to the fact that it would have been disclosed initially just for purposes of litigation. But that is an altogether separate question.

DOCTOR AND PATIENT

13.12 In the 5th century B.C. on the island of Kos in the blue Aegean the Hippocratic oath was formulated. And still today a doctor entering into practice takes the same oath. The oath itself reads in a typical translation as follows:

> "I swear by Apollo the physician, by Aesculapius, Hygeia and Panacea, and I take to witness all the gods, all the goddesses, to keep according to my ability and my judgement the following Oath:
>
> . . .
>
> All that may come to my knowledge in the exercise of my profession or outside of my profession or in daily commerce with men, which ought not to be spread abroad, I will *keep secret and will never reveal. . . ." (emphasis added)*

13.13 In contrast to the simplism of this attestation, there are to be found in recent jurisprudence such remarks as those of Eveleigh L.J. in the Court of Appeal judgement on *Gillick v. West Norfolk and Wisbech Health Authority*[7] (involving the question of whether contraceptive advice or treatment can be given by a doctor to a girl aged under 16 without the knowledge and consent of her parent(s):

> "I would add a word on confidentiality. A doctor's position is *not an easy one*. The courts recognise this . . . arguments which we have heard as to the difficulty which the duty of confidentiality imposes upon a doctor. *The alleged duty must be subject to exceptions* . . ." (at 446, emphasis added)

13.14 The underlying theme of these words is perhaps rueful. But they make the essential point that today the duty is not absolute; it is

7 [1985] 2 W.L.R. 413.

contingent upon disclosure not being required for other proper reasons. In the complexity of contemporary societal relationships, situations may arise which are far removed from the lesser sophistication of Ancient Greece. An example may be taken of the homosexual blood donor who is subsequently diagnosed by his doctor to be suffering from AIDS (auto-immune deficiency syndrome). The doctor knows of his patient's donor activities. Should he tell the blood transfusion authorities, in face of lack of patient consent and absence of any separate statutory compulsion, in order both to prevent further donations and try to track down existing ones? Judicial resolution of this particular problem is still awaited.

13.15 The subsequent ruling by the House of Lords in the *Gillick* case that such advice or treatment could be given, in certain circumstances, does not assist very much in ascertaining the overall contemporary bounds of the doctor's duty as regards patient confidentiality. No comprehensive definition of the exceptions is attempted in any of the speeches. About the most that can be said is that the majority view was clearly that, in the context of contraceptive advice or treatment for girls aged under 16, the doctor's duty lay to his patient (the under-age girl) and not to the parent(s).

Profit by doctor

13.16 Where on the other hand the doctor breaches the confidence for his own personal ends—say if he publishes for financial gain an account of the illnesses of his famous patients—there is little doubt but that the Court would intervene (at least whilst the patients are still alive). The rule can be traced back to 1820 when Lord Eldon, in the unreported case of *Wyatt v. Wyatt* expressed himself respecting an engraving of George III during his illness:

> "If one of the late King's physicians had kept a diary of what he had heard and seen, this Court would not in the King's lifetime, have permitted him to print or publish it."

13.17 The position may be different after the death of the patient on the basis that the confidential relationship is essentially a personal link between patient and doctor, which is inevitably broken by the patient's death. Ethical considerations may, however, in practice serve then to continue to restrict disclosure to a considerable extent.

8 [1985] 3 W.L.R. 830.

Records

13.18 Post mortem, or retirement, of the doctor the generally accepted view is, on the other hand, that his successors are still bound; hence, for example, the remaining partners in the practice may not disclose medical details to be found on the patient's record card even if the patient has never consulted them since the earlier doctor's time. To prevent such mishap (whether intended or not), periodic pruning of records may well be advisable, as indeed was recognised over two centuries ago by the surgeon in the *Duchess of Kingston's case*[9] (see para. 13.23 *infra*) when he said in evidence:

> "If I ever put down any thing in writing at the time, I might have destroyed it afterwards, according to my custom, which is to destroy papers that are of no use, and which might be *improper to be found after my decease*". (emphasis added)

13.19 Of course, the doctor who is negligent as regards his patient's records—say, one who entrusts his records disposal work to a casual operator who merely deposits them on the town dump where they can be readily picked up by the local scavengers—may well be liable for any consequential damage to his patient for reasons quite apart from the existence or not of any formal link of confidence. *Prima facie* the patient is a "neighbour" within the principle of *Donoghue v. Stevenson*.[10]

BMA Guidelines

13.20 In the 1981 edition of *The Handbook of Medical Ethics* (British Medical Association), the exceptions to the general principle of secrecy are put forward as follows:

> "(1) The patient gives consent.
> (2) When it is undesirable on medical grounds to seek a patient's consent, but is in the patient's own interest that confidentiality should be broken.
> (3) The doctor's overriding duty to society.
> (4) For the purposes of medical research, when approved by a local clinical research ethical committee, or in the case of the National Cancer Registry by the Chairman of the BMA's Central Ethical Committee or his nominee.
> (5) When the information is required by due legal process."

13.21 These categories provide a convenient starting-point for fuller discussion of the modern-day "doctor's dilemma". Exception No. 1 is of self-evident scope. Exception No. 2 covers, for example, the case where

9 (1776) State Trials (Howell's Collection) Vol. XX 355 at 571–2 and 576.
10 [1932] A.C. 562.

the patient would be tempted to commit suicide if he were made aware of the true nature of his illness; it may be proper there to disclose the position to a close relative, who is of course a third party so far as the original patient/doctor relationship is concerned. Exception no. 3 would cover the AIDS situation mentioned above. Exception no. 4 is of narrow scope and again self-explanatory; proper assessment of the clinical trials of a new drug may, for example, necessarily involve some degree of disclosure of results to third parties.

13.22 Exception no. 5 is of potentially wider scope, and may overlap with exceptions nos. 2 and 3 in any event. It can be divided, in principle, into the two limbs of (i) cases where disclosure is required by statute, and (ii) cases where disclosure is required by common law. As for (i), a primary example is provided by the requirement of the Public Health Acts[11] as regards notifiable diseases (cholera and the like). As for (ii), a primary example is provided by the rule that communications between doctor and patient lack privilege; situations can therefore arise in the course of legal proceedings where the doctor may, but not necessarily will, be liable for contempt if he refuses to answer questions concerning his patient. Refusal to answer does not necessarily involve contempt; the Court always has the option of holding that the public interest is, in the particular circumstances of the case, upheld better by refusal than compulsion. The principles enunciated in the modern leading case of *D. v. NSPCC*[12] (already mentioned at paras. 8.28–29) are likely to apply, even though that decision was concerned with social work practitioners rather than medical practitioners as such.

13.23 Case law on exception no. 5 can be traced back to *The Duchess of Kingston's case* in 1776 (prosecution for bigamy), where Lord Mansfield, in response to a demurral of the witness Mr. Caesar Hawkins (a surgeon) called by the Solicitor-General who said:

> "I do not know how far anything that has come before me in a confidential trust in my profession should be disclosed, consistent with my professional honour."

replied:

> "If a surgeon was voluntarily to reveal these secrets, to be sure he would be guilty of a breach of honour, and of great indiscretion; but to give that information in a court of justice, which by the law of the land he is *bound to do*, will never be imputed to him as any indiscretion whatever." (emphasis added)

11 E.g. Health Services and Public Health Act 1968 (1968 c. 46).
12 [1978] A.C. 171.

13.24 More recent cases include *Garner v. Garner*[13] (where a medical practitioner, who had treated a patient under a national scheme for dealing with venereal disease having regulations enjoining absolute secrecy, was compelled to give evidence as to his findings); *C. v. C.*[14] (where a medical practitioner was compelled to give evidence concerning venereal disease in his patient, in the course of divorce proceedings involving the same); *Nuttall v. Nuttall and Twyman*[15] (where a psychiatrist was compelled to give evidence concerning his patient, again in divorce proceedings); *Hunter v. Mann*[16] (where a medical practioner was charged with an offence under section 168(2)(b) of the Road Traffic Act 1972,[17] by failing to give information which might have led to the identification of the driver involved in a car accident). This list is not exhaustive.

HUSBAND AND WIFE

13.25 The law here has deep roots, even if not quite such long standing as in the case of confidence between doctor and patient. A starting landmark is provided by the decision of Lord Alvanley C.J. in 1802 in *Monroe & Twistleton*,[18] where an unsuccessful attempt was made to call evidence from the plaintiff's former wife, now divorced and remarried, concerning a contract for the board and lodging of the defendant's infant child:

> "To prove any fact arising after the divorce this lady is a competent witness, but *not* to prove a contract or anything else which happened *during the coverture*. She was at that time bound to secrecy; what she did might be in consequence of the trust and confidence reposed in her by her husband; and miserable indeed would the condition of a husband be, if, when a woman is divorced from him, perhaps for her own misconduct, all the occurences of his life entrusted to her *while the most perfect and unbounded confidence existed between them* should be divulged in a court of justice . . .; and it never shall be endured that the confidence which the law has created while the parties remained in the most intimate of all relations, shall be broken whenever . . . the relation has been dissolved." (emphasis added)

The attempt accordingly foundered on the issue of the spouse's competence, as distinct from that of compellability had competence existed.

13 (1920) 36 T.L.R. 196.
14 [1946] 1 All E.R. 562.
15 (1964) 108 Sol. Jo. 605.
16 [1974] 2 All E.R. 414.
17 1972 c. 20.
18 Peake's Add. Cas. 219 at 220.

13.25 The reasons for the law's concern to protect marital confidences is not hard to seek. It lies in public policy. There is a public interest in upholding the institution of marriage, and the preservation of confidence assists that aim. As it was put by the Court in the leading modern case of *Duchess of Argyll v. Duke of Argyll*[19] in 1964,

> "It has been said that the legal consideration of marriage—that is the promise to become and to remain man and wife—is the *highest legal consideration* which there is. And there could hardly be anything more intimate or confidential than is involved in that relationship, or than in the mutual trust and confidences which are shared between husband and wife. The *confidential nature of the relationship is of its very essence and so obviously and necessarily implicit in it* that there is no need for it to be expressed. To express it is superfluous, it is clear to the least intelligent." (emphasis added)

13.27 in the *Duchess of Argyll's* case the Duke was accordingly restrained from communicating to a newspaper:

> "secrets of the plaintiff relating to her private life, personal affairs or private conduct, communicated to the first defendant in confidence during the subsistence of his marriage to the plaintiff and not hitherto made public property."[20]

and the newspaper consequentially restrained from publishing the same, notwithstanding that the Duchess had already written articles for another newspaper including details—like the revelation that the Duke had been taking drinamyl tablets—which might be thought themselves to be objectionable. In this instance, the importance of the one equitable principle (preservation of confidence) served to override the other equitable principle that unclean hands are a bar to relief.

13.28 But if the parties effectively throw their private lives open to full public gaze, then by their own actions they destroy the nexus of confidence. This was the kind of situation involved in *Lennon v. News Group Newspapers and Twist*,[21] where the parties had previously engaged in what might be termed a press-article war concerning their prior form. As it was put by Lord Denning:

> "It seems to me as plain as can be that the relationship of these parties has ceased to be their own private affair. They themselves have put it into the public domain. . . . One only has to read these articles all the way through to show that each of them is making money by publishing the most intimate details about one another and accusing one another of this, that

19 [1967] Ch. 302 at 322.
20 At 306.
21 [1978] F.S.R. 573.

> and the other, and so forth. It is all in the public domain. I do not regard this as a breach of confidence at all . . ."[22]

The *Duchess of Argyll* decision was accordingly distinguished, and injunctive relief refused.

13.29 Although the jurisprudential emphasis has up to now been on the marital relation of traditional kind (a formal marriage between husband and wife), it would seem quite possible that the principles are capable of application also to less conventional forms of societal relationship—for example, co-habitation, homosexual marriage, polygamy and polyandry, or group living. A formal contractual relationship between the parties would not seem essential. In the *Duchess of Argyll's* case it was pointed out by the Court that although the marriage bond (in the traditional sense) includes contract, the relationship is really one of wider nature; and the Court's decision was founded upon such wider considerations, which can reasonably be argued to apply (according to circumstances) to relationships of these other kinds as well. But it is not yet clear as to precisely how far along this road the law is prepared to advance.

13.30 Mention should be made again, finally, of the exceptions to the principle of marital confidence to be found in the criminal law, under the Criminal Evidence Act 1898[23] and subsequent legislation. The scope of these exceptions (which may vary from time to time) and the case-law under them is beyond the scope of this book. They reflect the fact that in criminal matters there is a competing public policy—namely the detection of crime and pursuance of offenders—involved also.

PUPIL AND TEACHER

13.31 This represents an area of current controversy so far as questions of confidence are concerned. It is of course relatively rare for a teacher to be in the position of trying to obtain commercial gain as a result of his or her previous association with a particular pupil. This is not to say that the situation is unknown. The primary school teacher who has in her charge the 5-year-old of a leading actress may well have in her possession as a result of the child's innocent prattle lurid details of the actress' current home-life; the temptation to exploit those details may be strong. Likewise for the secondary school teacher in a position to reveal the minor youthful peccadillos of the now leading politician, up to now discreetly hidden in the school's punishment book. On normal principles of the

22 At 574–5.
23 61 & 62 Vict. c. 36.

action for breach of confidence, it may well be possible in circumstances of these kinds to obtain legal redress, since such subsequent use of the information could in each case be regarded as extra-ordinary, and hence unauthorised. The 5-year-old could hardly have capacity in the first place to authorise or not; the secondary pupil may well have been entitled to assume implicitly that those running the school will refrain from trying to take subsequent financial advantage of his current misfortune; he is, of course, unlikely to have been asked for permission on the point at the time.

13.32 The more common, and more difficult, problem arises in connection with the ordinary use of school and educatinonal records. There are two principal aspects to consider:

(i) the inherent accuracy of the records; and
(ii) subsequent reliance upon the same.

As for (i), a disgruntled teacher may—perhaps because the pupil has been rude—note in the records adverse information to that pupil; and it is unlikely, bearing in mind usual school conditions, that the correctness of the information will have been checked by others before entry. Should the pupil have the opportunity of subsequent access to the record, with a view to challenging its accuracy? After all, the record may subsequently be relied upon by the school in giving a subsequent report on the pupil to, say, a potential employer or to a university admissions office; these are examples of aspect (ii) of the matter. Use of records to prepare such references is of course in principle perfectly proper; there is, normally, a clear consent by the pupil to the reference being given; and the referor, say the head teacher or head of department, can hardly be expected to be personally omniscient of all present and past pupils under his aegis.

13.33 The law really still awaits development on these issues. But it is suggested that there is a substantial case for saying that such records should, at least insofar as they contain fact—for example that pupil X had to be suspended from school for misbehaviour Y times during his career there, rendered open to inspection and/or challenge by the pupil and/or parents. The position of expressions of opinion may be different, however.

13.34 A possible portent of a liberal attitude on the part of the Court in this area can, however, be seen in the recent case of *Thompson v. ILEA*.[24] The claim for access to the school records was made here by a

24 (1977) 74 LS Gaz 66.

third party. A pupil had suffered an eye injury while at school, allegedly by the wrongful act of another pupil. A claim for negligence was entered against the education authority, on the basis that they had failed to supervise properly that other pupil. A claim for privilege as to the school records of the other pupil was rejected, the argument that access would lead to lack of candour on the part of teachers in the future so far as records were concerned being decisively rejected.

CUSTOMER AND BANKER

13.35 This relationship has been discussed previously in Chapter 4. The position can perhaps be summarised by saying that there the customer enjoys confidentiality only so long as there is no other good reason for non-confidentiality.

CONFIDENTIALITY v. PRIVACY

13.36 Although the relationships discussed in this chapter are essentially all of private, as opposed to public or commercial, kind it must be emphasised that English law recognises no general right of privacy. The rights and obligations of the parties, in situations of the kind discussed in this chapter, all derive from the fact there is also between some kind of confidential relationship. In short, both private character and nexus are required for the law to step in. It follows that there can be situations in which subject-matter of inherently private kind can be revealed, against the wishes (declared or undeclared) of the party to whom the subject-matter relates, without any tort being committed by the revealer. For example, the prominent personality who accidentally drops his diary in a city street is unlikely to be able to succeed against the third party (quite unknown to him) who picks it up and sells its contents. Likewise in the case of the engineer who accidentally leaves behind in the railway carriage a copy of his latest research report; if by chance a competitor is sitting opposite and reads it, the former can hardly be heard to complain if the latter starts using the contents of the research to improve his own manufacture. In both instances the parties are legal strangers to each other at the time of communication, and there would seem to be little basis for implying between them any connection capable of giving rise in turn to a duty of confidence.

13.37 The likelihood of any general statutory right of privacy being created is low, at least at present. The Younger Report (Report of the

Committee on Privacy, 1972)[25] came down against the idea; they recommended instead, *inter alia,* that greater use be made of the action for breach of confidence. Because of the uncertainty as to the exact scope of the latter, the matter was referred to the Law Commission who in turn produced in 1980 the Report *Breach of Confidence*[26] to which reference has been made in a number of places in this book and which included the draft Breach of Confidence Bill reproduced in the Appendix.

25 Cmnd. 7341.
26 Cmnd. 8388.

CHAPTER 14

Journalists

14.01 Although the position of the journalist as regards protection of his confidential source is now essentially regulated by statute (section 10 of the Contempt of Court Act 1981,[1] already referred to in Chapter 7), the myths that tend to surround the topic merit the giving of some closer examination to its history. The statute is, in addition, quite new; its bounds have not yet been fully explored by the Courts; and it is possible that in exploring some or other of those bounds the earlier case-law may prove of value to the Court.

HISTORY

14.02 A starting point may be taken in the attempt before the Parnell Inquiry Commission of 1889 to force the editor of *The Times* to divulge the name of one of his contributors. As reported subsequently in *Attorney-General v. Mulholland*,[2] the exchange was:

> "(Q) Do you not know who the writer of the article was?
> (A) I do indirectly, not directly.
> (Q) Who was it then?
> (A) I do not know that I am bound to tell you.
> (Q) I ask you the question?
> (A) The conductors and the editor of *The Times* would be responsible for the statements contained in the paper, and I consider that that being so, counsel are not entitled to demand or to force from the conductors of *The Times* the names of the contributors.
>
> (Mr. Asquith, of Counsel:) I know of no such privilege . . ."

The President of the Commission eventually ruled, after discussion:

> "You are entitled to ask him as to specific statements which are made in some of these articles and to ascertain from him who is the writer, if he knows it. If he does not, you must take it that you have exhausted all the information you can get from this source."

1 1981 c. 49.
2 [1963] 2 Q.B. 477 at 490-91.

14.03 *Contra* to the above approach, which was in favour of compulsory obligation to disclose, there then arose a line of authority that in interlocutory proceedings involving matters of discovery and interrogatories a defendant newspaper or journalist would not be required to give the source of his information. Thus, in *Attorney-General v. Clough*[3] Lord Parker C.J. referred to this series of cases:

> "which have prevailed for 50 years or more"[4]

and discussed the various justifications which had been relied upon by the Court in favouring confidentiality and not disclosure, as follows:

> "In some cases the practice of not requiring an answer to such an interrogatory has been based on the fact that to require an answer will *disclose the defendant's witnesses.* In others, it has been put on the basis that it will *enable the plaintiff to sue* the people whose names are disclosed. In yet others, it is treated as a matter which is *oppressive,* and of course that would apply to the refusal to allow an interrogatory in any case, whether or not the defendant was a newspaper proprietor. But there is no doubt that one reason given, and this I think is the strongest way in which it can be put, was that given as a second reason in *Adam v. Fisher* . . . 'that a newspaper stood in such a position that it was not desirable on *grounds of public interest* that the name of a newspaper's informant should be disclosed' "[5] (emphasis added)

14.04 The conflicting views came squarely to a head in the two 1963 cases of *Attorney-General v. Clough* and, shortly thereafter, *Attorney-General v. Mulholland* already mentioned. Both were proceedings in contempt against journalists who had refused to disclose their sources for newspaper articles in proceedings under the Tribunals of Inquiry (Evidence) Act 1921[6] (the Vassall Tribunal); they were accordingly final trial proceedings rather than ones of mere interlocutory nature.

14.05 The journalist's explanation in the *Clough* case was eloquent:

> "My Lord, perhaps I may say a very brief few words on this. I feel personally that a special correspondent, even more than a general reporter, does rest on his sources of information to a very large extent on confidences from people in defence departments. This information came from a reliable, responsible source in Whitehall and I feel that if I disclose this source of information I would be breaking a trust. I feel that my future career as a defence correspondent would be jeopardised because nobody would then feel prepared to speak to me—or for that reason any other specialist defence correspondent—on an off-the-record basis for fear that their name might be disclosed at some later date. I am afraid, Sir, that I

3 [1963] 1 Q.B. 773.
4 At 789.
5 At 789.
6 11 & 12 Geo. V c. 7.

have firmly made up my mind that I am not prepared to disclose the name of this man, although he does exist, I can assure you."[7]

Lord Parker, C.J. in his judgement took the line that there was no fixed rule as to the journalist being privileged; it all depended on the facts of the case. Thus:

". . . in regard to the press, the law has not developed and *crystallised* the confidential relationship to which they stand to an informant into one of the classes of privilege known to the law. As I have said, it still, as I conceive it, would remain open to this court to say in the special circumstances of any particular case that public policy did demand that the journalist should be immune . . ."[8] (emphasis added)

14.06 In the *Mulholland* case, in a passage which was later described in 1980 in *British Steel v. Granada Television*[9] as being of "classic" nature, Lord Denning laid the emphasis upon the judge's responsibility in seeing that justice is done in the end from the standpoint of the community at large. His words were:

"But then it is said . . . that however relevant these questions were and however proper to be answered for the purpose of the inquiry, a journalist has a privilege by law entitling him to refuse to give his sources of information . . . It seems to me that the journalists *put the matter much too high*. The *only* profession that I know which is given a privilege from disclosing information to a court of law is the *legal profession*, and then it is not the privilege of the lawyer but of his client. Take the clergyman, the banker or the medical man. None of these is entitled to refuse to answer when directed to by a judge. Let me not be mistaken. The judge will respect the confidences which each member of these honourable professions receives in the course of it, and *will not direct him to answer unless not only it is relevant but also it is a proper and, indeed, necessary question in the course of justice to be put and answered.* A judge is the person entrusted, on behalf of the community, to *weigh these conflicting interests*—to weigh on the one hand the respect due to confidence in the profession and on the other hand the ultimate interest of the community in justice being done or, in the case of a tribunal such as this, in a proper investigation being made into these serious allegations. If the *judge determines that the journalist must answer, then no privilege will avail him to refuse.*"[10] (emphasis added)

BRITISH STEEL v. GRANADA TELEVISION

14.07 *British Steel v. Granada Television* concerned television journalism. The defendant television company had broadcast a programme concerning the strike then current in the steel industry, in which they had

7 At 776.
8 At 792.
9 [1981] A.C. 1096.
10 [1963] 2 Q.B. 477 at 489–90.

quoted from a number of confidential internal documents of the plaintiff corporation. The documents had apparently come into the hands of the television company in the first place quite properly; they had just been spontaneously delivered by the "mole" in the plaintiff corporation to the television company, without any payment or inducement being offered, although the television company had given a promise to the "mole" that no steps would be taken that might reveal or risk disclosure of his identity. The plaintiff corporation sued to compel disclosure. The balancing act which the Court has to perform in such circumstances was described very fairly by Lord Wilberforce as follows:

> "Courts have an inherent wish to respect this confidence, whether it arises between doctor and patient, priest and penitent, banker and customer, between persons giving testimonials to employees, or in other relationships. A relationship of confidence between a journalist and his source is in no different category: nothing in this case involves or will involve any principle that such confidence is not something to be respected. But in all these cases the court may have to decide, in particular circumstances, that the interest in preserving this confidence is *outweighed by other interests* to which the law attaches importance."[11] (emphasis added)

He went on, applying the principle to the facts of the case, to hold that the balance here lay strongly in the plaintiff's favour:

> "They suffered a grievous wrong, in which Granada itself became involved, *not innocently,* with active participation. To confine B.S.C. to its remedy against Granada and to deny it the opportunity of a *remedy against the source*, would be a significant denial of justice."[12]

The public interest in full information about the steel strike, and of the possible attitudes of HM Government and the plaintiff corporation to settling the same, was not enough to justify disclosure in any event under the "iniquity rule" reflected in the *Initial Services v. Putterill*[13] line of authority (see para. 5.18 *ante*).

14.08 The plaintiff's interest in finding the source of the leakage lay here of course in the fact that, as long as the "mole" remained undisturbed in his burrow, there existed the possibility of further leakages; the "mole's" possibly limited ability to pay damages which might compensate the plaintiff for the harm caused to them by the existing leakage (since obviously knowledge of the plaintiff's private views as to settlement would assist the strikers to force a harder bargain) would be a lesser factor. Excavation was the primary need, so far as they were concerned.

11 [1981] A.C. 1096 at 1168–69.
12 At 1175.
13 [1968] 1 Q.B. 396.

CONTEMPT OF COURT ACT 1981

14.09 Subsequent to the *British Steel* decision, Parliament intervened in 1981 to regulate formally the position of the journalists and the like. The relevant section 10 of the Contempt of Court Act has already been set out in full at para. 7.26 *ante*. Essentially, it now provides statutory protection for the journalist, editor and so on except in four cases where it is established to the satisfaction of the Court that disclosure is necessary (1) in the interests of justice or (2) national security, or for the prevention of (3) disorder or (4) crime.

14.10 The protection, if justified, extends both to interlocutory proceedings (say where the editor of the newspaper wishes to resist an application for discovery of the leaked document) and trial proceedings (say where the journalist refuses to answer a question in Court after ordered by the judge to do so); it extends also to publication generally, and not merely to printed publication in newspapers and the like; the scope of the statutory definition:

> ". . . includes any speech, writing, broadcast or other communication in whatever form, which is addressed to the public at large or any section of the public."

is clearly very wide; television reportage is obviously covered. A limitation of the protection is that tribunals or other bodies exercising the judicial powers of the State can also determine that one or other of the exceptions exist, in proceedings arising before them; to decree disclosure is not the sole prerogative of the Courts as such. Naturally, disclosure will only be ordered in any event where the identity or nature of the source is relevant to some issue in the proceedings being heard by the Court or other body in question.

"National Security" exception

14.11 The recent passage of the statute has meant that there has been only limited exposition of it so far. The leading case at present is that of *Defence Secretary v. Guardian Newspapers*[14] in 1984. It concerned a claim by the Secretary of State for Defence for the return from a newspaper of a document classified as "secret" and entitled "Deliveries of Cruise Missiles to RAF Greenham Common—Parliamentary and Public Statements". It had been originally prepared in the Ministry of Defence, and a copy had been handed in anonymously at the offices of the newspaper. As such, the newspaper had no direct knowledge as to who had made the copy and handed it in; the facts were of a rather different

14 [1985] A.C. 339.

kind to those arising in *British Steel;* nevertheless, return of the copy was desired in order that evidence as to the identity of the source might be ascertained by forensic tests on the document.

14.12 The classification of "Secret" was only second in the four grades of privity used for Governmental documents. These four grades were apparently defined in the following terms:

> "TOP SECRET. Information and material the unauthorised disclosure of which would cause exceptionally grave damage to the nation.
> SECRET. Information and material the unauthorised disclosure of which would cause serious injury to the interest of the nation.
> CONFIDENTIAL. Information and material the unauthorised disclosure of which would be prejudicial to the interests of the nation.
> RESTRICTED. Information and material the unauthorised disclosure of which would be undesirable in the interests of the nation."[15]

none of which refer to "national security", the relevant criterion under the 1981 Act, as such. Notwithstanding the omission, it was held (by a majority) that the Crown's evidence as to the impact of the document's contents was strong enough to enable the exception to be established; delivery up of the document was ordered.

Other exceptions

14.13 The other three heads of exception—interests of justice, prevention of disorder or crime—can be expected to generate further precedents in due course. The criteria are couched, as they stand, in terms similarly imprecise as the national security exception. One useful gloss, however, provided by Lord Diplock in the *Guardian Newspapers* decision concerns the "justice" exception; he said concerning this:

> ". . . in my view the expression 'justice', the interests of which are entitled to protection, is not used in a general sense as the antonym of 'injustice' but in the technical sense of the administration of justice in the course of legal proceedings."[16]

14.14 Whether the new statutory provision will, in the long run, clarify better than did the previous common law the demarcation line between what is permitted and what is prohibited in this arena still remains to be seen. The continuing presence of:

> "creatures who put conscience, greed or political advantage before their duty to respect confidences"

(as "moles" have been defined) will undoubtedly ensure that this is a field in which the law will not remain unexerted.

15 At 354.
16 At 350.

CHAPTER 15

Action for Breach of Confidential Information

GENERAL

15.01 Breach of confidential information is, fundamentally, a civil cause of action. Legal proceedings in respect of the breach have normally to be taken in the High Court (Chancery Division) in accordance with civil procedure generally. This book does not attempt to deal with civil procedure as a whole to any comprehensive extent; this can be ascertained from any of a number of textbooks, or from the standard work *The Supreme Court Practice* (the so-called "White Book"). Rather, this part of the book is devoted primarily to focussing upon (i) those aspects of civil procedure which can be of particular practical significance so far as ordinary actions for breach of confidential information are concerned (Chapter 15) and (ii) the remedies available to the plaintiff in the case of such a breach (Chapter 16).

15.02 It is only in the minority of cases, where the breach gives rise also to an offence, that criminal procedure plays a part as well. An example here would be that of the checkweigher who divulges a trade secret of his employer in contravention of section 3(5) of the Checkweighing in Various Industries Act 1919 (see para. 1.04 *ante*); this represents a summary offence in respect of which the checkweigher may be punished under the criminal law if convicted. The employer might well be able, separately, to sue him civilly since the whole purpose of the statutory provisions is clearly to protect the employer's legitimate trade secrets. The criterion set out in the leading modern case of *Island Records v. Corkindale*[1] that:

> "the essential requirement for the conferring of a civil remedy by a penal provision was that the offence created must consist of a failure to perform a defined duty which the statute imposes on the potential defender for the benefit of a particular class of person."

is likely to be fulfilled. An instance where the existence of potential criminal liability might not be immediately suspected lies in the area of improper dealings by trustees with landed subject-matter—say a noble

1 [1978] F.S.R. 505 at 517.

estate. Under section 4 of the Theft Act 1968 [2] a person cannot normally steal land, except, *inter alia:*

> "(2)(a) when he is a trustee . . . and he appropriates the land or anything forming part of it by dealing with it *in breach of the confidence* reposed in him; . . ." (emphasis added)

15.03 It has also now been held that confidential information is not intangible property within the meaning of section 4(1) of the Theft Act 1968—see the 1978 Divisional Court decision of *Oxford v. Moss*,[3] concerning the "borrowing" of an examination paper at Liverpool University. Although the *Oxford* decision has been widely criticised and may be overruled in future by a higher Court, the position remains at present that the civil action provides the primary source of legal relief so far as the ordinary breach of confidential information is concerned. It has been suggested[4] that more use could be made, in appropriate circumstances, of the law of criminal conspiracy (as in *R. v. Hall and Merkin*[5]) and the Prevention of Corruption Acts 1906[6] and 1916,[7] but this also is for the future.

15.04 Outside the traditional area of the equitable action, and in the area of what might be compendiously termed "statutory confidence", the emphasis on the criminal aspect of the law may naturally increase. The relevant statute may formally impart both civil and criminal liability; for example, the Data Protection Act 1984 (see Chapter 10) both (a) gives an affected "data subject" rights of compensation against the "data user" in respect of inaccurately recorded personal data, loss or unauthorised disclosure of data, and (b) endows the Data Protection Registrar with potential criminal sanctions against those who contravene the "data protection principles".

15.05 Alternatively, the statute may be concerned primarily with criminal liability, leaving civil liability, if any, to be dealt with at common law; an example here is provided by the Official Secrets Acts 1911–1939 (see Chapter 13). The fact that the Crown does not normally proceed civilly against the convicted traitor who has sold missile technology or other commercially valuable secrets to a foreign hostile power does not mean that it lacks the inherent right to do so; it is a question of policy.

2 1968 c. 60
3 68 Cr. App. R. 183.
4 T. Eisenschitz, "Trade Secrets and the Criminal Law" (1984) 9 E.I.P.R. 266.
5 *loc cit.*
6 6 Edw.VII c. 34.
7 6 & 7 Geo. V c. 64.

15.06 The possibility of including, in the ordinary case, additional claims for other legal breaches should not be overlooked. A given breach of confidentiality may, in the case of an employee, involve also a breach of his employment contract which may in turn affect the employee's position so far as unfair dismissal, redundancy payments and the like under statutory employment law is concerned; similarly with consultancy contracts. There might also be a breach of copyright or other intellectual property right involved (see Chapter 6), say where a rival concern markets a product made in accordance with purloined engineering drawings passed to them by the dishonest employee.

15.07 Such additional claims may provide a plaintiff with multiple causes of action; they can represent alternative shots in his locker, in case the parent claim for breach of confidence should fail. But they may not necessarily lead to corresponding multiplication of damages; the Court may be concerned to prevent overlapping in this respect. The matter of damages generally is more fully discussed in the succeeding Chapter 16.

PARTIES

15.08 In the case of an action for breach of confidential information relief may normally be sought against both:

(1) the party who makes the unauthorised disclosure, and
(2) the party who receives the unauthorised disclosure.

15.09 The potential liability of party (1) is self-evident. The making of the unauthorised disclosure represents the actual tortious step; it is the third and culminating requirement of the *Coco v. Clark* test (see paras. 2.21 and 5.01 *ante*), the first and second requirements (confidential quality of the information, obligation to maintain confidence in that information) representing, rather, the necessary conditions precedent to any act of unauthorised disclosure.

15.10 The potential liability of party (2) may both involve subtler considerations yet be in practice more significant; if the unauthorised disclosure has been made by a disgruntled employee who is, financially, a man of straw, the prospects of recovering any damages awarded against him may be remote; an injunction against future repetition of the unauthorised act may be of little value once the secret is already out. Often, it will only be the recipient of the disclosure who is in a position to compensate effectively the original owner of the information; in the typical case of a disgruntled employee, the rival concern to whom he passes the information may well be of a substantial character.

15.11 Whilst party (2) may be able in certain circumstances to take advantage of defences not available to party (1)—say the defence of innocent purchase and use (see Chapter 5)—it is clear that he will be liable if he positively procured the commission of the unauthorised disclosure by party (1) in the first place. Party (2) then becomes a joint tortfeasor along with party (1). This can be regarded as established by the leading case of *Hivac v. Park Royal Scientific Instruments and others* [8] in 1946 (the "others" being the employees in question), involving the manufacture of midget valves for deaf aids, where Greene M.R. said:

> "The defendants secretly *procured* five employees of the plaintiffs to come and work for them, and to put at their disposal their skill and experience for the purpose of enabling the defendant company to get its business going and to become successful in their particular field. . . . . The question we have to decide for the purpose of this interlocutory appeal is whether or not the five employees were committing a breach of their obligation to their employers in using their spare time for the purpose of assisting a company which they must have known was either in competition, or proposing to enter into competition, with their employers; and, if so, whether the defendants *procured* that breach." [9] (emphasis added)

15.12 Where party (2) is a company (and particularly if it is one whose wealth consists only of a nominal share capital and/or intangible assets—perhaps one specifically set up to act as a vehicle for the undertaking of manufacturing activities based on the information), further questions may arise concerning the personal liability of individual directors and the like.

15.13 The question of personal liability of directors for the torts of company employees is itself a complex area of law; a full discussion is not presented here. The classic statement of the law is that contained in the speech of Atkin L.J. in *Performing Right Society v. Ciryl Theatrical Syndicate* [10] in 1924:

> "*Prima facie* a managing director is *not* liable for tortious acts done by servants of the company unless he himself is privy to the acts, that is to say unless he *ordered or procured* the acts to be done." (emphasis added)

8 [1946] 1 Ch. 169.
9 At 172.
10 [1924] 1 K.B. 1 at 14.

But it is clear that in this field "each case depends upon its own particular facts"[11]; another useful judicial comment in this connection is contained in *White Horse Distillers v. Gregson Associates:*[12]

> "The facts of each case must be broadly considered in order to see whether, as a matter of policy requiring the *balancing of the two principles of limited liability and answerability for tortious acts or conduct,* they call for the director to be held personally liable." (emphasis added)

A frontal attack upon the *Ciryl Theatrical* principle was rejected recently by the Court of Appeal in *Evans v. Spritebrand.*[13]

15.14 It follows in short that the precise circumstances in which those running party (2) (assuming it to be a company) came into possession of the confidential information are significant. These circumstances may well be unknown to the plaintiff at the time of issuing proceedings; they may become clearer in some cases at the interlocutory stage of discovery of documents, although in other cases they may be only fully elucidated at trial. Hence it may well be prudent as a precaution to cite individual directors of the company, as well as the company itself, as co-defendants in the first place. A director of the defendant company who was previously an employee of the plaintiff may naturally be in a considerably more vulnerable position in this respect than one who had no previous association with them. This is illustrated in such decisions as *Cranleigh Precision Engineering v. Bryant*[14] (swimming pools) and *Industrial Furnaces v. Reaves*[15] (air heaters).

INTERLOCUTORY INJUNCTION

15.15 A matter which is often of considerable interest is the possibility of obtaining an interlocutory injunction; that is, an injunction granted by the Court in advance of trial as a freezing measure. If the breach of confidential information is only threatened (as where an employer gets wind of rumours that his chief engineer is about to move out to a rival, taking with him the latest information as to the employer's new plant for making optical fibres, or that a misguided distillery worker is about to reveal publicly the secret herbs of liqueur X), the grant of such an injunction may indeed be the plaintiff's only really effective form of relief. Where granted in advance of any actual breach, it is termed a *quia timet*

11 *Wah Tat Bank v. Chan Cheng Kum* [1975]. A.C. 507 (P.C.) at 515.
12 [1984] R.P.C. 61 at 91.
13 [1985] 1 W.L.R. 317.
14 [1966] R.P.C. 81.
15 [1970] R.P.C. 605.

interlocutory injunction, *quia timet* meaning literally "because he fears"; where granted after breach but before trial it is just a regular interlocutory injunction.

General principles affecting grant

15.16 The leading modern decision on the grant (and, conversely, the refusal) of interlocutory injunctions is that in *American Cyanamid v. Ethicon*[16] in 1974, a case involving the alleged infringement of a patent for an absorbable surgical suture. Much of the language of this decision (given by Lord Diplock) is of an intricate nature. But it can be said to focus upon the point that, by granting an interlocutory injunction, the Court is not coming to a concluded view on the merits of the case; indeed, if anything, the Court should positively abstain from making any such kind of pronouncement, one way or the other, since the facts have not yet been established (evidence is normally given by affidavit only in interlocutory proceedings, to the exclusion of cross-examination). It follows that the plaintiff (the applicant for the interlocutory injunction) need not show that he has a *prima facie* winning case. The hurdle is lower; he need only show a *prima facie* arguable case. Whether, having surmounted this hurdle, he then gains an interlocutory injunction depends on the so-called "balance of convenience". One of the introductory passages in Lord Diplock's speech sets the scene:

> "The object of the interlocutory injunction is to protect the *plaintiff* against injury by violation of his right for which *he could not be adequately compensated* in damages recoverable in the action if the uncertainty were resolved in his favour at the trial; but the plaintiff's need for such protection must be weighed against the corresponding need of the *defendant* to be protected against injury resulting from his having been prevented from exercising his own legal rights for which *he could not be adequately compensated* under the plaintiff's undertaking in damages if the uncertainty were resolved in the defendant's favour at the trial. The court must *weigh one need against another* and determine where *'the balance of convenience'* lies." (emphasis added)

15.17 It is clear, following *American Cyanamid,* that many of the earlier decisions in this area suggesting that the plaintiff has a heavier burden to carry as regards the strength of his case—for instance, the 1964 dictum in *Donmar v. Bart*[16a] that:

> ". . . . . . the applicant must establish a *probability* or a *strong prima facie* case that he is entitled to the right of whose violation he complains . . ." (emphasis added)

—are now of doubtful authority.

16 [1975] R.P.C. 513 at 540–543.
16a [1967] 1 W.L.R. 740.

15.18 Although "balance of convenience" is the conventional legal expression, the phrase is not one of happiest kind. It suggests that the Court is motivated by considerations of procedural simplicity. This is not so. The balance is one of interim justice, during the period up to trial. This point has recently been emphasised by the Court of Appeal in *Francome v. Mirror Group*, involving telephone eavesdropping of a well-known jockey. To quote from the judgement of Donaldson M.R:

> ". . . I stress, once again, that we are *not* at this stage concerned to determine the final rights of the parties. Our duty is to make such orders, if any, as are appropriate pending the trial of the action. It is sometimes said that this involves a weighing of the balance of convenience. This is an *unfortunate expression. Our business is justice, not convenience.* We can and must disregard fanciful claims by either party. Subject to that, we must contemplate the possibility that either party may succeed and must do our best to ensure that nothing occurs pending the trial which will prejudice his rights. Since the parties are usually asserting wholly inconsistent claims, this is difficult, but we have to do our best. In so doing, we are seeking a *balance of justice,* not of convenience."[17] (emphasis added)

Factors affecting balance of convenience

15.19 There is no set list of factors which must be considered by the Court in determining where the balance of convenience lies; each case must be determined on its own facts. But it is normal to take into account at least the following:

(1) *The relative financial strengths of the parties.* If the defendant is a man, or company, of straw, and hence unlikely to be good for any damages that may be eventually awarded, then such poverty may be a good reason for stopping him now; if, *contra,* it is the plaintiff who is of this type then his financial weakness may be to the defendant's advantage because of doubt as to whether he is good for the cross-undertaking in damages normally required should the grant of the interlocutory injunction turn out, at trial, not to have been justified.

(2) *Delay.* This is largely self-explanatory; the Court is obviously less likely to interfere pre-trial in a case where the plaintiff has (without good excuse) effectively lulled the defendant into thinking that interlocutory action will not be taken than in a case where he has acted promptly; thus interlocutory relief was refused in *Mayflower Products v. Derek Bailey*[18] (ripple air mattresses—7 months delay) and *Flexiveyor Products v. Owens*[19] (flexible conveyors—10 months delay).

(3) *Trade and commercial considerations.* These are perhaps given

17 [1984] 1 W.L.R. 895 at 898.
18 I. P.D. 7118.
19 I. P.D. 7120.

greater weight today than in previous eras; will employees be immediately thrown out of work if the interlocutory injunction is granted? Will existing capital investment likewise be stultified during the pre-trial period? Will valuable export orders (particularly if they have given the defendant a toe-hold in a new market) be lost? Conversely, will the plaintiff's existing trade be destroyed by price-cutting from the defendant? This may well be so if the body of confidential information has taken the plaintiff much time and expense to assemble in the first place, so that his own selling prices need to recoup those costs. There may well of course be others. In the somewhat unusual case of *Standard Telephones & Cables v. Plessey Semiconductors*[20] (circuit drawings and the like) a special factor within the *American Cyanamid* sense lay in the effect which interlocutory relief might have on an innocent third party customer of the defendant.

(4) *Public interest.* If the nature of the confidential information is such as to have implications for the public generally, apart from the private interests of the individual warring parties, then this may be a highly pertinent factor (for either side). Examples on this point already mentioned include *Fraser v. Evans*[21] (political report), *Francome v. Mirror Group*[22] (racing conversations) and *Lion Laboratories v. Evans*[23] (intoxication measuring device).

And to some extent (if other factors prove indecisive) the Court may also consider:

(5) *Relative strengths of the parties' respective cases in fact and/or law,* bearing in mind that evidence in interlocutory proceedings is normally given on affidavit only, and hence has been untested by cross-examination; in *Aveley Cybervox v. Boman*[24] (language laboratory designs) the latter was even positively disapproved of, due to absence at this stage of the pleadings (which otherwise normally define the issues arising in the action) and the consequential discovery of documents thereon.

(6) *Status quo.* This means, essentially, keeping the parties in their pre-dispute as opposed to post-dispute position; the relevant date for this purpose is normally that of the period immediately preceding issuance of the writ, although if there is significant delay by the plaintiff it may be pushed forward to the period immediately preceding the issuance of the relevant notice of motion (*Garden Cottage v. Milk Marketing Board*[25]), by which time the defendant's commercial position may naturally have

20 1 P.D. 7010.
21 [1969] 1 Q.B. 349.
22 [1984] 1 W.L.R. 892.
23 [1985] 1 Q.B. 526.
24 [1975] F.S.R. 139.
25 [1983] 3 W.L.R. 143.

altered; he may have become established in the trade. To take advantage of this consideration, a plaintiff may therefore have both to sue promptly and apply for interlocutory relief promptly thereafter.

15.20 In the particular instance of breach of confidential information there may well be the further persuasive factor (particularly if the application for interlocutory relief is made *quia timet*, in advance of any actual unauthorised disclosure) that by injuncting the defendant the plaintiff's secrets may never be let out of the bag in the first place. Confidential information is, inherently, property of a different kind compared to other species of intellectual property; so long as confidentiality enures, the information may be priceless to the owner; but once disclosed to others it may be effectively valueless in his hands. A defendant who infringes a patent, or a copyright, or who passes off his goods as those of the plaintiff, is unlikely to effect such a dramatic reversal in the plaintiff's fortune.

Specimen case

15.21 The decision in *Potters-Ballotini v. Weston-Baker*[26] represents a specimen case which illustrates neatly some of the conflicting considerations which may arise, and is now reviewed in greater detail.

15.22 The dispute here concerned the manufacture of ballotini, which are tiny small glass beads used for various industrial purposes such as marking white lines on roads (since they reflect the lights of the cars), or cleaning jet engine blades. The plaintiffs were the only manufacturers in the United Kingdom.

15.23 Two key men, the general manager and the works manager, had left the plaintiff's employment and clandestinely built, along with others and with the assistance of finance from private and governmental sources, a rival plant costing around £¼m. The plaintiffs applied for interlocutory relief, on the ground that the new plant (which appeared externally to be strikingly similar to the plaintiff's plant) incorporated their confidential information; the employment contracts of the two men had stipulated that neither would use any confidential information acquired by them during employment until one year after termination (and the time limit had not yet run out). Proceedings were begun as soon as the plaintiff had received news of the plant, which was pre-production. But by the time that the application for interlocutory relief was heard, production had begun. The Court refused the interlocutory injunction,

26 [1976] R.P.C. 202.

notwithstanding what might be considered as the regrettable nature of the conduct of the two men, and the refusal was upheld on appeal. The appeal judgements indicate that the following points were influential in deciding that the balance of convenience lay with the defendants:

(1) There was uncertainty as to exactly how much of the information used in building the new plant was in fact objectively confidential; there were other rival plants abroad, and some information at least was clearly in the public domain already. This uncertainty was relevant because an injunction, being a restraint upon the defendant for which proceedings in contempt can be brought if broken, must be clear in scope for the Court to grant it.

(2) The "springboard" doctrine (see paras. 5.09 ff) was of limited duration; by the time of trial, the springboard here might well have lost its bounce.

(3) Even in respect of the information which was objectively confidential, there was difficulty in separating out those items which constituted part of the employee's own knowledge and expertise, and those which belonged truly to the plaintiff ex-employer. The Court is slow to prevent a skilled employee from practising his art.

(4) Some of the defendants, e.g. the contractor who had built the new plant, had not committed any breach of confidence in the first place, never having been in confidential relation with the plaintiffs but being only in third party capacity instead.

(5) If the defendants were injuncted now, the plant would be stopped and the effect upon them would clearly be disastrous; they might be unable to restart even if they were to succeed at trial. Moreover, if they were injuncted now, and continued to lose at trial, the prospects of the plaintiffs actually being able to obtain the likely level of damages appeared (in the circumstances, the two employees—at least—being just individuals and the plant expensive) to be rather remote.

(6) Conversely, if the plant were allowed to continue and make profits, the prospects of the damages being paid, if the defendants were to lose at trial, were considerably better.

ANTON PILLER ORDERS

15.24 Another matter, which is often allied to the grant of an interlocutory injunction, is that of an Anton Piller order. An Anton Piller order is, essentially, an order granted by the Court on *ex parte* application by the plaintiff for immediate inspection of the defendant's premises and seizure of documents, drawings and the like—that is to say, without the defendant being informed until the plaintiff arrives to execute the order. If the defendant refuses to permit the inspection to take place, he renders himself liable to proceedings in contempt. The order is usually applied for before proceedings have been started at all, that is, at the stage when the defendant is only a potential defendant.

15.25 The purpose of the Anton Piller order is to prevent a dishonest defendant from destroying records and the like which would otherwise under the regular Court procedure have to be shown to the plaintiff at the later stage of mutual discovery of documents; *ex hypothesi* such an order may be of peculiar usefulness in confidential information cases, since it may be impossible to tell for sure from the defendant's rival finished product as to whether manufacture had taken place with the assistance of the plaintiff's confidential information or not. It is a relatively new practice.

15.26 The order is a relatively new practice and takes its name from the case of *Anton Piller v. Manufacturing Processes*[27] in 1975. The plaintiffs here were German manufacturers of electrical machinery; they sold in the United Kingdom through the defendant agents. Two employees of the agents ascertained that confidential details of the plaintiff's power units were being revealed behind their backs to rival German manufacturers; taking their courage in both hands, they went to Germany to acquaint the plaintiffs with what was happening. A new frequency converter was about to be introduced by the plaintiffs, and if details of this also were to be leaked back to the rival manufacturers, the plaintiff's market for the new machine would be severely affected. The plaintiffs accordingly commenced proceedings for *ex parte* relief; the High Court was prepared to grant interlocutory relief of the usual kind, restraining the defendants for the time being from acting further in breach of confidence, but no more. As regards the existing breaches, however, the plaintiffs were fearful that:

> "........ if the English company were given notice of this application, they would take steps to destroy the documents or send them to Germany or elsewhere, so that there would be none in existence by the time that discovery was had in the action."[28]

15.27 The Court of Appeal, under Lord Denning's aegis, held that the Court could give in appropriate circumstances the kind of search and seizure order requested. But it was made clear that these circumstances had to be exceptional. The order was not to be used as some kind of convenient routine tool for assisting early evaluation by the plaintiff of the strength of his case. To quote from the judgement of Ormrod, L.J:

27 [1976] R.P.C. 719.
28 At 723.

"The proposed order is at the *extremity* of this court's powers. .... There are three essential pre-conditions for the making of such an order, in my judgement. *First,* there must be an *extremely strong prima facie* case. Secondly, the damage, potential or actual, must be very serious for the applicant. *Thirdly,* there must be clear evidence that the defendants have in their possession incriminating documents or things, and that there is a real possibility that they may destroy such material before any application inter partes can be made."[29] (emphasis added)

15.28 In the period immediately following the creation of the jurisdiction there was a tendency—quite understandably—on the part of plaintiffs to abuse it. This in turn engendered a judicial reaction. In *Systematica v. London Computer Centre,*[30] a copyright case where the defendant was operating his business quite openly and there was nothing to show by way of underhand nature, the Court explicitly observed:

"A situation is developing where I think rather *too free a use* is being made by plaintiffs of the Anton Piller provision." (emphasis added)

and made it clear that unnecessary applications of this kind are made at the plaintiff's peril so far as costs are concerned. In the same vein is the dictum of Lawton L.J. in *Hytrac Conveyors v. Conveyors International*[31] that:

"Those who make charges must state right at the beginning what they are and what facts they are based upon. They must *not* use Anton Piller orders as a means of finding out what sort of charges they can make." (emphasis added)

15.29 The question of whether or not the defendants are likely to have technological manufacturing secrets of their own on the premises in any event is also relevant since, as pointed out in *Thermax v. Schott Industrial Glass*[32] :

"Since Anton Pillar orders give compulsory rights of inspection, once those inspections have taken place the information procured from it is in the hands of the other side and the situation is irreversible."

In short, the defendant may have a bagged cat of his own just as the plaintiff has (or thought he had); the Court should be astute to prevent mutual de-bagging.

29 At 726.
30 [1983] F.S.R. 313 at 316.
31 [1983] F.S.R. 62 at 70.
32 [1981] F.S.R. 289 at 298.

PLEADINGS TO TRIAL

15.30 Such peculiarities as there are in an action for breach of confidential information, as compared to a civil action in the High Court generally, tend to spring from the very nature of the subject-matter involved—namely its confidential nature. The plaintiff may, for example, wish to try and preserve this confidence as against the world generally whilst simultaneously proceeding against a particular party, the defendant, for its misuse; his victory otherwise might be Pyrrhic only. The defendant likewise may be in a comparable position; he may wish to argue that the product in suit has been made solely with the assistance of his own independently created body of technical know-how. Some of the procedures which the Court may adopt in these circumstances have already been dealt with in earlier Chapters—particularly in Chapter 7. It is convenient here just to recapitulate briefly as to the incidents of the action as a whole, from issuance of writ to hearing at trial, and the bearing of confidentiality thereon.

Pleadings

15.31 A plaintiff will at some stage, either in his original statement of claim or in response to a request by the defendant, have to provide "particulars" of his claim; a defendant must be apprised of the case which he has to meet. In the words of O. 18 r. 7(1) of the Rules of the Supreme Court 1965 (as amended):

> ". . . every pleading must contain, and contain only, a statement in summary form of the *material facts* on which the party pleading relies for his claim or defence, as the case may be, *but not the evidence* by which those facts are to be proved, and the statement must be as brief as the nature of the case admits." (emphasis added)

and in r. 12(1):

> ". . . . . . . every pleading must contain the *necessary particulars* of any claim, defence or other matter . . .",

the function of the particulars being variously defined (to quote from the list given in *The Supreme Court Practice*)[33] as:

> "(1) to inform the other side of the nature of the case they have to meet as distinguished from the mode in which that case is to be proved; . . .
> (2) to prevent the other side from being taken by suprise at the trial; . . .
> (3) to enable the other side to know what evidence they ought to be prepared with and to prepare for trial; . . .

33 1985 Edition at Note 18/12/2 (page 279).

(4) to limit the generality of the pleadings or the claim or the evidence;. . .

(5) to limit and define the issues to be tried, and as to which discovery is required;. . .

(6) to tie the hands of the party so that he cannot without leave go into any matters not included. . . ."

15.32 A similar obligation exists on the part of the defendant also; if he fails to provide adequate particulars in his defence, he may be faced with a request for further and better particulars from the plaintiff. Just as the defendant must be apprised of the case which he has to meet, so correspondingly must the plaintiff be apprised of the defence which he has in turn to overcome. Questions as to the extent of necessary detail in pleadings, in order to give adequate particulars (according to the nature of the given case) and of the distinction between material facts (which must be pleaded) and evidence (which must not) constitute procedural topics in their own right; there is an extensive body of case law in existence. The primary point for present purposes, however, is that confidential information of technological kind (trade secrets) may give rise to special difficulties of its own at the pleading stage, particularly so far as the plaintiff is concerned. These include (a) unwillingness of the plaintiff to reveal too much as to the information which he alleges has been taken and used, (b) uncertainty as to exactly what the defendant is doing—for example, if a manufacturing process is involved which is unascertainable from mere inspection of the finished product as sold, and (c) similar unwillingness of the defendant (assuming that he is asserting independent evolution of comparable confidential information of his own or like defence) to reveal too much concerning the same. One or both of the parties may have a vested interest in keeping the pleadings vague.

15.33 Thus, in *Printers and Finishers v. Holloway,*[34] the plaintiff's statement of claim read (in relevant part) as follows:

> "The processes and materials used by the Plaintiffs in their said business for the flock printing of textiles are secret and all information including instructions, documents, drawings and photographs relating thereto and to the plant, machinery, tools and equipment used by the Plaintiffs therefor are and at all material times have been confidential information the property of or possessed by the Plaintiffs. Such information is hereinafter referred to as the 'Plaintiffs' confidential information."

A request for particulars elicited such further generalities as:

> "Flock is cut from continuous rayon filament into exactly uniform lengths by flock cutting machines made specially for the Plaintiffs according to a

34 [1961] R.P.C. 77.

> design supplied by United Merchants. The construction of the said flock cutting machines is secret."

and

> "The methods of bleaching and dyeing and preparing the flock and the chemicals used therefor are secret."

The plaintiff in short was still attempting to evade his proper responsibilities. At this date (1960) flockcutting machines and flock-bleaching and dyeing methods were clearly not unknown in the art generally; the defendant was therefore entitled to be told of the particular features in these machines and methods for which the plaintiff was asserting secrecy.

15.34 The Court of Appeal cut the Gordian knot in this instance by ordering that delivery of particulars should await completion of discovery of documents (normally a later stage in the action, undertaken once the pleadings have closed). Such discovery can of course be done under terms (if appropriate) restricting disclosure of the contents of the documents to independent experts, legal advisers and the like only and excluding the opposite party himself.

15.35 An alternative technique followed in, for example, *Sorbo Rubber Sponge Products v. Defries* [35] (manufacture of sponge rubber) and *Zink (John) v. Wilkinson* [36] (flare stacks) is to require the opposite party to give suitable undertakings (as regards return of particulars when proceedings terminated, no further use or communication of the particulars, etc.) before their delivery.

Discovery, inspection and the like

15.36 The techniques adopted by the Court for preservation of confidentiality at these stages has already been discussed quite extensively in Chapter 8.

Trial procedure

15.37 The *in camera* course has, likewise, been already discussed in Chapter 7.

35 47 R.P.C. 454.
36 [1973] R.P.C. 717.

Defences

15.38 The accent in much of the book so far has been on the plaintiff—upon what his rights in respect of his confidential information may be, and how he may enforce them. The defendant's position represents the other side of the coin; and it is convenient to collate here, at the end of this chapter, the various grounds which he may be able to rely upon in defending himself against any action brought by the plaintiff. These grounds are limited to those normally arising in the ordinary action for breach of confidential information. They are not necessarily all potentially applicable in all cases; for example, the defence of "loss of springboard" is hardly meaningful in relation to a claim by a patient for the unauthorised disclosure by his doctor of the patient's medical history, although it may be particularly pertinent in the case of technological information. There is naturally some overlapping in any event; many of the later more specific defences may be regarded as sub-divisions of one or other of the first three. Where the plaintiff's claim arises under statute, e.g. under the Data Protection Act (see chapter 10) or the Rehabilitation of Offenders Act (see chapter 11) a quite different situation may arise; statutory defences may be available as an alternative, or in addition.

15.39 The ordinary defences include (this list is not exhaustive):

(a) lack of confidential quality of the information;
(b) no confidential obligation;
(c) no unauthorised use of the information;
(d) employee's existing expertise;
(f) expiration of the "springboard";
(g) independent evolution of the information;
(h) innocent use of the information following innocent acquisition of the same;
(i) public interest in disclosure;
(j) disclosure authorised by statute (even though plaintiff not claiming under statute);
(k) disclosure authorised by Court order;
(l) estoppel;
(m) release or waiver;
(n) laches, acquiescence and/or delay;
(o) use permitted by contract;
(p) no negligent disclosure.

15.40 The existence of other defences, e.g. privilege, obligation unenforceable under EEC law (say, because the information is the subject-matter of an agreement void under Article 85(1) of the Treaty of

Rome) has been mooted.[37] But the position is not yet entirely clear. The law of confidential information is still not explored to its limits.

15.41 By the same token, the list of possible defences (together with any future extension of the same) just given provides the plaintiff with a touchstone to be applied (so far as may be feasible) to his given facts prior to initiating any action. Of course, not all the possible defences can be accurately assessed at this juncture; defence (g) for example (independent evolution) represents an issue upon which the plaintiff by definition is unlikely to have many facts available to him; other defences, for example defence (i) of public interest, are of inherently more elusive character, rendering estimation in turn the more difficult. But for the common case of possible suit against an ex-employee in respect of technical or business secrets, the questions of terms/nature of the employment, nature of the information involved, and the circumstances whereby the plaintiff employer acquired that information are clearly fundamental. The last of these, in particular, may necessitate in a technical case an extensive review of the progress of the relevant art both within and without the employer's enterprise. Litigation in this area is an expensive pastime, and not to be entered into lightly.

37 *Breach of Confidence* (The Law Commission, 1981) Cmnd. 8388 at paras. 4.68–4.70.

CHAPTER 16

Remedies

GENERAL

16.01 Since the action for breach of confidence was originally developed in the Courts of Equity, and prior to the fusion of the systems of law and equity in 1875, it necessarily follows that the remedies available have equitable roots. It was, for example, only in 1858 under the Chancery Amendment Act[1] (Lord Cairns' Act) that the Courts of Equity were empowered to award damages in addition to or in place of an injunction at all; and only recently, the landmark being generally taken to be the case of *Seager v. Copydex (No. 2)*[2], has it become accepted that damages—as opposed, say, to an injunction or account of profits—are available in the action for breach of confidence.

16.02 Where a given action involves additional and/or alternative claims to the claim for breach of confidence, then the additional and/or alternative relief appropriate to those claims (if proven) may be available as well. The possibility of there being associated with the breach of confidence such infractions as breach of contract, patent infringement or copyright infringement has been mentioned before.

16.03 Thus if there is a breach of contract present also, a successful plaintiff has the potential remedy of damages for that breach under ordinary common law principles. If there is patent infringement, the remedies available are those statutorily defined in section 61(1) of the Patents Act 1977[3]; for copyright infringement, the provisions of Part III of the Copyright Act 1956[4] as amended (sections 17 to 22) apply. There is of course overlapping as between the kinds of relief available under these various other heads, but it is important to realise that there is no identity. Section 18(1) of the Copyright Act, for example, provides that the copyright owner is to be regarded as the owner of any infringing copy, and this in turn enables damages to be obtained on a conversion scale;

1 21 & 22 Vict. c. 27.
2 [1969] R.P.C. 250.
3 1977 c. 37.
4 4 & 5 Eliz. II c. 74.

this scale will normally be much higher than damages available for possible breach of contract arising out of the same course of behaviour. The provision can be particularly onerous on a defendant who has, for example, infringed copyright by making manufactured articles from engineering drawings supplied to him, at his instigation by an employee of the company owning the drawings; yet there is no equivalent provision in the Patents Act or under regular contract law. Again, under section 17(3) of the Copyright Act, the Court has power to award additional damages having regard to the "flagrancy" of the infringement; there is no counterpart in section 61(1) of the Patents Act, or contract law, but the provision is comparable to the possibility of awarding exemplary or punitive damages in tort law under the principle of *Rookes v. Barnard*,[5] and which is considered[6] to apply also to breach of confidence.

16.04 The Court will, however, normally take steps to ensure that the defendant is penalised only once in respect of his wrongful act; the plaintiff may be compelled to make some kind of election as between the legal rights in respect of which he is suing. For example, in *Nicrotherm Electrical v. Percy*,[7] where there had been previous collaboration between the parties in respect of developement of a pig rearer, including the preparation of working drawings of a prototype machine, the Court of Appeal said:

> "But it would not, I think, be right that the Plaintiffs should be able to prosecute both the enquiries for damages at the same time against the Appellant. They must, in my view, make up their minds whether they desire to proceed upon the basis of breach of copyright or upon the basis of breach of confidence, and should be entitled to proceed only upon that *one* of the two enquiries which they may select."[8] (emphasis added)

And in *Seager v. Copydex (No. 2)* the comment was made by the Court in course of argument:

> "You cannot have damages for breach of confidence and for infringement of your patent. These are alternative remedies and you would have to elect."[9]

16.05 The remedies now intrinsically available for breach of confidence *simpliciter* can accordingly be listed as:

(a) declaration
(b) injunction

5 [1964] A.C. 1129.
6 *Breach of Confidence* (The Law Commission, 1981) Cmnd. 8388; para 4.83.
7 [1957] R.P.C. 207.
8 At 214.
9 [1969] R.P.C. 250 at 255.

(c) destruction or delivery-up
(d) damages
(e) account of profits.

This is not to say that all of remedies (a) through (e) are available in a given case; remedies (d) (damages) and (e) (account of profits) are always alternatives; and there may be individual restrictions as regards remedies (a) (b) and (c), depending upon the circumstances of the case. It must not be forgotten that the action for breach of confidence is, in principle, an action to enforce an equitable right and equitable remedies are, in general, discretionary. Nevertheless, it is common to ask for all of them at the pleading stage, in the statement of claim.

DECLARATION

16.06 A declaration was, traditionally, an equitable remedy only, although it is now available as a remedy in civil law generally; it is concerned, as the name implies, with declaring the rights of the parties.

16.07 In the present context, it is probably true to say that its scope is somewhat limited; a successful plaintiff will normally be more concerned to gain an injunction (restraining further breaches) and damages or an account of profits (in respect of any benefit which the defendant has obtained as a result of the existing breach of confidence). But there are some instances in which it has independent value. One is where the defendant has attacked the confidential quality of the information relied upon by the plaintiff; he may, for example, have argued unsuccessfully that the plaintiff's manufacturing process was already public property in face of teachings in textbooks and the like; a positive declaration that the process is still a valid trade secret may assist the plaintiff in subsequent litigation against others, or even against the same defendant—say if the latter starts using a fresh process of his own as to which the plaintiff's information has provided the "springboard". Another arises in connection with employee contracts; a plaintiff may have a standard form of employment contract restricting the employee in certain respects from working for competitors in the same field; if he succeeds in having the terms of the restrictive covenant upheld in an action against a particular employee who leaves, then a declaration to the effect that the terms are valid may help in similar actions at a later date against similarly tied employees.

16.08 Some of the limits on its invocation were exposed in the case of

Malone v. Metropolitan Police Commissioner[10] (tapping of confidential telephone conversations). A declaration to the effect that interceptions and monitoring of the plaintiff's telephone lines violated Article 8 of the Convention for the Protection of Human Rights and Fundamental Freedoms[10a] (which entitled everyone to "respect for his private and family life, his home and his correspondence") was refused on the basis (i) that the Convention had the mere status of a treaty which was not justiciable as such in England and (ii) that even if the Court did have jurisdiction, the matter should be dealt with by the bodies set up by the Convention for that purpose. Again, in *Seager v. Copydex (No. 2)*, the defendant's application for a declaration that he could freely manufacture his "Invisigrip" carpet grip (since no injunction against future use of the same had been granted at the trial of the action) was refused in the Court's discretion; the furthest the Court would go was:

> "It is sufficient for us to say that, on a satisfied judgement for damages, the confidential information belongs to the defendants."[11]

INJUNCTION

16.09 This again, like the declaration, was traditionally an equitable remedy although now granted in legal proceedings generally. It is in principle available in the form of a final injunction to a successful plaintiff in an action for breach of confidence, in order to restrain further breaches; it is also available to restrain a threatened breach of confidence, at the interlocutory stage; the principles applicable to the grant of interlocutory injunctions have been discussed in the previous Chapter 15. In some cases, it is the injunction which is more desired by the plaintiff than any damages or other form of relief. A well-known local personality who fears that his doctor is about to reveal to the district newspaper that he is suffering from a venereal disease is probably concerned above all else with preventing the disclosure; damages could hardly compensate if the news were to leak out and he were hence compelled to resign his political candidature. Likewise, the owner of some secret formula for making custard powder, instant tea or the like may know that the employee who was about to tell all is himself penniless (and hence incapable of paying any damages which might be awarded against him), or that once the secret was out it would be hopeless in practice to try and proceed against all the multitude of competitors (in the United Kingdom and abroad) who would immediately market a similar product.

10 [1979] Ch. 344.
10a Cmnd. 8969.
11 [1969] R.P.C. 250 at 256.

16.10 Availability in fact of the injunction, and if so for how long and against whom, can in practice, however, prove to be more uncertain. The action for breach of confidence embraces a large variety of circumstances, some of which are clearly suitable for injunctive relief (as for example those of the kind just mentioned above) while others may not be so suitable. The Court will be unwilling, in particular, to grant an injunction which serves no useful purpose; if the employee has already revealed the formula of the custard powder, etc (as distinct from being about to so reveal), then his capability for damaging his employer may have come to an end; if he has in fact no more secrets to reveal, there is little justification for any injunction purporting to prevent from doing so if he did. But to injunct in such circumstances the competitor who procures the breach of confidentiality (and assuming that the disclosure has gone no further than the competitor) does have real purpose.

16.11 Possible duration of any injunction can give rise to difficulties. The position has to be compared to that of final injunction granted in the case of, say, patent or copyright infringement (which of course may be associated with the breach of confidential information in the first place). Both copyright and patent protection have determinate lives; the term(s) is set by the corresponding applicable statute. Hence a final injunction, even if expressed in perpetual form, is bound to become unenforceable, and hence effectively terminated, once the copyright or patent has expired in due course by effluxion of time. A trade secret, on the other hand, has no such temporal limitation in theory; it can notionally persist for ever.

16.12 In practice, the confidential information may have been already revealed by the time the case comes to be tried; this is particularly so where the information relates not to some process, the nature of which cannot be ascertained by analysis or inspection of the final product, but instead to some new article of commerce which by its very nature immediately discloses the information. An example is provided by the carpet grip involved in *Seager v. Copydex*[12]; as soon as it was sold by the defendant, the constructive features of the original inventor's grip which had been taken by the defendant were by definition put into the public domain; to injunct a particular defendant in such a type of case, when all other manufacturers are free to exploit (because the knowledge has become public property—and assuming no patent conflict by the side), may hardly be very sensible. Although he may have erred, and have to pay for his sins accordingly, is it right that he should also be put

12 (No. 1) [1967] R.P.C. 349.

henceforth on a permanent disadvantage as compared to competitors? Other examples arise where the action is based upon the "springboard" principle; the springboard eventually loses its spring, although the precise term for such loss may well vary from case to case; if the resilience has already been substantially dissipated during the interval between issue of proceedings and trial, the Court may be reluctant to order an injunction extending over a few more months only. It may well be more appropriate to regard the damages paid by the defendant simply as the purchase price of the confidential information, as in *Seager v. Copydex (No. 2)* already mentioned, where Lord Denning said:

> "Once a lump sum is assessed and paid, then the confidential information would belong to the defendants in the same way as if they had bought and paid for it by an agreement of sale. The property, so far as there is property in it, would vest in them. They would have the right to use that confidential information for the manufacture of carpet grips and selling of them. If it is patentable, they would be entitled to the benefit of the patent as if they had bought it. In other words, it would be regarded as a real outright purchase of the confidential information. The value should, therefore, be assessed on that basis, and damages awarded accordingly."[13]

16.13 There may be other perfectly good reasons as to why the Court should, in its discretion, refuse a final injunetion—just as in cases involving other kinds of equitable rights. It is not possible to consider the question exhaustively here; suffice it to say that unconscionable behaviour on the part of the plaintiff himself in connection with the information itself, or the suit, is always regarded unfavourably; equity normally demands the so-called "clean hands"; so is excessive delay on the part of the plaintiff in initiating or pursuing the action. Oppressive effect generally—say where the chance of any further breach is small—provides another category of reason.

DESTRUCTION OR DELIVERY-UP

16.14 As regards delivery-up, the Court would normally be prepared to order the return to the plaintiff of any documents and the like incorporating the confidential information of which the defendant has made unauthorised use. These documents could of course emanate in the first place either from the plaintiff or the defendant; the plaintiff may have transcribed his confidential information onto a modern equivalent of the tablets of stone (in memoranda, drawings, specifications, production instructions, photographs, videotapes, etc as the case may be) which has subsequently reached the defendant in improper circumstances; alter-

13 [1969] R.P.C. 250 at 256.

natively, the information may have been transmitted orally in comparable improper circumstances, with subsequent reduction into documentary form by the defendant. Such delivery-up does no harm of its own account to the defendant, in the ordinary case.

16.15 Obtaining delivery-up of products made with assistance of the confidential information—in other words, of the physical embodiment of the confidential information—can depend upon other factors as well. There may be a question of quantum; if the product as sold by the defendant is a complex machine, of which 9/10ths has been manufactured from publicly available or the defendant's own private knowledge and only 1/10th with the assistance of the plaintiff's confidential material, the Court may be reluctant to decree this. The consequential harm to the defendant might be out of all proportion to the harm suffered by the plaintiff in allowing the defendant's remaining stock to be marketed. Damages, in respect of the infringing part of the machine, would be expected to suffice.

16.16 As for destruction, as an alternative to delivery-up of products incorporating the confidential information, the Court may naturally be unwilling to order the destruction of valuable machinery without good cause. The point was canvassed in the well-known case of *Saltman Engineering v. Campbell,*[14] where it was reported that in the course of the discussion as to relief.

> ". . . their Lordships expressed reluctance to make any order which would involve the destruction or sterilisation of tools which might serve a useful purpose, since under Lord Cairns' Act the Court could award damages, to cover both past and future acts, in lieu of an injunction."[15]

and the eventual order was confined to delivery-up of the drawings the subject of the breach of confidence, together with an inquiry as to damages arising therefrom. The relevant part of Lord Cairns' Act has now been re-enacted in the Supreme Court Act 1981[16] (section 50); it is accordingly to be expected that this approach will be retained by the Court in future.

DAMAGES

16.17 Since breach of confidence ranks as a tort, the fundamental principle in the assessment of damages is the same as in tort generally—

14 65 R.P.C. 203.
15 At 219.
16 1981 c. 54.

namely, that they should compensate the plaintiff for the harm caused to him by the defendant's acts. This is assuming that other heads of liability (for example, associated breach of contract or copyright, patent infringement) are absent and that there is no justification for exemplary or punitive damages (which would in practice be uncommon). The difficulty lies in applying that compensation principle to the variety of actual commercial circumstances which may surround the plaintiff's and defendant's activities. A plaintiff who makes his living by researching in a particular technical area with a view to licensing out or selling that information is clearly in a different position to one who manufactures and sells the product as well; the tortious acts of the defendant, if he has reached the market, may drastically affect these sales also. If it is a "springboard" type of case—in other words, if the defendant will be in a position in any event shortly after conclusion of trial to make and sell freely because the springboard will by then have sprung—there may hardly be any justification for alleging that the defendant's acts have caused long-term loss to the plaintiff; he would have had to have faced the competition in any case; *contra*, perhaps, where the confidential information has been successfully kept secret and exploited for many decades, as in the instance (if the advertising claims are correct) of certain beverages (alcoholic or otherwise). The damages may also be increased if they are to be given as substitute for an injunction; in other words, the Court may have to assess damages both in respect of past infringement (of known scale) and future infringement (on an unknown scale). It is not entirely clear as to whether, in actions for breach of confidence ouside the commercial/industrial sphere, there can be awarded additional damages for mental distress and the like—say in the case of unauthorized disclosure of some personal confidence.

16.18 The most comprehensive discussion in recent times of the principles applicable in practice to assessment of damages has been that of Lord Denning in *Seager v. Copydex (No. 2)*, as follows:

> ". . . The value of the confidential information depends on the *nature* of it. If there was nothing very special about it, that is, if it involved no particular inventive step, but was the sort of information which could be obtained by enploying any competent consultant, then the *value of it was the fee which a consultant would charge for it*; because in that case the defendants, by taking the information, would only have saved themselves the time and trouble of employing a consultant. But, on the other hand, if the information was something special, as for instance if it involved an inventive step or something so unusual that it could not be obtained by just going to a consultant, then the value of it is much higher. It is not merely a consultant's fee, but the price which a willing buyer—desirous of obtaining it—would pay for it. It is the *value as between a willing seller and a willing*

buyer. In this case Mr. Seager says the information was very special. . . . *Furthermore*, if he is to be regarded as a seller, it must be remembered that he had a patent for another carpet grip called KLENT; and, if he was selling the confidential information (which I will call the INVISIGRIP information) then the sales of KLENT might be adversely affected. The sales of the KLENT would be reduced owing to the competition of the INVISIGRIP. So he would ask for *a higher price for the confidential information in order to compensate him for the reduction in the KLENT*. In these circumstances, if Mr. Seager is right in saying that the confidential information was very special indeed, then it may well be right for the value to be assessed on the footing that in the usual way it would be remunerated by a royalty. The court, of course, cannot give a royalty by way of damages. But it could give an equivalent by a calculation based on a capitalisation of a royalty. Thus it could arrive at a lump sum."[17] (emphasis added)

Winn L.J. in the same case added the pertinent comment:

". . . That is, that since the basis on which damages are to be recovered in this case is a tortious basis, where there is insoluble doubt between any two possible versions or assessments, when the tribunal of fact is pursuing the factual issues, it should be borne in mind that there is a general principle that *omnia praesumuntur contra spoliatorem*." (All things are presumed against a robber.)[18]

16.19 The Court accordingly ordered that the inquiry as to damages should proceed upon the basis of a capitalised lump sum royalty, the lump sum to reflect the fact that the defendants were to have future unrestricted use of the information as though they had purchased it outright—*vide* the passage quoted earlier at para. 16.12. The capitalised royalty was, in other words, to reflect both existing and future use of the information.

ACCOUNT OF PROFITS

16.20 An account of profits is an alternative to an inquiry for damages. The plaintiff has to make his choice. Moreover, it is a choice which he has to make at the conclusion of trial (assuming that he has been successful), a time at which he may be uncertain as to which avenue will be more advantageous to him financially; he may have to make the best guess that he can, based upon the material which has emerged either during the discovery stages or during the course of trial. If he asks for an account, hoping that it proves the superior avenue, he cannot later back-track and ask for an inquiry instead when he finds out the account will prove

17 [1969] R.P.C. 250 at 256.
18 At 258.

minimal benefit—due, say, to the inefficiency of the defendant in utilising the improperly acquired confidential information.

16.21 The basis of the two kinds of relief is quite different. For an account of profits, the test is the actual profit (large or small) made by the defendant out of the information: this may be smaller, equal to or larger than the loss which has been suffered by the plaintiff as a result of the competition provided by the defendant. Generally, the test for an inquiry as to damages is that of the harm suffered by the plaintiff as a result of the unauthorised use of the information and consequential competition; this harm may likewise be smaller than, equal to or greater than the defendant's actual profit out of the information. Much may depend upon the defendant's manufacturing and/or selling efficiency, as just mentioned, and also upon the general financial circumstances operative in the industry or trade in question. For an industry requiring high capital investment but with low margins, an account may prove less desirable than for an industry with lesser capital requirements but higher risk and margins.

16.22 The account of profits is a traditional equitable remedy and has accordingly figured perhaps rather more prominently in actions for breach of confidence than might be otherwise expected—at least until relatively recent times. This is notwithstanding the fact that the plaintiff usually has a clearer idea by the conclusion of trial as to what his own losses are than what his adversary's profits were; he will probably have a fair idea, for example, as to how many sales he himself has lost as a result of the defendant's activities and how these translate into profits lost, machinery running under-used, employee redundancies and the like, or alternatively, as to the royalty which he would have charged had he in fact been approached by the defendant for a licence at the time and been willing to grant the same; the relevant facts and figures on these matters are largely already in his own domain. Nevertheless, the account does still have value for dealing with a defendant who has—perhaps rather cynically—estimated in advance that the damages likely to be awarded upon an inquiry, upon the notional royalty approach or otherwise, would be very much less than his anticipated profits.

16.23 The proper accounting basis to be employed for the account of profits may in itself provide substantial difficulty. This is illustrated in the case of *Peter Pan Manufacturing v. Corsets Silhouette*,[19] involving post-termination continued use by the defendant of confidential information which he had received from the plaintiff under a licence agreement.

19 [1963] R.P.C. 45.

16.24 The successful plaintiffs had asked that:

> ". . . an account be taken of the profits made by the defendants in the manufacture and sale of brassieres of the said style U.15 and brassieres of the said style U. 25."

The defendants in reply had argued that instead:

> ". . . an account be taken of the profits made by the defendants by the wrongful use of confidential information supplied by the plaintiffs to the defendants in the manufacture and sale of brassieres of the said styles U.15 and U. 25."[20]

The difference between these two accounting formulas is substantial. Under the first, the defendant has to hand over his entire profit on the goods; under the second, he merely has to hand over that part of his total profit which exceeds the profit which he would have made in any event if he had manufactured the goods without the aid of the confidential information—in other words, only the extra profit which arose from the use of the confidential information.

16.25 The Court opted for the first formula, in the circumstances of the case, on the basis that the defendants would never have been able in fact to manufacture the article at all without the assistance of the confidential information. And as for what amounted to "profit", the Court decreed here the simple calculation of:

> ". . . what has the defendant expended upon manufacturing the goods? What has he received on their sale? and the difference is profit."[21]

Whether such a rough-and-ready approach would always be followed today (the *Peter Pan* decision is now over twenty years old) may be less certain; accounting techniques have become more sopisticated since. The decision may also be inapplicable in instances where the confidential information played only a minor part in the manufacture of the entire article, or performance of the entire process as the case may be, or where the defendant could in any event have manufactured or performed without reliance upon the confidential information as a *sine qua non*, by employing already known technology.

16.26 Outside the commercial/industrial sphere, the usefulness of the account of profits as a remedy alternative to damages may again vary widely. At the one extreme, say the case of the former maid who sells personal secrets of her mistress's pre-marital excapades for a large sum to a newspaper, the profits could be, so far as the maid is concerned, the

20 At 58.
21 At 60.

whole of the sum passing; if the newspaper were sued as co-defendant, and it could be shown that circulation figures went up that particular issue as a result of the story, the additional profits generated thereby might also be retrievable; the newspaper in such circumstances might have difficulty in persuading a Court that it genuinely believed the maid to have had her mistress's permission to make such revelations, so as to render them in turn a mere innocent purchaser. At the other extreme, say the case of the employee who for misguided but altruistic beliefs discloses to a journalist that his employer has plans to shut a branch factory in an area of existing high unemployment, the revelation may have been made purely gratuitously; if so, there would be no profit to bite upon.

16.27 Such examples illustrate once again the at times sinuous, yet flexible and far-reaching, nature of the action for breach of confidence which it has been the author's purpose in this work to endeavour to expound.

APPENDIX

Draft Breach of Confidence Bill

This Appendix reproduces the draft Breach of Confidence Bill prepared by the Law Commission in their Report *Breach of Confidence* (Cmnd. 8388, 1980) which has been mentioned at various places in the main text. The Appendix includes the side-notes written for the Bill by the Law Commission, but excludes their separate accompanying explanatory notes for each section; the latter are lengthy, in some places.

Generally speaking, the Bill is self-explanatory and directed to enunciating a statutory law of breach of confidence in terms akin to those of the existing common law; much of the phraseology is couched in general terms, in an attempt to provide some flexibility. To quote from the Commission's Report:

> "However, we should emphasise that the legislative framework which we envisage would allow the Courts wide scope in applying its principles to differing situations and changing social circumstances."
>
> (Para 6.1)

The proposal to provide for an "adjustment order" (clause 15) in order to deal with the position of an innocent third party acquirer of the confidential information which has been disclosed in breach, who has incurred expenditure in connection with its exploitation (capital investment in new plant, additional premises, market surveys, advertising and the like) prior to being informed of the illicit origin of the information, is of interest; it may be regarded as providing new law. Mention may also be made of clause 16 providing for application of the "head start" or "springboard" doctrine; of the possibility of damages for mental distress under clause 14(1)(b); of the duty of an authorised communicatee to take reasonable care of the information passed, under clause 8(1)(b); and of the availability of tort defences generally in any action for breach, under clause 12(5).

Elsewhere, some emphasis has been added to assist appreciation of the Bill's provisions. A skeletal concordance with relevant chapters of this book has also been inserted against the Arrangement of Clauses. The provisions have to be considered, in any event, against the background of statutory legislation enacted since the date of the Report in some of the pertinent legal areas—particularly, the Contempt of Court Act 1981 (Chapter 7) and Data Protection Act 1984 (Chapter 10).

ARRANGEMENT OF CLAUSES

Preliminary

New statutory obligations of confidence.

1.—(1) The provisions of this Act have effect for the purpose of—

(*a*) providing for obligations of confidence, within the meaning of section 8, to be imposed on persons acquiring information in the circumstances mentioned in sections 3 to 6; and

(*b*) providing for proceedings to be brought under this Act in respect of breaches of such obligations, and for the remedies available in those proceedings.

(2) In consequence of the provisions of this Act, any principles of equity or rules of the common law by virtue of which obligations arise in respect of the acquisition of information in circumstances of confidence, or by virtue of which relief may be granted in respect of the disclosure or use of information in breach of confidence, are (subject to subsection (3)) abolished.

(3) Nothing in subsection (2) has effect in relation to—

(*a*) contractual obligations to treat information confidentially so far as enforceable by proceedings for breach of contract; or

(*b*) proceedings for contempt of court.

Information to which the Act applies.

2.—(1) An obligation of confidence can arise under this Act only with respect to information which is *not in the public domain;* and references to information in any of sections 3 to 6 are accordingly references to such information.

(2) Information in the public domain includes information which is public knowledge or accessible to the public (whether or not on payment of a fee or subject to any other restriction); but, for the purposes of this Act, information which is capable of being extracted from any matter in the public domain (whether a document, product, process or anything else) is not in the public domain on that ground alone if such extraction would require a significant expenditure of labour, skill or money.

(3) For the purposes of this Act, information not already in the public domain which is orally disclosed in such a way as to be generally available to those present at the proceedings of any court—

(*a*) does not come into the public domain if the court is sitting in private; but

(*b*) comes into the public domain if the court is in open session and publication of the information is not prohibited in the circumstances by any statutory provision or by an order or direction of the court (having the power to make such an order or direction).

(4) In subsection (3) "court" includes a judge, tribunal and any person exercising the functions of a court, judge or tribunal; and the reference to a court sitting in private includes a court sitting in camera or in chambers.

Circumstances in which obligations of confidence arise

Undertaking to treat information confidentially.

3.—(1) A person who has acquired information from another person shall owe the other an obligation of confidence under this section with respect to the information if—

(*a*) he has *expressly undertaken* to the other to treat the information, or a description of information within which it falls, confidentially; or

(*b*) an undertaking by him to the other to that effect is, in the absence of any contrary indication given by him to the other, to be *inferred* from the nature of any relationship between the parties or from his conduct in relation to the other.

(2) A person who has acquired information on behalf of another person shall, if either paragraph (*a*) or (*b*) of subsection (1) is applicable, owe to the other person an obligation of confidence under this section with respect to the information.

(3) For the purposes of this section it is immaterial whether the undertaking given by a person (expressly or by inference) was given at the time when he acquired the information in question or at some other time, whether before or afterwards.

(4) A person who has acquired information from another person and is, or in all the circumstances ought to be, aware that the information was supplied by the other on behalf of a third person shall be treated for the purposes of this section as having acquired the information from that third person as well.

(5) It is declared that subsection (1) applies in relation to the following, namely—

(*a*) the acquisition by a person from another person of information supplied to him by the other in accordance with any requirement to do so imposed by or by virtue of any statutory provision, or so supplied in connection with an application under a statutory provision for the grant of any benefit or permission;

(*b*) an undertaking within paragraph (*a*) or (*b*) of subsection (1) which is an express or implied obligation of a contract.

Acquisition of information disclosed in or for purposes of legal proceedings.

4.—(1) Where information, or any document or other matter containing information, is required to be disclosed to a person for the purposes of any legal proceedings (pending or otherwise)—

(*a*) by an order or direction of a court, or

(*b*) by rules of court,

then, on acquiring the information as a result of it or the matter containing it being disclosed in pursuance of that order or direction or those rules, that person or any other person to whom the disclosure is made on his behalf shall owe an obligation of confidence under this subsection with respect to the information to the person required to make the disclosure.

(2) Where information is disclosed in legal proceedings—

(*a*) at a time when the court is sitting in private otherwise than in chambers, or

(*b*) if this subsection applies to that disclosure in accordance with subsection (3), at a time when the court is sitting in chambers,

any person who thereupon acquires the information shall owe an obligation of confidence under this subsection with respect to the information to the person making the disclosure.

(3) Subsection (2) applies to a disclosure of information at a time when the court is sitting in chambers in the following cases, namely—

(*a*) where the proceedings relate to a breach of an obligation of confidence under this Act or to a breach of a contractual obligation to treat information confidentially and the information disclosed is material to the proceedings;
(*b*) where the proceedings relate to any secret process, know-how, discovery or invention and the information disclosed is material to the proceedings;
(c) where it appears to the court proper that the information disclosed should be protected by means of an order under this paragraph and the court accordingly by order directs that subsection (2) is to apply to the disclosure.

(4) If a person acquiring information as mentioned in subsection (1) or (2) is or in all the circumstances ought to be aware that the person in whose favour an obligation of confidence arises under that subsection made the disclosure in question on behalf of a third person, the person acquiring the information shall owe an obligation of confidence under that subsection with respect to it to the third person as well.

(5) In this section "court" has the meaning given by section 2(4); and the reference in subsection (2)(*a*) of this section to a court sitting in private includes a court sitting in camera.

(6) Nothing in this section prejudices the exercise by any court of any power to prohibit or punish contempt of court (whether in relation to its own proceedings or otherwise).

Improper acquisition of information.

5.—(1) Subject to the provisions of this section, a person who improperly acquires information from another person shall owe an obligation of confidence under this section with respect to the information—

(*a*) to the person from whom the information is so acquired, and
(*b*) if that person is at the time when it is so acquired holding it on behalf of some other person, to that other person as well.

(2) For the purposes of this section a person acquires information improperly if—

(*a*) he acquires it as a result of doing any of the following acts without authority (express or implied), namely—
  (i) taking, handling or interfering with any document, record, model or other thing containing the information,
  (ii) taking, handling or interfering with anything in which any such thing as is mentioned in sub-paragraph (i) is for the time being kept,
  (iii) (without prejudice to the generality of the foregoing) using or interfering with any computer or data retrieval mechanism,

whether, as regards any such act, the absence of authority relates to his doing it at all or only to the manner or purpose in or for which he in fact does it; or

(*b*) he acquires it as a result of using any violence, menace or deception; or
(*c*) he acquires it while somewhere where he has no authority (express or implied) to be; or

(*d*) he acquires it by means of the use of—
  (i) a device made or adapted primarily for the purpose of surreptitiously carrying out the surveillance of persons, their activities, communications or property, or
  (ii) subject to subsection (3), any other technical device capable of being used for carrying out such surveillance, whether surreptitiously or overtly,

provided that (in either case) he would not in the circumstances have acquired the information but for his use of the device in question.

(3) A person's acquisition of information by means of the use of a device within subsection (2)(*d*)(ii) is not improper for the purposes of this section if a reasonable man in the position of the person from whom the information is acquired would have appreciated the risk of, and taken precautions adequate to prevent, its being acquired by means of the use of a device of the kind in question; and nothing in that sub-paragraph is to be read as referring to a device designed to bring vision or hearing so far as possible up to a normal standard.

(4) In the case of information acquired as a result of using or interfering with a device mentioned in subsection (2)(*a*)(iii), any person by or on behalf of whom the information was supplied to the device shall be regarded for the purposes of subsection (1) as a person from whom the information is acquired (and subsection (1)(*b*) accordingly does not apply).

(5) Where two or more persons ("participators") have jointly participated in the acquisition of information from another person, any participator—

(*a*) who has personally acquired the information from the other person, and
(*b*) whose acquisition of it was not improper under subsection (2) apart from this subsection,

shall nevertheless owe an obligation of confidence under this section to the other person with respect to the information as from such time as the participator is aware, or ought in all the circumstances to be aware, of any act done by any other participator in connection with the acquisition of the information which, if done by the former participator, would have rendered his acquisition of the information improper under subsection (2).

(6) In any case where a person's acquisition of information falls within subsection (2) but the information was acquired by him—

(*a*) in the course of the lawful exercise by him of any official function to acquire information for the purposes of protecting the security of the State, or of preventing, detecting or investigating crime, or
(*b*) in pursuance of any statutory provision,

nothing in this section or section 6 imposes on him or on any other person directly or indirectly acquiring it from him any liability under this Act in respect of the disclosure or use of that information in so far as it is disclosed or used—

(i) for any such purposes as are referred to in paragraph (*a*) of this subsection or for the purpose of bringing any related legal proceedings, or
(ii) for any purpose expressly or impliedly authorised, in relation to information acquired in pursuance of the statutory provision referred to in paragraph (*b*) of this subsection, by that or any other such provision.

Acquisition by third party of information subject to an obligation of confidence.

6.—(1) If, while an obligation of confidence under section 3, 4 or 5 is owed by any person ("the original acquirer") to another person with respect to any information—

(*a*) the information is acquired from the original acquirer (by whatever means and whether directly or, through successive acquisitions, indirectly) by any third person, and

(*b*) the third person becomes aware, or ought in all the circumstances to have become aware, of the material facts or circumstances giving rise to the obligation of confidence owed by the original aquirer or otherwise that an obligation of confidence has arisen with respect to the information under the preceding provisions of this Act,

then, as from the relevant time under subsection (2), the third person shall owe an obligation of confidence under this section with respect to the information to the other person mentioned above.

(2) The relevant time referred to in subsection (1) is whichever is the later of the following, namely the time when the third person acquires the information and the time when he becomes, or ought to have become, aware as mentioned in paragraph (*b*) of that subsection.

(3) Where a person dies (or, if not an individual, ceases to exist) while owing an obligation of confidence under section 3, 4 or 5 with respect to any information, then, unless that obligation of confidence thereupon ceases to have effect in accordance with subsection (2) of section 9, the information shall for the purposes of this section continue to be subject to that obligation of confidence, as if it were still owed by that person, until such time as that person would have been released from it by virtue of subsection (1) or (2) of section 9 if still alive or (as the case may be) still in existence.

No obligation of confidence where information acquired in course of work merely enhances personal skills, etc.

7. Nothing in the preceding provisions of this Act has the effect of imposing an obligation of confidence on any individual with respect to any information which—

(*a*) is acquired by him in the course of his work (whether under a contract of employment or as an independent contractor or otherwise), and

(*b*) is of such a nature that the acquisition of it by him amounts to *no more than an enhancement of the personal knowledge, skill or experience used by him in the exercise of his calling.*

Obligations of confidence

Duties arising out of an obligation of confidence.

8.—(1) For the purposes of this Act an obligation of confidence owed under any provision of this Act with respect to any information shall, subject to subsections (3) and (4), impose the following duties on the person who owes the obligation, namely—

(*a*) a duty not to disclose or use the information except to the extent (if any) to which he is for the time being expressly or impliedly authorised to do so by the person to whom the obligation is owed; and (*b*) a duty to *take reasonable care* to ensure that the information is not disclosed or used except to the extent mentioned in paragraph (*a*).

(2) Accordingly, any reference in this Act to a breach of an obligation of confidence is a reference to an act or omission in breach of one or other of the duties subsisting with respect to the information in question in accordance with subsection (1).

(3) Nothing in subsection (1)—

(*a*) prevents a person who owes an obligation of confidence under section 3 with respect to information supplied as mentioned in subsection (5)(*a*) of that section from disclosing or using it to such extent as is, in relation to information supplied in pursuance of the statutory provision in question, expressly or impliedly authorised by or by virtue of that or any other statutory provision;

(*b*) prevents a person who owes an obligation of confidence under subsection (1) or subsection (2) of section 4 from disclosing or using the information in question for the purposes of the proceedings referred to in that subsection; or

(*c*) prevents a person who owes an obligation of confidence under section 6 with respect to information directly or indirectly acquired from a person such as is referred to in paragraph (*a*) or (*b*) of this subsection from disclosing or using the information to the extent to which the latter may do so by virtue of that paragraph.

(4) Where a person owing an obligation of confidence under section 3, 4 or 5 with respect to any information has been expressly or impliedly authorised by the person to whom the obligation is owed to disclose or use the information to any extent, nothing in subsection (1) of this section prevents a person who owes an obligation of confidence under section 6 by virtue of that obligation of confidence from disclosing or using the information to an extent which will not result in a more extensive disclosure or use of the information than has been so authorised.

Termination of obligations of confidence.

9.—(1) A person who, under any provision of this Act, owes another person an obligation of confidence with respect to any information shall cease to owe the other person an obligation of confidence with respect to the information—

(*a*) if he is expressly or impliedly released by the other person from such an obligation; or

(*b*) in so far as an order of the court under section 15(2) has the effect of releasing him from such an obligation; or

(*c*) if the information comes into the public domain.

(2) Where in the case of an obligation of confidence under section 3 the relevant undertaking within subsection (1)(*a*) or (*b*) of that section was given, expressly or by inference, for a particular period of time (including a period expiring on the occurrence of any event), that obligation of confidence, and any obligation of confidence owed under section 6 by virtue of it, shall cease to be owed at such time as that period expires.

(3) For the purposes of subsection (1)(*c*) of this section it is immaterial whether the person responsible for the information coming into the public domain was the person to whom the obligation of confidence was owed, the person who owed it or some other person.

(4) Subsections (1) and (2) of this section are without prejudice to—

(*a*) any claim in respect of a person's breach of an obligation of confidence which was committed before, or as a consequence of which, he ceased to owe that obligation in accordance with this section;

(*b*) the power of the court to grant relief in respect of such a breach in the circumstances mentioned in section 16.

Proceedings for breach of confidence

Proceedings for breach of confidence.

10.—(1) A breach of an obligation of confidence owed under any of the preceding provisions of this Act is a tort and, subject to the following provisions of this Act, proceedings may be brought in respect of such a breach by any person to whom the obligation is owed in like manner as any other proceedings in respect of tort.

(2) Proceedings brought by virtue of this section are referred to in this Act as proceedings for breach of confidence.

Plaintiff's claim liable to fail unless upholding of confidentiality is in public interest.

11.—(1) A defendant in proceedings for breach of confidence shall not be liable to the plaintiff in respect of any disclosure or use of information by the defendant in breach of an obligation of confidence if—

(*a*) the defendant raises the issue of public interest in relation to that disclosure or use in accordance with subsection (2); and

(*b*) the plaintiff is unable to satisfy the court that the public interest relied on by the defendant under that subsection is outweighed by the public interest involved in upholding the confidentiality of the information.

(2) For the purposes of subsection (1) a defendant raises the issue of public interest in relation to a disclosure or use of information if he satisfies the court that, in view of the content of the information, there was, or (in the case of an apprehended disclosure or use) will be, at the time of the disclosure or use a public interest involved in the information being so disclosed or used.

(3) A public interest may be involved in the disclosure or use of information notwithstanding that the information does not relate to any crime, fraud or other misconduct.

(4) When balancing the public interests involved for the purposes of subsection (1) the court shall have regard to all the circumstances of the case, including—

(*a*) the extent and nature of the particular disclosure or use in question as compared with the extent and nature of the disclosure or use which appears to be justified by the public interest on which the defendant relies;

(*b*) the manner in which the information was acquired by the defendant and (in the case of an obligation of confidence under section 6) the manner in which it was acquired by the original and any subsequent acquirer of it; and

(*c*) the time which has elapsed since the information originally became subject to the obligation of confidence owed by the defendant or (in the case of an obligation of confidence under section 6) became subject to the obligation of confidence by virtue of which that obligation arose.

Defences

12.—(1) In any proceedings for breach of confidence in respect of a disclosure or use of information it is a defence to prove—

(*a*) that, at the time of the defendant's acquisition of the information which gave rise to the obligation of confidence in question, he was already in possession of the information, or

(*b*) that he subsequently came into possession of it by independent means,

and, in addition, that at the time he disclosed or used the information the defendant did not, in connection with his previous or (as the case may be) subsequent awareness of the information, owe any other obligation of confidence of which that disclosure or use constituted a breach.

(2) In any proceedings for breach of confidence in respect of a disclosure or use of information it is a defence to prove that the disclosure or use was required or authorised to be made by or by virtue of any statutory provision.

(3) In any proceedings for breach of confidence in respect of a disclosure of information it is a defence to prove that the disclosure was made on such an occasion as attracts, for the purposes of the law of defamation, an absolute privilege in respect of statements made thereon.

(4) Without prejudice to the generality of subsections (2) and (3) it is a defence in any proceedings for breach of confidence in respect of a disclosure of information to prove that the disclosure was required to be made by a court in pursuance of any power to order the disclosure of information.

(5) Defences *generally available in tort proceedings* are, in accordance with section 10(1), available in proceedings for breach of confidence.

Remedies

Remedies in proceedings for breach of confidence: general.

13.—(1) The following relief may be granted by the court in proceedings for breach of confidence—

(*a*) an injunction restraining the defendant from any apprehended breach of an obligation of confidence (with or without, in a case to which section 15(1) applies, an adjustment order under that subsection providing compensation for the defendant);

(*b*) damages in accordance with section 14;

(*c*) an account of the profits derived by the defendant from the breach;

(*d*) an adjustment order under section 15(2) regulating the respective rights and liabilities of the plaintiff and the defendant in so far as the defendant is not to be restrained by injunction;

(*e*) an order for the defendant to deliver up or destroy anything in which the information to which the breach relates is contained.

(2) With the exception of paragraph (*b*), the relief mentioned in subsection (1) is at the discretion of the court.

(3) Nothing in this section prejudices any jurisdiction of the court to grant ancillary or incidental relief.

Damages.

14.—(1) The damages which may by virtue of section 13(1)(*b*) be awarded to a plaintiff in proceedings for breach of confidence are, subject to the provisions of this section, damages in respect of either or both of the following matters, namely—

(*a*) any pecuniary loss suffered by the plaintiff in consequence of the defendant's breach of an obligation of confidence owed to him; and

(*b*) any mental distress, and any mental or physical harm resulting from such distress, suffered by the plaintiff in consequence of that breach.

(2) The court shall not in respect of the same breach of an obligation of confidence both award the plaintiff damages under subsection (1)(*a*) and order that he shall be given an account of the defendant's profits therefrom.

(3) The court shall not award the plaintiff any damages under subsection (1)(*b*) unless it appears to the court that a person of reasonable fortitude in the position of the plaintiff would have been likely to suffer mental distress in consequence of the defendant's breach.

Adjustment orders.

15.—(1) Where in any proceedings for breach of confidence—

(*a*) the court proposes to grant an injunction against a defendant restraining him from an apprehended breach of an obligation of confidence owed under section 6, but

(*b*) it appears to the court that, prior to the time when he became subject to that obligation, he incurred any expenditure in connection with exploiting the information to which the breach relates,

then, if the court thinks fit, it may (in addition to granting the injunction) make an adjustment order under this subsection requiring the plaintiff to make to the defendant such contribution towards that expenditure as appears to the court to be just and equitable.

(2) Where in any proceedings for breach of confidence the court has power to grant an injunction against a defendant restraining him from an apprehended breach of an obligation of confidence but considers that it would be inappropriate in all the circumstances to do so to any extent, the court may, if it thinks fit, make an adjustment order under this subsection for the purpose of regulating, as regards such future exploitation by the defendant of the information in question as it is not proposing to restrain, the respective rights and liabilities of the plaintiff and the defendant.

(3) An adjustment order under subsection (2) may require the defendant to pay to the plaintiff one or other of the following, namely—

(*a*) such sum in lieu of an injunction as appears to the court to be appropriate in all the circumstances, or

(*b*) a royalty in respect of the future use by the defendant of the information in question calculated on such bases as appears to the court to be appropriate, the defendant's use of the information being for such period and on such terms as the court may specify in the order,

together with (in either case) such contribution as appears to be just and equitable towards any expenditure which the plaintiff has already incurred in connection with exploiting the information in question and which is likely to become wasted expenditure as a result of the defendant being allowed to exploit the information in future.

(4) The court may in any adjustment order under subsection (2) determine any incidental question relating to the extent to which either of the parties is to be free to exploit the information in question.

(5) In any case where the court proposes to make—

(*a*) an award of damages under section 14(1)(*a*) in respect of the defendant's breach of an obligation of confidence, and

(*b*) an adjustment order under subsection (2) of this section in respect of future exploitation by the defendant of the information to which that breach relates,

the court, when determining whether to make the plaintiff an award under subsection (3)(*a*) or (*b*) of this section, and if so the amount of any such award, shall take such account of any element of that award of damages which reflects future loss to the plaintiff as it thinks appropriate for the purpose of doing justice between the parties.

(6) Any reference in this section to expenditure incurred by a person in connection with exploiting information includes expenditure incurred by him in connection with acquiring it.

Remedies in respect of future use of information which is no longer subject to an obligation of confidence.

16.—(1) The court may, if it thinks fit in the case of a defendant in proceedings for breach of confidence who has committed a breach of an obligation of confidence under this Act, grant relief under this section in respect of the future use by him of the information to which the breach relates notwithstanding that such use will occur at a time when the information has, or is likely to have, come into the public domain (and accordingly ceased to be subject to an obligation of confidence).

(2) The relief which may be granted by the court under this section in the case of such a defendant is—

(*a*) an injunction for such period and on such terms as appear to the court to be necessary to prevent the defendant from enjoying an advantage in the exploitation of the information in question over persons able to exploit it only as from its coming into the public domain (granted with or without, in a case to which section 15(1) applies, an adjustment order under that subsection); or

(*b*) an adjustment order under section 15(2), but only in respect of such period of future use by the defendant as, in the view of the court, the defendant is likely (in so far as not restrained under paragraph (*a*) from exploiting the information) to enjoy an advantage in its exploitation over persons able to exploit it only as from its coming into the public domain.

(3) Section 15 shall in its operation for the purposes of this section have effect as if, in each of subsections (1) and (2) of that section, for the words "an injunction against a defendant restraining him from an apprehended breach of an obligation of confidence" there were substituted "an injunction under section 16(2)(*a*) against a defendant who has committed a breach of an obligation of confidence".

Special provisions as to county court.

17.—(1) A county court may in proceedings for breach of confidence grant the plaintiff an injunction or a declaration notwithstanding that he does not seek any relief other than an injunction or a declaration.

(2) A county court may in proceedings for breach of confidence make an adjustment order under subsection (1) of section 15 whatever the amount required to be paid by virtue of it by the plaintiff, but shall not have power to make an adjustment order under subsection (2) of that section by virtue of which the defendant is required to pay such a royalty as is mentioned in subsection (3)(*b*) of that section.

Transmission of benefit of obligations of confidence

Transmission of benefit of obligations of confidence.

18.—(1) Subject to subsection (2), nothing in this Act prevents the benefit of an obligation of confidence under this Act from being assigned to a person other than the person in whose favour the obligation of confidence has arisen in so far as it is, in any particular case in view of the nature of the information to which the obligation of confidence relates, capable of being so assigned in accordance with the general law as to the assignment of rights.

(2) No proceedings for breach of confidence shall be brought in respect of mental distress, or mental or physical harm resulting from such distress, suffered by any person other than a person in whose favour an obligation of confidence has arisen under this Act.

(3) Any reference in this Act (whether express or implied and however worded) to the person to whom an obligation of confidence is or was owed includes (subject to subsection (2) and so far as the context so permits) a person to whom the benefit of the obligation of confidence has been assigned.

(4) In this section references to assignment include assignment by operation of law.

Operation of Act in relation to proceedings in contract

Operation of Act in relation to proceedings in contract.

19.—(1) Section 11 (plaintiff's claim liable to fail unless upholding of confidentiality is in public interest) shall have effect in relation to proceedings for breach of contract in respect of a breach of a relevant contractual undertaking as it has effect in relation to proceedings for breach of confidence, but with the following modifications, namely—

(*a*) any reference to an obligation of confidence shall be read as a reference to a relevant contractual undertaking;

(*b*) the reference in subsection (1)(*b*) to upholding the confidentiality of the information shall be read as a reference to upholding the contractual undertaking in question; and

(*c*) subsection (4)(*b*) and so much of subsection (4)(*c*) as relates to an obligation of confidence under section 6 shall not apply.

(2) Subject to subsection (1), any relevant contractual undertaking may be enforced by proceedings for breach of contract in all respects as if this Act had not been passed.

(3) In this section "relevant contractual undertaking" means an express or implied contractual undertaking not to disclose or use information.

General

Interpretation.

20.—(1) In this Act, unless the context otherwise requires—

"the court" means the High Court or, subject to section 17(2) of this Act and section 39 of the County Courts Act 1959 (which contains financial limits on jurisdiction), a county court;

"proceedings" includes proceedings by way of counter-claim, and references to a plaintiff or defendant in proceedings shall be construed accordingly;

"statutory provision" means any enactment, whenever passed, or any provision contained in subordinate legislation (as defined in section 21(1) of the Interpretation Act 1978), whenever made.

(2) References in this Act to information in, or coming into, the public domain shall be construed in accordance with subsections (2) to (4) of section 2.

(3) References in this Act to an obligation of confidence shall be construed in accordance with section 8, and references to the person to whom such obligation is owed shall be construed in accordance with section 18(3).

Supplemental.

21.—(1) Sections 3 to 6 have effect in relation to acquisitions of information taking place before the commencement of this Act as well as to those taking place thereafter, but an obligation of confidence under section 6 shall not be owed in respect of an acquisition of information taking place before that commencement unless it would have been owed in respect of that acquisition if this Act had at all material times been in force.

(2) Section 19 has effect in relation to contractual undertakings given before or after the commencement of this Act.

(3) Section 10(1) and 19(1) have effect, however, only in relation to a disclosure or use of information taking place after the commencement of this Act; and accordingly nothing in this Act affects any cause of action accruing before this Act comes into force.

(4) The Limitation Act 1980 shall apply in relation to a claim for damages in respect of mental distress suffered as mentioned in section 14(1)(*b*) of this Act as it applies in relation to a claim for damages in respect of personal injuries within the meaning of the Act (references to "injury" and cognate expressions in that Act being construed accordingly).

(5) Nothing in this Act affects the operation of section 1 of the Law Reform (Miscellaneous Provisions) Act 1934 (survival of causes of action against, or for the benefit of, a deceased's estate).

Application to the Crown.

22.—(1) This Act shall bind the Crown, but as regards the Crown's liability in tort shall not bind the Crown further than the Crown is made liable in tort by the Crown Proceedings Act 1947.

(2) Without prejudice to the generality of section 21(1) of that Act (nature of relief in proceedings by or against the Crown), references in sections 15 and 16 of this Act to the granting of an injunction restraining a defendant in proceedings for breach of confidence shall, in relation to the Crown where it is a defendant in such proceedings, be read as references to the granting of such equivalent declaration with respect to the rights of parties as the court is empowered to grant by virtue of proviso (*a*) to the said section 21(1).

Citation, commencement and extent.

23.—(1) This Act may be cited as the Breach of Confidence Act 1981.

(2) This Act shall come into force at the end of the period of three months beginning with the day on which it is passed.

(3) This Act extends to England and Wales only.

Index